Alice Hescox

ABOVE: Left to right: 14in (35.6cm) *Baby Grumpy,* in pink, sitting. *Jeannette Gustin Collection.* 15in (38.1cm) *Baby Grumpy,* standing. *Sherryl Shirran Collection.*

TITLE PAGE: Left to right: 16½in (41.9cm) *Bubbles,* 15'' (38.1cm) *Bubbles* collection of *Virginia Tomlinson.*

Cover: Back row, left to right: 15in (38.1cm) *Dolly Dumpling,* 30in (76.2cm) *Bubbles,* 17in (43.2cm) *Baby Grumpy.* **Front row, left to right:** 14in (35.6cm) *Baby Dainty,* 12in (30.5cm) *Grumpykins,* 14in (35.6cm) *Hard-to-Break Grumpy,* 14in (35.6cm) *Aunt Dinah's Boy.*

EFFANBEE DOLLS

by Patricia N. Schoonmaker

HOBBY HOUSE PRESS, INC.
900 Frederick Street
Cumberland, MD 21502
(301) 759-3770

DEDICATION

To my husband, John, for his photographic skills, as well as all manner of help, encouraging me on at times when I felt the task would never be finished. Indeed, research **is** open-ended.

The author in about 1920 with a composition doll which did not survive her early affections.

ISBN: 0-87588-213-7

TABLE OF CONTENTS

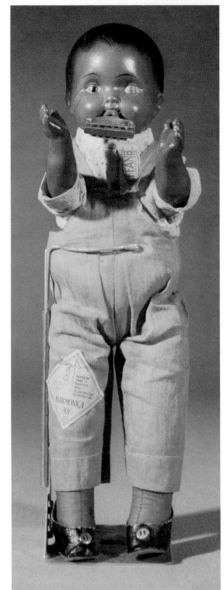

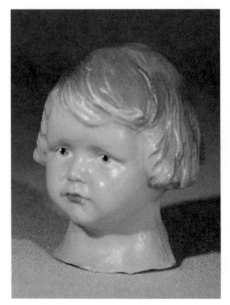

ABOVE: 12in (30.5cm) infant doll shown in 1915 Effanbee catalog, possibly *Little Walter*. See *Illustrations 36* and *37. Rhoda Shoemaker Collection.*

ABOVE RIGHT: 14½in (36.9cm) *Harmonica Joe.* See *Illustrations 276* through *278. Betty Johnsen Collection.*

BELOW RIGHT: *Pouting Bess* composition Hard-to-Break type of head. See *Illustrations 39* through *42. Pearl Morley Collection.*

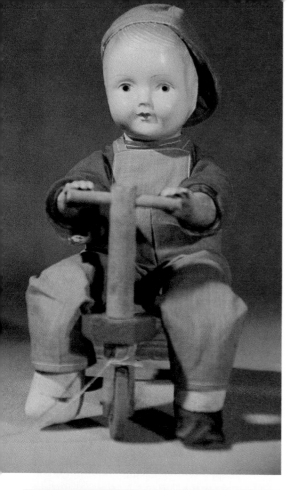

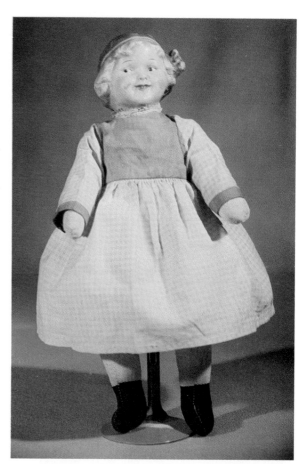

LEFT: 12in (30.5cm) Dragabout toy. See *Illustrations 272* and *273. Frances James Collection.*

RIGHT: 12in (30.5cm) all-original *Coquette.* See *Illustrations 31* through *35. Francine P. Klug Collection.*

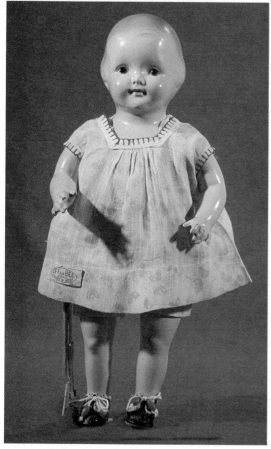

LEFT: All-original *Baby Dainty.*

RIGHT: 24in (61cm) *Rosemary.* See *Illustrations 367* and *368. Joyce Olsen Collection.*

ACKNOWLEDGEMENTS

One is **especially** grateful for the help of fellow researchers who have busy lives and research projects of their own. Dorothy S. Coleman sent research data. John Axe furnished photographs and other information. Loraine Burdick is an indispensable helper with source material or old catalogs not in our own files. Jan and Howard Foulke have been supporting and sharing with rare doll photographs, some of which will be in Volume II. Rhoda Shoemaker loaned early rare dolls to be photographed. Pat Smith, at my request, promptly furnished an address which led to a collector's rare all-original doll for photographing and examination.

We were most appreciative to be allowed access to "the stacks" at the Library of Congress, Washington, D.C., a privilege no longer easily granted; for our time spent in the conference room at *Playthings* magazine in New York, New York, checking early material missing elsewhere; and for our friendly reception at the Effanbee showroom in New York. Mr. Arthur Keller expressed interest in this forthcoming book.

The collectors were generous beyond measure. Many shipped dolls to be set up in our own lights; others, at our suggestions, became top-notch photographers. Their names are credited, along with their doll photographs, as well as are any other persons who did photography. For still other people who supplied information or pictures not used due to the bulk of material, we are just as appreciative of their contributions.

Many thanks to our editor, Virginia Ann Heyerdahl, ever so helpful and encouraging, and to everyone at Hobby House Press, Inc., who has had a hand in the work on the book.

INTRODUCTION

In our privately published 1971 paperback book, *The Effanbee Patsy Family and Related Types,* we reprinted a letter received from Julia Klein, Effanbee Doll Corporation, written in September 1969.

The company stated at that time that they had no literature **at all** on Effanbee dolls manufactured before 1958. Ms. Klein wrote, "At that time we moved our plant from Manhattan to Brooklyn. Unfortunately, the case containing printed matter, dated many years back, was lost and has never been located by the movers."

Many is the time we mourned the loss of that "treasure trove" to a researcher! Yet we would not give up the quest to uncover the lost history of this prestigious American company whose quality dolls were so loved by the children who owned them, and later by the preservers of history, the doll collectors.

We first threw out the challenge for help in 1971, and this still stands. What **different** bit of doll history can you contribute? An all-original doll, an original label or tag, a folio of advertising?

While writing for the **Doll Reader** magazine over a number of years, I became more experienced in the difficult but most interesting task of doll researching. (I am still learning.) My column, "Compo Corner" has kept me in touch with many people who take as much joy and interest in the composition dolls as I do. In fact, we have had the vicarious thrill of hearing details of each new discovery of some beginning collectors who attack the search with boundless energy and enthusiasm. Since the value has risen so dramatically over the years on these bits of Americana, an individual cannot possibly afford to buy all the dolls one would like to, in order to examine and photograph them, as one once could. So the participation of others has been immensely appreciated, and will be for future volumes.

Our aim was not merely to find lost material but to show a doll to the reader as though he/she had actually examined it by seeing the body type and marking, or original tags where available. We also wanted to make it possible to know how to properly dress these early dolls. So many are found without original clothing and are often, unknowingly, overdressed for the period.

Another writer may have arranged the material in a different manner than we have done. We strove for the **convenience** of the reader. Some dolls with a definite, strong identity have been grouped all together. Hence, for example, a few dolls which could have gone into the Mama Doll chapter can be found elsewhere. We separated the Hard-to-Break *Grumpy* dolls from the wood pulp *Grumpy* dolls to better clarify the difference as well as to put them into their own time period.

We have made three trips to the Library of Congress to spend long hours searching *Playthings* and *Toys and Novelties* trade magazines, and we have other source material as well in our *Doll Research Projects* files begun in 1956. Various other researchers have contributed valuable information on this same topic, which the collectors have absorbed like ink to a blotter. Now it is **our** pleasure to share with you, the collector, and the Effanbee Company this first section of collected source data and dolls brought together in one volume.

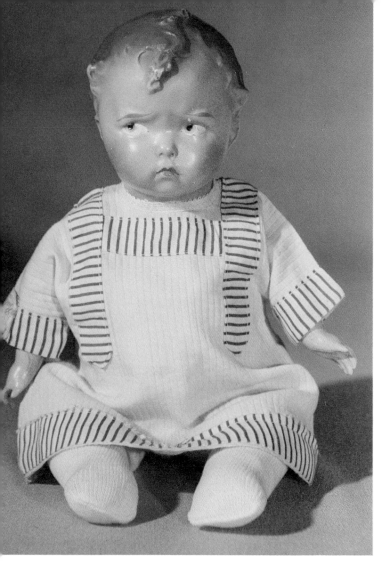

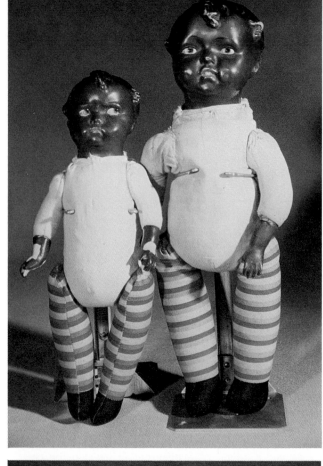

ABOVE: 14in (35.6cm) *Baby Grumpy.* See *Illustrations 84* and *85. John Axe Collection.*

ABOVE RIGHT: 15in (38.1cm) *Grumpy Aunt Dinah* with 12in (30.5cm) black *Grumpy* called *Baby Snowball.* See *Illustration 109.* Doll on left, *Pearl Morley Collection.*

BELOW RIGHT: Rare all-original black *Baby Grumpy* with black cloth legs.

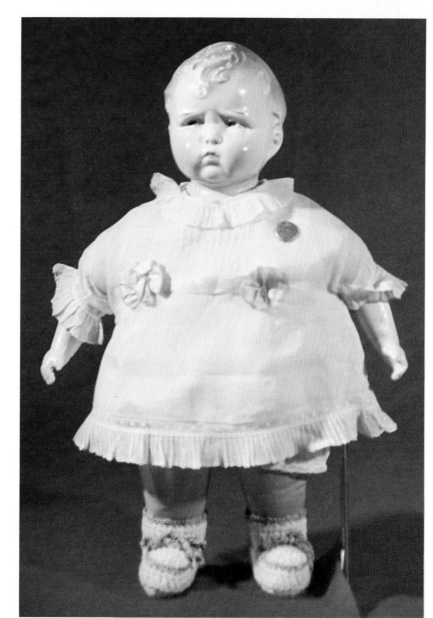

RIGHT: 17in (43.2cm) first wood pulp *Baby Grumpy* from 1923.

BELOW: Rare all-original infant *Baby Grumpy* from 1925.

I. Company History

Ten Years of Progress

It is such a revelation to delve into old records; if one reads far enough, names are not merely names anymore. The principals begin to "flesh out," their hopes and ambitions become very real. We were surprised to realize that Mr. Bernard Fleischaker was only 35 years old in 1920 when the firm had made decided successes since its inception in 1910. **Quality** was the keynote, or at least the firm was striving for it.

The major emphasis in this particular writer's style of research is **the dolls themselves,** but a greater understanding and appreciation of the tremendous effort that went into their creation adds zest to collecting. These dolls, however simple, are little segments of American history.

We have decided to print, in its entirety, a *Playthings* article of February 1920 as well as a series of articles from the same source, which began in April of the same year, so that the reader might read firsthand this enlightening material.

No doubt Effanbee arranged for this series of articles "Little Visits to a Doll Factory" to be printed. They contain a wealth of information that would have been lost to doll collectors and historians, had they not been written.

We have had a series of sketches enlarged for the book which presents the reader with a much more realistic idea of these pioneer efforts. There are three views of the Effanbee establishments. A proud banner, "Effanbee," flies atop the buildings. "Fleischaker &

Baum Manufacturers of Effanbee Dolls" is lettered on the front of the building. "Dolls Effanbee Dolls" is lettered on the Green Street and Wooster Street entrances. Ten thousand dolls could be turned out a day in 1920 with 40 hot press machines.

The Company

1910: Bernard E. Fleischaker and Hugo Baum form a partnership.
1923: Morris Lutz joined the firm.
1940: Hugo Baum passed away.
1941: Partner B. E. Fleischaker moved to California and started a new company.
1941: Bernard Baum, Hugo's son, and Walter F. Fleischaker, Bernard's brother, ran the New York business.

World War II struck a terrible blow to the doll industry. Rubber could not be used for *Dy-Dees,* imported human hair could not be had, metal for sleep eyes was not always available. Even better quality materials for costuming were in short supply. Ingenuity made it possible to carry on, but by the war's end in 1946 the company was in financial straights. Noma Electric bought the firm in 1947 and kept it until 1953. The compositin doll era was more or less finished by this time.

A Romance of the Business World

Fleischaker & Baum Celebrate Their Tenth Anniversary of Sucessful Doll Making.

Ten years ago a new doll factory was launched on Manhattan Island—the popular dolls of the day were manufactured, "unbreakable American character dolls," dolls long on strength but rather short in other respects, which fact can be frankly admitted today when American dolls are standard for doll quality throughout the world.

In the old days the worth of a doll would be demonstrated by rapping it sharply upon the head with a hammer and if the head contained sufficient "bone" and did not break it was a "good doll." Likewise if a doll could be dropped out of a five story window and land on its head without smashing, it was a—doll.

It is a long cry from those days to the days of the 1920 American doll and no history of U. S. A. doll making

would be complete without reference to the famous "Effanbee."

For this reason in these days when American dolls have come into their own and when a line of "Effanbee" standard celebrates its tenth year of progress it seems fitting to print the photos of Bernard Fleischaker and Hugo Baum and to print a few lines relative to these doll experts and their immediate associates in the upbuilding of the business.

Bernard Fleischacker, a young man thirty-five years of age, was born in "Old Kentucky," where his family has lived several generations. He came to New York in 1907, went into the novelty business on lower Broadway, later moving to Union Square, where he became associated with Hugo Baum, who had been in the notion business.

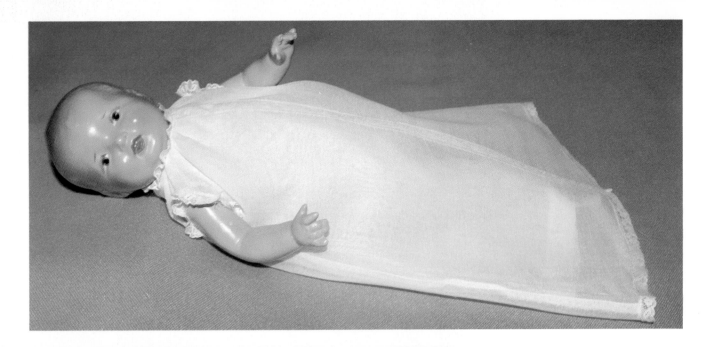

ABOVE: 12in (30.5cm) special edition *Bubbles;* painted eyes; different arms; open/closed mouth with two painted teeth; all original clothes, long christening dress. *Alice Wardell Collection.*

LEFT: 16½in (41.9cm) all-original *Bubbles* with replaced ribbons. *Ozella Roach Collection.*

RIGHT: 25½in (64.8cm) black life-size *Bubbles,* sitting; brown metal eyes; composition legs. *Frances James Collection.*

BELOW: Four versions of the smallest 13in (30.5cm) *Bubbles.* Dolls on the left and the right, *Alice Wardell Collection.* Doll second from left, *Bea Anderson Collection.*

Illustration 1. Hugo Baum.

Illustration 2. Bernard Fleischaker.

Hugo Baum was born overseas and came to America as a boy. At first he had hard work to get a foot-hold and tried many openings until he found a real partner in Mr. Fleischaker.

Ten years ago the firm began the manufacture of dolls. They realized from the very beginning that in order to be successful they would have to manufacture quality merchandise. The firm moved to 79 Fifth Avenue and remained there two years, afterward moving back to Union Square. From Union Square a move was made to 45 East Seventeenth Street in the Everett Building, their present palatial salesroom.

As a result of increased business the firm was forced to occupy larger factory quarters at 42 Wooster Street, and from year to year added one loft to another until they occupied the entire Wooster Building. In 1917 they leased 45 Greene Street, occupying the lower floor. In 1919 the firm bought the entire building, 42 to 44 Wooster Street, and also the one at 45 Greene Street. The concern is now rebuilding the structure on Greene street, adding 100,000 feet of floor space, and in addition to that the business is compelled to rent additional lofts.

Walter Fleischaker, brother of Bernard, and a member of the firm, has general charge of all territory in the states. The South and the West Indies are cared for by J. I. Hackel, another member of the firm. W. A. G. Le

Boutellier, Walter Millius and Irving Stark complete the traveling force.

F. W. Trumpore, formerly the well-known buyer for the Claflin stores, is able to render splendid service as year-round New York salesman at 45 East Seventeeth Street. J. C. Ruben is the factory manager and Miss Kitty Fleischmann, formerly assistant buyer for Gimbel Bros., is the designer of doll dresses, doll novelties and art supervisor of Effanbee products generally.

The young men of this firm are full of live ideas and have succeeded in developing their business by giving the public what it wants. Both Fleischaker and Baum are high-powered business men who accomplished what they wanted by starting out right. As a result, in a short time they produced goods that need not fear competition from any country of the world. This firm is of the opinion that the American manufacturers of dolls have made more progress in the production of dolls in a few years then Germany has in a hundred years.

Despite their great business success, these young men remained democratic and unspoiled. They are examples of what can be accomplished in America through tireless industry. Their growth also shows how a large business can be developed in a comparatively few number of years through energy and the application of modern ideas.''

From *Playthings,* February 1920.

Little Visits to a Doll Factory

by a **Veteran Buyer**

Note:—During the period of our experience as makers of EFFANBEE Dolls we have frequently had applications from heads of the principal establishments throughout the country for permission to allow groups of toy department sales people to visit our factories for the purpose of seeing how dolls are made. We have found that this interested the sight-seeing individual and helped to bring the art of selling dolls in the retail stores to a higher degree of efficiency than it had been previous to the visit. The curiosity of the majority of the public to learn something about this subject is almost universal and, indeed, the craft is quite as fascinating to the workers themselves as to strangers in the mysteries of the business.

Illustration 3. A view of the sales office at 17th Street. The Effanbee banner flies over the building. Note the lettering on the top of the second, third and fourth floors which reads, starting at the fourth floor: "FLEISCHAKER & BAUM//MANUFAC-TURERS OF//Effanbee DOLLS."

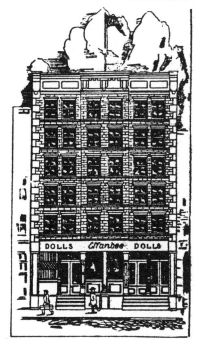

Illustration 4. This is the front of the building, the Greene Street entrance with the General Office on the first floor. The six upper floors were used for manufacturing and the basement was used for storage of raw materials.

It is unlike most trades in which the operations are mechanical and the product mere merchandise. A doll is a miniature imitation of a human being and no matter how one doll may be made to look like its mate of the same style, there is always some slight difference that makes it individual and interesting. It is for the purpose of entertaining and educating the trade who cannot find time or cannot, through force of circumstances, visit our factories that this series of articles which we shall publish in monthly installments is undertaken. The articles will continue until the subject covering the technique of our ancient trade has been at least superficially covered. We wish to state, however, that while these articles will not be exhaustive, they will be sufficiently liberal in scope to insure the reader of a valuable insight into the business of making dolls.

Our series will be entitled "Little Visits to a Doll Factory," and our call this month will take us to the door of the factory with just a peep inside to see what we shall see.

On Monday morning we left our hotel and subwayed downtown, emerging from the cellar railroad at Canal Street. There were in our crowd Miss Stevens, my assistant, and Madge White, one of the girls from the doll department, and myself. I have been in the business for nearly 35 years and have been across the water twenty times in the capacity of doll and toy buyer. For the last five years I could not go on account of the war, and I may say truthfully, that I am glad of it now, for I learned more in those years about American Toys and Dolls than I had gathered in all the years before, and this information I turned to my own good and the good of my employers.

When we came up out of the station and got our bearings I found that we were just a short distance from our objective destination, and headed northward with the girls.

I had not told them that we were going to a doll factory when we started out, as I intended to make a kind of surprise visit of it, so I kept them guessing until we were half way between the station and the factory entrance.

As we walked I inquired causually about the doll stock on hand back home and led up to the subject of dolls and their makers as we went on. By the time we had reached Greene and Grand Streets, we were interested in a discussion that threatened to become an argument as to the most approved types of dolls and how they were taking with the public.

"Well, I'll tell you what girls," I said. "I have asked for permission to visit a factory where dolls are made and that's where we are going now. You will see for yourselves just why every type has its place and importance in the business—and that rag dolls, stuffed dolls, kid body and composition dolls are in demand each for a different purpose."

Just at this point we came to and stood at the entrance of the EFFANBEE Factory at 45 Greene Street. Madge and Miss Stevens were interested in watching the employees enter as it was still early when we arrived, while I busied myself for a few moments looking over my memorandum book.

What seemed to surprise her and Miss Stevens was that the operatives did not look like the usual run of factory help. They came in a steady stream of all ages. The men had the appearance of business men rather than of factory workers, and the girls for most part rather above the average.

I asked the superintendent who stood at the door and smiled good morning to his people as they

Illustration 5. This is the back of the building, the Wooster Street entrance of the building from where the shipping was conducted. The Effanbee banner flies over the building. The building ran through an entire city block.

Illustration 6. He gave it a rub of his thumb here and there.

entered, how many there were employed in the buildings and he told me there were some 500 just then but later in the season there would be a great many more. "You see we have about 100,000 square feet of floor space," he said, "and we employ a large force in every department. On the first floor we have our General Office on the Greene Street end of the building and on the Wooster Street end our shipping department is conducted.

"There are six floors that extend through the entire block from Greene to Wooster Street. The upper floors are used exclusively for manufacturing and in the basement is our storage room for raw material and stock."

Just then the heads of the firm, B. E. Fleischaker and Hugo Baum came in and greeted us warmly. "We beat you to it this morning," I laughed as Baum laid his hand on my shoulder.

"Yes," he admitted, "that was because B. E. and I were uptown at the sales office at 17th Street this morning before we came down here, otherwise we would have been down before you were out of bed."

We all joined in a little chat in the private office of the firm for a half hour or so while Baum in his usual jolly vein entertained us with yarns about folks and events and then B. E.—that's Fleischaker—took us in hand and told us what he expected to show us. "First of all," he explained, "I'll take you to our modeling department and show you how doll heads and bodies are evolved."

Dolls for "The Female of the Species"

Before we went up to the modeling rooms, B. E. that's Fleischaker—gave us a short talk on child life and the principle of the play instinct and the value of dolls as educators for the female of the species. Then as we went up to the studios where the sculptors and artists were at work, he also told us something about the temperament and peculiarities of the modelers which interested us very much.

Like all men of their profession, they wore their hair rather long. Some of their fine heads were curly-locked and some wore wavy pompadours. Each was clad in the usual painter's smock and they all wore flowing black bow ties. The chief artist sang little snatches from operas in a high falsetto every now and then which seemed to give zest to his appetite for work.

The studio on the top floor reminded Madge of a photograph gallery and she asked whether there was a camera for taking pictures included in the apparatus which the artists used.

"Wouldn't it be fine to have a group picture of our party taken to send back home," she exclaimed, "To be printed in the paper with a story about our visit to this factory." "Don't be ridiculous," put in Miss Stevens, "this is not a trip to Niagara Falls, this is where we learn about dolls." The side chatter of the girls failed to draw my attention, for I became interested at once in a young man who stood at his work, hardly noticing our entrance. A half finished model of a doll's head in some kind of white clay was perched on the work bench before him. He gave it a rub of his thumb here and there and with some small instruments, a number of which lay handy, he added minute bits of clay where they were needed to round out the features, or he scraped a bit off where it was not needed.

Madge Meets a Pair of Soulful Italian Eyes

There were several artists at work in the room, each on a different object—and round about on shelves were hundreds of casts of all manner of doll parts—heads, bodies, hands, feet and what not, in all sizes and shapes. It reminded me more of an art museum than a photograph gallery, and I remarked it to the girls. Madge was too much interested in the work of one of the artist just then, however, to notice what I said. She divided her time 75-25 to the young man who was just starting operations on a lump of clay which was beginning to show signs of evoluting into the trunk or body of a doll. It was certainly interesting to watch him slice and pat his clay into the semblance of a graceful little figure. I am not sure whether in the division of her time tho' that the 75-25 did not go the greater part to the young man. I'll admit he was rather good to look at with his soulful Italian eyes, and Madge isn't such a bad looker either. The young man himself had an eye for beauty for I noticed that he took a long time to explain his work to her.

"This body," he told her, as his big black eyes snapped with animation, "will be an exact reproduction in clay of the drawing I have here. The drawing was made by a celebrated artist and is, as you see, shown from three different views or angles. When my model is finished it will be cast in plaster of paris and from the

Illustration 7. Our artist was soon ready for the next operation

Illustration 8. Forty hot presses line the walls.

plaster the dies will be made." Miss Stevens could not understand just how the cast was to be made and turned to B. E. for information. "I'll let him make a cast for you from this new head which our chief artist has just finished," he said, and at once gave directions for the performance.

Like a Potter of Old He Moulds His Doll

The chief carefully removed the new clay head from its little pedestal and oiled it carefully all over with a small feather brush. Bringing a pan he dumped into it a quantity of white plaster of paris and mixed it with water to a stiff paste. When all was ready he poured the mass into a small square box about four inches deep and six inches in length and width. Before it "set" or began to harden he carefully lifted the oiled clay head and pressed it gently and firmly face down into the soft plaster and let it stand.

While we waited the girls conversed with the artists while B. E. and I traded experiences and discussed the doll and toy business generally. Our artist was ready for the next operation again in about half an hour and we were all attention to witness the next process.

He produced his little pot of oil again and dipping his feather brush into it oiled the smooth edge of the plaster that extended to the sides of the box and prepared a second box of plaster exactly like the first. When this was done he picked up the first box from which the back half of the head now protruded and turning it over without removing it from the box, pressed the back of the head just as gently as he had done in the first place with the face half, into the second box.

The Doll Maker Is the Sculptor of Commerce

It took another half hour or so for that second half to harden and as the edges had been oiled the two halves came apart easily when the hardening was complete. Of course, all this was not new to me, but Madge and Miss Stevens were as pleased as two children when the clay head was removed to see how clean and perfect the negative mold looked when it was opened. The artist explained the details of making additional models from the cast which was simply a reversal of the formula just gone through. When the model is intended for direct die making he told them the clay model is made directly of plaster.

It was nearing noon by this time, and as I could not give our entire day to our highly entertaining visit, I proposed that B. E. and I take the girls to lunch, but the artist had forestalled us and had already invited Madge and Miss Stevens to lunch, so we left them to themselves and went out for a stag dinner over on Broadway, at which Baum joined us.

Toy Buyers Swap Stories at Luncheon

It was almost two o'clock when I left B. E. and Baum, the day before having enjoyed our noon luncheon immensely. At the restaurant we met Kearney of Buckly. Brothers, and Carlton, his valuable assistant. If you have never met Kearney, you have an interesting experience still awaiting you.

Big, rotund, whole-hearted, Kearney is a tonic to tired nerves, and Carlton is just as clever as his superior in his own quiet way. The banter and crossfire of conversation kept us all in excellent humor all through the meal, and we parted most reluctantly. I went uptown to meet Miss Stevens and Madge, as we had previously agreed, though it had been my intention to stop on the way uptown for a short call on my friend Stegman at Lacy's. We had lingered too long at our luncheon, however, so I had no time to spare. I hurried over to the Waldorf, where Miss Stevens and Madge had promised to meet me, and arrived there just on time. The girls were full of praises for the young artists who had taken them to lunch and deluged me with a glowing account of their adventure. We spent the remainder of the afternoon looking over some lines of goods we were short on back home and returned to our hotel rather tired with the day's work and entertainment.

10,000 Dolls a Day Is Effanbee Factory Capacity

The next morning at nine o'clock we were again at the EFFANBEE Doll factory but this time B. E. and Baum were there before we arrived. We joked them a little about their early arrival and both of them took the good-natured grilling with feigned embarrassment. Baum took us at once to the hot press department, where we found the men already an hour at work at their presses. There were about forty of these ranged against the walls of the great floor, in the middle of which a huge automatic mixing machine rumbled and groaned as it turned over and over on its axis.

Illustration 9. Automatic mixing machine.

Baum Describes "The Hot Press Room"

Baum conducted us to the middle of the floor and pointed out to us a pile of something that looked like wet sand that had just been removed from the mixer. "That," he said, "is the first step in the making of a doll. We place a quantity of pulp into this receptacle and mix it with chemical binders so that it will hold together when put into the presses. If these chemicals were not there, the pulp would crumble like dust when it is pressed. After it is well mixed, the men take it in buckets to their machines and here you see it pressed into its first recognizable shape."

Madge and Miss Stevens registered surprise and truly feminine curiosity, and I will confess that, although I had seen dolls made several years ago, the improvements in their manufacture had left me almost a total stranger to the art and I was very much interested in the way they were now made with modern equipment.

The presses were fitted with upper and nether bronze dies, each of which were about sixteen by twenty-four inches on the surface and nearly four inches thick. I should have guessed that each would weigh approximately sixty pounds.

Dies and Gas Flames Are needed to Make Beautiful Dolls

The upper dies are made to fit into the lower ones in such a manner that when a layer of the sand-like pulp was packed on top of the lower set it leaves a proper thickness for the particular part that is to be stamped into shape. Above the upper die a double row of tiny gas flames sent down their blue flames to heat the die, and underneath the lower die a similar double row of blue blazes sent up heat from below.

A long lever at the side of the machine when pressed down by the operator brought the two dies together, like the jaws of a giant animal, and from between came the hissing and sputtering of the damp pulp as the flame-heated dies baked it dry.

"It takes about six minutes to bake a setting," explained Baum, "and when one setting is removed from the press another is put in at once. Each part of the doll is made in halves and these halves are then set together for the next process."

Each Press Makes One Complete Part

You will see that on some of the presses we make heads and on others arms and bodies. No press makes a complete doll at one operation, but each makes a complete part, such as the front and back of a head, or the front and back of a body, or upper or lower leg.

Madge wanted to know why all the parts were brown in color when they came out of the press, but Miss Stevens wisely advised her to wait and see how the coloring was done, as it certainly could not be done in the hot press, and Baum promised he would show us how it was done on our next visit.

"It is, I think, quite different from what you will expect, and I assure you a most entertaining demonstration," he said.

Why Madge Missed the Matinee

Miss Stevens and Madge had determined to witness a matinee performance, after I left them yesterday, as they had heard that a pretty little girl carried an EFFANBEE Doll in the play, but as there were no suitable orchestra seats to be had, they decided to return to the factory and to continue their sight-seeing.

"Really," declared Madge, "the doll factory is as good a show as any we can go to, and we can see the play when the company comes to our city. But the EFFANBEE factory must be seen in New York."

The heads of the firm were in their private offices when the girls returned to the factory, and with them was Miss Corcoran, of the great firm of Light Bros., of Philadelphia. They were evidently discussing the details of some important matters, for neither B. E. nor Baum could spare the time to take the girls through the factory in the afternoon.

Illustration 10. Walter Fleischaker, brother of Bernard Fleischaker, and a member of the firm.

Walter Plays Host to the Ladies

Fortunately, though, another member of the firm, in the person of Walter Fleischaker, was at the factory just then, and B. E. introduced him to the girls, cautioning him to take good care of them and to explain anything about the making of the dolls which the girls might wish to know.

Their guides heretofore were excellent demonstrators, but none of them were as expert in entertaining the ladies as Walter.

Madge exchanged significant glances with Miss Stevens as they acknowledged their introduction to the dashing Walter, and received his smiling nod in return.

"Isn't he grand?" whispered Madge to Miss Stevens as they trailed behind him on their way up to the grinding and polishing department.

"Did you notice the dimples when he smiles?" returned Miss Stevens, softly. "I am glad we did not go to the theatre," she confided.

Effanbee White Clad Crew

Stepping out of the elevator which carried them to the fourth floor, long rows of workers in white overall suits seated at benches greeted their eyes. At the far end

Illustration 11. The grinding wheels.

Illustration 12. Filling and polishing.

of the great floor, lines of the same white clad young men sat on high stools before rapidly revolving emery wheels. A hum of machinery and clicking of pulley belts as the connected edges passed over the pulleys gave life to the picturesque scene. Walter led the way toward the far side of the floor.

Half way toward the grinding wheels they stopped a few moments to watch the "stickers" at work gluing the front and back halves of doll parts together which had been delivered to them from the hot presses. These operations were wonderfully dextrous and rapid. From long practice they had become expert in the handling of the parts, and their hands fairly flew. The large trays beside each man into which the "stickers" dropped the glued parts in a remarkably short time filled the trays with neat rows of doll heads or doll bodies. A stout young man passed in front of Madge carrying a filled tray high above his head and avoided a collision of the tray with her hat by a fraction of an inch as it tilted with the movement of his body.

Madge dodged and laughed, and Walter good-naturedly shook a warning finger at the young man and shouted, "Look out!" There had been no damage, though, and they followed the tray to see what would be done with its contents. He set it down between two "grinders" and went back for another load, and the busy grinders attacked the contents of the tray at once.

Doll Making at Close Range

Deftly they applied the seamed edges of the parts to the abrasive wheels and ground off the rough edges, while the small bits from the half-finished heads flew into metalic receptacles arranged to catch the small chips which the grinding wheels bit from the seams. As each tray of parts was finished it was again shouldered by a new set of carriers and taken to the filling department where any small roughness that still appeared on the parts was examined and every little depression or unsightly crevice filled with a prepared composition and the entire piece treated to a thorough rubbing with emery cloth and fine sand paper.

"This operation," Walter explained, "is called polishing, and when the fillers and polishers again return the pieces to the trays their work is indeed well done, for each one takes pride in turning out work which his inspector will compliment him on. Not a blemish

remains when the polishers have smoothed the last fleck of dust with the little fine-haired brush which they use for the purpose; and be it body, leg, arm or head on which they may be working; the job is as nearly perfect as it can be made."

As Miss Stevens and Madge had been sight-seeing at the factory all morning and the greater part of the afternoon, they were well nigh tired out, particularly as they had been on their feet all that time, and when Walter suggested that they visit the next floor to inspect the dipping department, they unwillingly declined, for their aching limbs refused to carry them further; so it was agreed that they would see that operation the following day. Walter conducted the girls back to the office, and Miss Stevens thanked him for his attention and kindness, to which Madge added "me, too." By rare good luck, Walter's chauffeur entered the front door just as they came in from the rear, and Walter caught his signal that the car was at the door.

A Long Motor Ride

It did not require much persuasion on Walter's part to induce the girls to accept his invitation for a spin uptown in the car, especially as he had assured them that he would drop them safely at their hotel after the ride. It was a jolly and tired party that piled into the big, dark blue car, and the order from Walter to the chauffeur sent it ahead on a longer journey than any of them had intended to make that day.

The ride uptown and through Central Park invigorated all of them, and the almost noiseless purring of the motor hardly indicated the swift movement of the machine. They chatted like old friends and laughed heartily at Walter's witty sallies. None of them paid the least attention to a gray touring car that had followed them through Central Park and was still behind them as they struck the old Boston Post Road; neither did they notice how gradually the distance between the two cars was closing as evening approached.

They had no idea that it would be many days before any of the party would see the factory again nor the time I would have to find Madge and Miss Stevens.

Watching and Waiting

At the customary dinner hour that evening, I waited in the lobby of our hotel for Miss Stevens and Madge to make their appearance as usual and grew somewhat

impatient at the delay, but attributed it to the feminine failing of lingering too long with dressing and primping. I paced the floor for awhile and then sat down and passed the time watching the ebb and flow of the human tide about me.

A half hour of this decided me to call their room by telephone to ascertain the reason for their tardiness. I was surprised and annoyed when the switchboard operator informed me that "they don't answer." I thought for a few minutes and took a few more turns up and down the lobby, wondering what could be the matter. Twice in the next half hour I repeated the telephone performance, with no better result than at first, before it occurred to me to inquire of the clerk whether he had seen them come in.

"No, the key to their room is still in the box," he told me politely, "and I am sure they have not been here since they left this morning." As it was now after seven I was alarmed lest something may have happened to prevent their safe return.

A Restful Night

I called B. E. at his residence by phone immediately and inquired whether he knew where the girls were. It was a relief, indeed, to learn that they had left the factory in Walter's car and that they were probably safe in his care. I was eased and thanked him and went out to dine by myself. They had not yet appeared when I came back, so I conjured myself into a conclusion that Walter had taken them out for the evening and with no more serious thought than that they should have let me know where they had gone, and a natural fretfulness on account of the situation, I turned in for the night and for a good snooze.

Doubts and Fears

The next morning alarm and worry again seized me when I discovered their continued absence and I hastened down to the Effanbee Factory to solve the mystery if possible. Walter was not there nor had any other member of the firm arrived, excepting Julius Hackel. Bland and docile, easy of speech and manner, Julius is one of those fellows who immediately set you at ease. His geniality and reassuring conversation smoothed my doubts and fears and at his suggestion to make a short trip through the dipping department of the factory

until some of the other members of the firm arrived, I readily acceded. So we left word at the office to send Walter to us as soon as he should arrive.

An Expensive Mixture

On the fifth floor the pungent odor of fresh harmless chemicals permeated the big room. It was not an unpleasant smell yet I do not think a lady would select it as a perfume for her kerchief. The contents of dozen copper caldrons like those employed in great hotels for cooking soups and broths were being stirred by men with paddles while around each caldron were wound steam coils to keep the liquid warm. The beautiful flesh colored mixture which they stirred is made up of harmless pigments and ingredients chief among which is glycerine which is very expensive and without which this mixture cannot be made. It is used to give the doll its skin and is called "dip," because the parts are dipped into it instead of its being applied with a brush like paint, and then placed on racks to harden.

When the doll parts which have been filled and polished are ready for this process they are brought in trays to the dippers and each piece is treated to a pink bath and then set on a wooden pin, which stick up like large nails on rack-like tables, and left there until the hardening is complete. Then they are again passed to polishers, who rub them down with fine emery cloth, so that every detail and feature is smooth. Next comes the trimmer, who cuts off along the edges all the ends of the "dip" which in its fluid state ran off during and after dipping. So precious is the dip liquid that every particle which has run off and rests on the table is removed and remelted in the pots for use again.

Why Effanbee Dolls Are Beautiful

Hackel told me that one of the reasons why Effanbee Dolls all had that smooth and beautifully natural finish was due to the frequent rubbing and polishing that each piece was subjected to, for I noticed that after the dipping process the polishers again plied the emery cloth and brush to every part of the dipped piece. "The dip used on Effanbee Dolls," said he, "is not the same as that used by the great number of doll makers. Our secret formula is one that our chemist perfected for us after many months of experimenting, and its peculiar quality is that the detail and character of the finer lines of the head and body are accented, while in most others this is entirely overlooked and the features blurred.'' I had often wondered why Effanbee Dolls had achieved such wonderful success, and why they are so generally preferred, and this was indeed a revelation of considerable importance to me. I knew that I had always liked Effanbee Dolls for their dainty appearance, but I failed to understand why they were such particularly bright looking dolls.

Just as we were entering the spraying department, the office boy approached us and said that Walter had arrived, and we hurried down to the office at once to learn what had happened to Miss Stevens and Madge.

I made an earnest effort to annihilate time in my haste to reach the office on the ground floor and left Hackel to follow me by the slower but more convenient means of the elevator. Walter was there, but without the girls. He eyed me curiously and waited for the verbal fire which he seemed to expect on my entry. He did not have long to wait. I talked fast, and propounded questions as rapidly as he answered. The only thing I learned with certainty was that Miss Stevens and Madge had disappeared.

Where Did the Girls Go?

Try as we would, neither of us could solve the mystery. Over and over we examined every possible theory which might put us on the right track. It was useless. The artists who had shown so much interest in the girls and who had taken them to lunch a few days before, were at their work in the studio. Clearly they were not involved. This we ascertained beyond doubt or question. Our first impulse was to notify the authorities, but on second thought and consideration we concluded that this course would not be the wisest just then. The story might get into the papers and I felt some reluctance in letting it be known back home that I had not exercised sufficient care in guarding them. One day of waiting could do no great harm in any event, so it was decided to wait until evening at least for developments.

Madge White Has an Uncle

Seiman, of Grand Rapids joined us in the office just as we were about to leave. He is an old friend of mine from my home state, and I was mighty glad to see him and tell him my troubles, particularly because he knew the girls. What I did *not* know was that he was an uncle of Madge White. He heard the story from the beginning, and promised to give us his aid in finding the girls. ''They'll turn up all right,'' he assured me. ''No fear for

that.'' I thought I detected a twinkle in his eye, but a second look convinced me of his earnestness. ''We'll just remain here this morning,'' he said, ''and if we hear nothing by noon I'll give you some information that might help.'' He refused to be drawn out any further, and as he was Madge's uncle, I thought it wise to be guided by his advice.

Swapping Stories

It looked very much as if the morning would be wearisome and difficult. There was nothing to do but wait. Seiman appeared less worried than any of us, and we were soon talking shop, as buyers will, who are in New York on buying expeditions.

We discussed our successes with EFFANBEE Dolls, and agreed that quality plus had been the factor which had built up the business of the firm. Walter described to us many of the newly-invented machines which had been installed to improve the appearance of their dolls. He conducted us to the upper floors of the factory, to let us see for ourselves, and to demonstrate how these machines were used.

''When we first began the manufacture of sleeping eye dolls,'' he said, ''we found it necessary to cut the eye openings by hand. It was a slow and tedious performance. Apparently it was a trifling thing, but actually each small and seemingly unimportant detail, carefully done, helps to make perfection more easily possible in the finished article. This is now done by an automatic eye cutting device.''

The Effanbee ''Eye-Opener''

He pointed out a machine and seated himself before it, pressing the pedal with his foot a few times to demonstrate the manner in which it was worked. Two steel cutting dies, their edges shaped to represent the curve of the upper and lower lid of the eye, are set side by side in the machine and are so arranged that when power is applied to the pedal these dies move downward and exactly meet the indications for the eyes on the head of the doll, which the operator places in position to receive them. With one clip, both apertures are punched. When the head is removed from the machine, the thickness of the head substance does not permit the placing of the eyes sufficiently close to the surface to make them look natural. The inside of the head is therefore applied to what is known as a ''phrasing machine,'' which shaves it down from the inside of the lids, thinning them, to natural proportions. This also

Illustration 15. The eye cutting machine.

Illustration 16. The cold press

permits the fitting of the eyes in such a manner that they will open and close easily and make the doll look very lifelike.

The Electric Phrasing Machine

The phrasing machine itself is a very simple contrivance, being merely a shaft, on the end of which a small steel ball with a cutting surface revolves swiftly by electric power.

When the thinning process is finished, an expert, with a steady hand and the help of a fine file, carefully finishes the edges of the eyelids, and this is all that is needed to prepare the head for the next stage of the work.

How Doll Hands Are Made

A short distance from where we were standing, half a dozen stalwart men were operating several cold press machines. When the trade was in its infancy, these had been used for making doll heads and doll hands, but now doll hands alone are made on them.

A mass of dark gray composition, for all the world in shape like a prepared baking of bread dough, lay on the work bench before each man. In making the hands, a small portion of the dough is taken from the mass and rolled out in the shape of a band about four inches wide and twelve inches long. This is laid on the face of the bronze die, and bronze cores placed. Another strip of the dough is placed on top, and the remainder or top part of the die superimposed to complete the whole piece. The set is then placed into the levered cold press and subjected to a heavy pressure.

Cold Press and Hot Press Analyzed

It takes about seventy-two hours for the hardening or seasoning to be completed, after the hands have been pressed into shape, before they can be dipped. This seasoning is simply to allow the moisture to evaporate from the composition.

Illustration 17. View of doll factory showing the doll heads being taken out of the molds. *Toys and Novelties,* January 1927.

There is considerable difference between the dies of the hot press and those of the cold press. The hot press dies are made with an upper and lower half, which fit *into* each other in such a manner as to produce a solid half piece at each pressing. The hot press pieces represent the front half and the back half of a part and must be joined together with glue to make the complete piece. The cold press dies produce one entire part complete by means of the core.

Walter had one of the men make a number of different sizes of hands so that we could observe the work and see how the hollow was made by removing the bronze core, when the hand, bearing the small part of the forearm, was removed from the presses.

In my judgment, the cold press will remain for many years as the most suitable type of machine for making doll hands. It seems particularly well adapted to that sort of work. Each machine is capable of turning out from three to six pairs of hands about every three minutes, according to the size.

A Die Cost as Much as an Automobile

A set of dies, which consists of two pieces, costs about a thousand dollars, and from five to seven sets are needed for a full complement. I did not require pencil and paper to figure that the investment for this part of the work alone represented a neat sum, and I am sure that the machinery necessary to equip a factory of the size and efficiency of the EFFANBEE plant must be considerable.

Seiman was impressed with the clocklike movements of the men and the regularity with which the finished hands dropped into the receiving basket as they were taken from the dies.

Walter Receives a Telegram

It was rapidly nearing noon, and although I was entertained and interested by Walter's demonstrations, my mind kept constantly reverting to Miss Stevens and Madge; and I wondered whether by any chance Seiman might know something of their whereabouts. It was at least comforting to known that Madge's uncle did not show any great anxiety concerning her and Miss Stevens.

We were engrossed in conversation regarding projected inventions and newly patented processes when an office boy handed Walter a telegram which had just been received. I looked anxiously at Walter as he ripped open the envelope containing the message.

Author's note: *Playthings* or the Effanbee company inadvertently omitted the ending of this article, "Little Visits To A Doll Factory" story and went on with other topics.

Illustration 18. An air brush artist painting the cheeks pink and making the head brown. *Toys and Novelties,* January 1927.

Illustration 19. An electric oven used for baking dolls' heads. This illustration was obtained from a library photograph file with no date or source included. It surely appears to be from the *Saturday Evening Post* and may be inside the Effanbee factory. The huge ovens held a great many pieces at once. In the background are racks completely to the ceiling for waiting pieces.

MANUFACTURING HISTORY

1910: Partnership is formed by Bernard E. Fleischaker and Hugo Baum.

1910 to 1911: No record available on which dolls were sold at this time.

1912: *Foxy Teddy Bear,* composition head, plush body
The Fairy Brand Character Dolls
Baby Dainty (an infant)
Johnny-Tu-Face
Little Walter
Miss Coquette ⎤ ⎡same mold, differ-
Naughty Marietta ⎦ ⎣ent costumes

1913: Begin to use EFFanBEE *Eff* (for Fleischaker) *an Bee* (for Baum)

1913: *Betty Bounce*
Baby Bright Eyes, Jr.
Bobby (Baby Huggims in 1915)
Baby Dainty — with pacifier
Pajama Baby (costume name for *Baby Dainty)*

1914: *Jumbo Baby*
Baby Grumpy
Baby Grumpy, Jr.
Baby Dainty (an infant)
Betty Bounce
Tango Kiddies (*Betty Bounce* with red, blue or green hair)

1915: *Reversible Rag Doll* (see the 1915 catalog reprinted)
Sleep eye dolls
12 new *Grumpys*

1916: *Bright Eyes*
Dorothy Dainty (infant with pacifier)
Uncle Sam
Columbia

1917: *Mary Jane* — wood pulp
War Nurses — wood pulp
Bathing Bud — wood pulp
Grumpy — Hard-to-Break composition

1918: *Bathing Bud* — wood pulp
Baby Dainty — infant
Dolly Dumpling
Our Baby
Christening Babies, some with pacifier
Baby Catherine
Sammie the Soldier
Jackie the Sailor
Lady Grumpy (standing girl with wig)
Lady Grumpy's Brother (standing boy with wig)
The *Coquette* (standing girl, molded hair)
Jumbo Infants (painted eye, mohair wig)

1918: *Baby Blanche* — standing girl, pursed mouth, wig
(*Sweetheart Boy/Girl* — costume versions of *Baby Blanche)*
Katie Kroose Girl/Boy — costume versions of *Baby Blanche*

1919: Buy American Campaign begins
Mary Jane, wood pulp head
Mary Jane, bisque head by Lenox Potteries
Riding Hood Bud
Valentine Bud
French Baby
Infants, toddlers, *Christening Babies*

1920: Buy American Campaign continues
Mary Jane — wood pulp
Kid body dolls
Composition dolls
Grumpy returns
Bisque baby doll
Rag dolls

Buy American-Made Toys

S ANTA CLAUS—the good American that he is—this year has turned to Uncle Sam for his toys. In fact the pair of them have been working together for months and months for our American kiddies.

They have planned and arranged and built really wonderful things. They are original—there is a host of new toy ideas.

They are conceived and built by American men and women —they are not the thoughts or work of foreign countries.

American-made toys are best for the children because each toy is perfect. The design is right, the craftsmanship is careful—there are more to pick and choose from. They are educational—they are amusing.

This Christmas make children happier with American-made toys.

This season—this coming New Year—resolve to support American industries—to protect American trade.

Patronize the toy store that shows the circle of Uncle Sam and the laughing, happy children. You will find there the greatest assortment of Christmas and all-year-round toys— the best ones, too.

Patronize the toy store that displays these signs

This space is contributed in the cause of American industries by the Toy Manufacturers of the U. S. A. Flatiron Building, New York

Illustration 21. Advertisement urging the purchase of American-made toys for Christmas. *The Ladies' Home Journal,* December 1919.

American-Made TOYS

Toy Hours Build Patriotism

T HAT is, if the kiddies have American-Made Toys to play with. The splendid teachings, the 100 per cent "Americanism," that boys and girls absorb in school and at home, can be furthered and enriched if the play hour—the toy hour is surrounded by real American things.

Buy American-Made Toys

Give your children the original conceptions—the careful craftsmanship of American men and women, not the thoughts of foreign countries. Toy stores—the far-seeing patriotic ones everywhere, are displaying the sign

of American-Made Toys. Look for it— look for the circle of Uncle Sam with the happy children on his knee. It represents a national benefit—a great big help—a real toy joy, to the coming generation.

"Made in U. S. A." is the guarantee of American-Made Toys —the best that are procurable.

This space is contributed to the cause of American Industries by the Toy Manufacturers of the U. S. A., Flatiron Building, New York City.

Illustration 20. Advertisement expounding the virtues of American-made toys. *The Ladies' Home Journal,* November 1919.

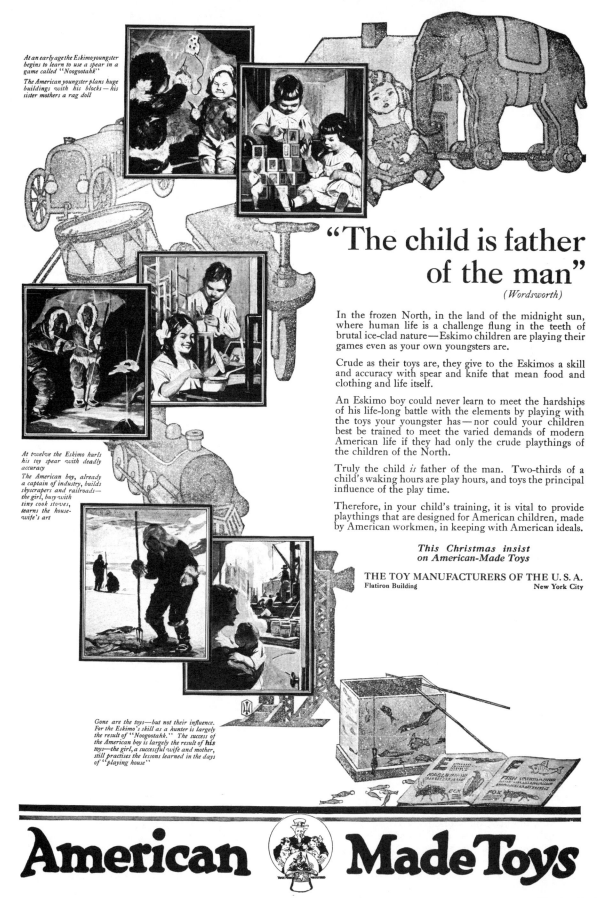

At an early age the Eskimo youngster begins to learn to use a spear in a game called "Noogootahk"

The American youngster plans huge buildings with his blocks — his sister mothers a rag doll

At twelve the Eskimo hurls his toy spear with deadly accuracy

The American boy, already a captain of industry, builds skyscrapers and railroads— the girl, busy with tiny cook stoves, learns the house-wife's art

Gone are the toys—but not their influence. For the Eskimo's skill as a hunter is largely the result of "Noogootahk." The success of the American boy is largely the result of his toys—the girl, a successful wife and mother, still practises the lessons learned in the days of "playing house"

"The child is father of the man"

(Wordsworth)

In the frozen North, in the land of the midnight sun, where human life is a challenge flung in the teeth of brutal ice-clad nature—Eskimo children are playing their games even as your own youngsters are.

Crude as their toys are, they give to the Eskimos a skill and accuracy with spear and knife that mean food and clothing and life itself.

An Eskimo boy could never learn to meet the hardships of his life-long battle with the elements by playing with the toys your youngster has — nor could your children best be trained to meet the varied demands of modern American life if they had only the crude playthings of the children of the North.

Truly the child *is* father of the man. Two-thirds of a child's waking hours are play hours, and toys the principal influence of the play time.

Therefore, in your child's training, it is vital to provide playthings that are designed for American children, made by American workmen, in keeping with American ideals.

This Christmas insist on American-Made Toys

THE TOY MANUFACTURERS OF THE U.S.A.
Flatiron Building   New York City

American Made Toys

Illustration 22. Yet another advertisement urging that American-made toys be bought for Christmas. *The Ladies' Home Journal,* December 1920.

The most familiar doll of this period is *Baby Grumpy*, which had a cloth body stuffed, for lightness, with ground cork. The heads, especially in large sizes, were quite heavy as the material was very dense. *Playthings* in 1920 described early Effanbee dolls as having been of a concrete-type composition. Some have interpreted this to mean a rough, coarse finish but it could not be further from the truth. Side seams were not polished on these early efforts but the finish was excellent. Denivelle's method was said to be the most expensive, and more of them seemed to have survived in good shape then have Horsman's Can't Break 'Em dolls, one of which was *The Campbell Kid*.

Dorothy Coleman, in the 1973 souvenir book of St. Petersburg, Florida, wrote a fascinating report on the work of Otto Ernst Denivelle. The trade magazine *Playthings* calls him a "famous doll maker and pioneer among doll makers."

Mrs. Coleman stated that around 1910 two young men just out of school, Otto Ernst Denivelle and his brother, were experimenting with formulas for making composition dolls. While still in school, Mr. Joseph Kallus would go on weekends to work with these brothers. After the death of his brother, Otto carried on the work alone.

Eventually Otto Denivelle's secret formulas were used in the making of their dolls (DECO's dolls) for Effanbee, according to the 1915 Effanbee catalog. "Deco" was the marking used by Denivelle on his dolls, or at least on some of them. Some dolls marked "Deco" have been found with all-original clothing bearing Effanbee cloth labels.

There was a *Baby Dainty*, an infant at this period; *Little Walter; Johnny-Tu-Face; and Naughty Marietta*, a *Coquette*-type inspired by the German Heubach bisque doll. Later, nearly every company doing early compositions had a *Coquette*-type. (Louis Amberg & Son called theirs *Laughing Marietta*.)

By 1913 *Betty Bounce* was offered, and new in 1914 was the much sought after *Baby Grumpy*, as well as a *Catholic Sister*, and *Jumbo Infant* (12in [53.3cm] long) dolls. All these had the ground cork-stuffed cloth torsos. Using a magnifying glass, one can see a *Catholic Sister* displayed in the illustration titled "A Corner of Our Sample Room." There also seem to be *Baseball Players* not shown in the catalog. In 1916 Hugo Baum designed *Uncle Sam* and *Columbia*. *Mary Jane*, a typical ball-jointed German style doll came along in 1917, as well as nurses with red cross emblems on their uniforms.

By 1918 the wood pulp formula was adopted. First examples were *Dolly Dumpling* and *Baby Bud* as well as an all-composition infant. These do not seem to be the work of Denivelle or those of the earlier period, but no records remain to be certain. No doubt the wood pulp formula would be changed from time to time and improved over the years. No composition doll could top the perfection of the later *American Children*, the Brus of the composition doll world.

Effanbee Catalog, 1915

Nothing seems more precious to a researcher then the survival, intact, of an old trade catalog. So little is known of the formative years of the American doll industry that it was decided to print the entire 1915 catalog.

Six thousand two hundred heads a day were said to be molded by Effanbee. By the size of the heads in comparison to the men, the doll on page 7 of the catalog appears to be for a 21in (53.3cm) model, *Our Baby* marked "108." These large dolls with ground cork-stuffed bodies and Hard-to-Break heads are seldom found. Mr. Morris Lutz of Effanbee stated that so many dolls were sent to South America that the early doll catalogs were printed in Spanish editions as well as English. So many versions of large babies are not commonly found and may have been the great bulk of what was sent to South America.

The largest standing dolls were 15in (38.1cm) tall, mainly dressed in simple cottons in the style of the period. The most expensive were large babies, some with glass eyes, with lace-trimmed lingerie clothes or a lamb's wool brush suit, cap, sweater and leggings. Few of these seem to have survived.

On page 11 *School Girl* is a costume name for *Pouting Bess*, that is "*Pouting Bess* as a schoolgirl." The doll named *Billy Boy* appears to be *Baby Huggims* with standing legs. *Brick Bodkins*, on page 13, with an open/closed mouth and teeth is a non-grumpy version of the same child used for modeling *Baby Grumpy*. His black counterparts are *Aunt Dinah* and *Uncle Mose*, rather youthful looking for adult models. (Their child, *Baby Grumpy* in black face, is named *Baby Snowball*.)

Baby Ethel appears to be the same as *Baby Huggims* with a change of costume. The very first use of the name *Baby Dainty*, a sober infant, seems to derive from the lacy clothes, a bit fancier than the others. The mouth is cut open for a pacifier.

Baby Ethel (*Huggims'* mold), *Kutie* and *Baby Blanche* came with painted molded shoes and socks. The author has never located one of these particular models. Possibly they were exported.

No inches are given in this catalog but as many as five sizes were available on some baby models. One doll had a curly mohair wig and another had glass eyes. This would be common later on but was rare in this Hard-to-Break (Effanbee's Can't Break 'Em type) era.

On page 18 are character face *Jumbo Girl* and *Jumbo Boy*, the girl not yet located. There is a *Jumbo Boy/Soldier* version as well. The *Tiny Tads* are miniature versions of other dolls, *Coquette* and *Betty Bounce* are recognizable. Babies at the top of page 19 are from the same mold as the 1915 *Baby Dainty* but not designated such. Those in the bottom row have mohair wigs. On page 20 *Baby Darling* appears to be a version of *Baby Dainty*. *Baby Bobbins* is another version of *Baby Huggims* but with the body having composition legs with molded shoes and socks. *Imperial Baby*, number 1190-4, being royal, has fancier clothes and what appear to be real leather slippers—such as used on bisque dolls of the day.

The novelty toys on page 21 must have been a child's delight on Christmas morning. There were other Wiggle Waggle toys besides the dog. Note electric eye teddy bears were made.

The author has spent time with a magnifying glass pouring over the Sample Room illustration on page 22. There appear to be uniformed baseball boys and a Catholic nun, as well as white and dark teddy bears and a dog which is not on a wiggle waggle platform. A salesman proudly shows off a baby doll model.

On page 23 men and women can be seen sewing small garments, while others are dressing the dolls. The painting and spraying department shows men apparently spraying color on the heads and others seated doing fine work by hand.

DOLLS

Ancient and Modern

Dolls of the Ancients.

Since prehistoric times little girls have been fascinated by dolls, and ethnologists are continually learning more about the playthings of the children of centuries ago.

In a recent excavation near the ancient city of Antenoe in Egypt, Prof. Thomas A. Whittemore of Tufts College found a rag doll with movable arms and a head of wood.

Dolls were also common in ancient Greece and Rome. The Vatican and Museum Carpequa both have dolls in their collections which were found in the Catacombs.

In Syria, the little girls had mechanical dolls which were manipulated by pulling a string, thus moving the arms and legs much after the fashion of jumping jacks.

In Australia dolls of wax were made by the natives, and even the Red Indian tribes and Eskimos of Alaska were fond of dolls.

The inventive mind of the Ancient Greeks created dolls of wax and clay which were decorated with bright colors and had movable limbs and clothes that were made to put on and take off. They were exquisitely dressed and were made to represent gods and heroes.

Most of our knowledge of dolls of long ago has been gained by the ethnologists who found these toys of past ages in ancient tombs. It is believed that as children of the olden times married when they were very young they played with their dolls until just before their wedding day; and if unfortunately some little girl died before she grew up, her dolls were buried with her.

Throughout history dolls have nearly always taken baby form, and to the present day it is a known fact that when a fortunate little girl has the privilege of selecting a doll for herself, she always selects one that is true to nature and resembles a real infant.

Children are also fond of calling their dolls by name and the word doll is believed to be an abbreviation of the English Dorothy or the Scotch Doroty.

Dolls of the United States.

During the 19th century Germany supplied almost the entire world with dolls, making the heads from their native clay which is abundant in certain parts of the country and is called Bisque. The Germans had practically a monopoly of the doll business until a few years ago, when American ingenuity evolved a new material far superior to the German Bisque in wearing quality.

Each American firm has its own method of manufacturing heads and we shall endeavor to give a brief description of the way ours are made under the DENIVELLE method, which is the most expensive method known on account of the tremendous manufacturing plant required.

However, owing to the strict economy observed in conducting our business, our enormous output, and the fact that we are satisfied with small profits, we are enabled to furnish these high class heads at prices as low as those demanded for merchandise of much inferior quality.

Effanbee Dolls

The heads are made by a secret formulae of special materials which require boiling for hours and when the composition is ready it is then poured into Plaster of Paris moulds to cool.   When the moulds are opened the heads are inspected by experts who reject any that are imperfect.   Only the very best ingredients are used in making the composition and as soon as a mould becomes scratched the least bit it is replaced. This insures the heads being perfectly smooth, and enables us to paint them without first applying a coating to cover the defects.   That is the reason EFFANBEE dolls never peel.   The paint is applied with air brushes and does not contain any poisonous zinc or lead pigments.   In every department the greatest care is exercised to insure against unsanitary or unhealthful methods or materials.

After the flesh color, the hair and the cheeks are sprayed on with compressed air brushes; the heads are ready for the artists who paint the mouth, the eyes and the eye brows by hand.

The heads are then taken to the assembly room where they are sewed on to the bodies.   The dolls are dressed, packed and shipped to the four corners of the earth.

We regret that through lack of space we are not able to give complete descriptions of our dressmaking department, assembly and shipping departments, but we believe the illustrations herein will give you an idea of the thoroughly scientific and efficient factory that produces EFFANBEE DOLLS.

The EFFANBEE DOLLS illustrated in this booklet are but a few styles selected from a line which is being improved daily and which always contains the latest novelties. EFFANBEE DOLLS are true to life, they are sweet faced, typical American children, dressed in the nattiest and most becoming costumes that can be imagined. Each doll is packed in a pasteboard carton and is guaranteed to be made under sanitary conditions and of the most durable and expensive materials and by the most modern machinery. Each doll is guaranteed to give satisfactory wear.

When buying a doll or any stuffed toy, look for the EFFANBEE label.

EFFANBEE dolls are sold by the prominent dealers in toys throughout the civilized world. If your dealer cannot supply you, send us his name and we will see that you get the doll you desire.

MOULDING ROOM—Where 6200 heads a day are moulded

Dorothy Dainty No. 1121

This beautiful infant with rosy cheeks, curly wig, elaborate lace trimmed dress, pacifier in mouth. True to life in every particular.

Price, $1.25

1089   **1142**   **1143**

Baby Grumpy is a wonderful reproduction of a charming baby in a passing moment of petulancy. The artist has caught the transcendent mood in a manner truly remarkable and every mother will see her child in "BABY GRUMPY."

1090   **1116**   **1143B**

Baby Grumpy comes clothed in a large assortment of costumes and is made in two sizes at **65c.** and **$1.25.**

1151   **1120**   **1118**

Baby Huggims hasn't a grouch in the world.   This doll is dressed very similar to Baby Grumpy and has been called "Baby Grumpy in Good Humor."

1189   **1152**   **1008H**

Baby Huggims sells everywhere at **$1.25.**

1155	1005	1147
COQUETTE	JOHNNY JONES	POUTING BESS

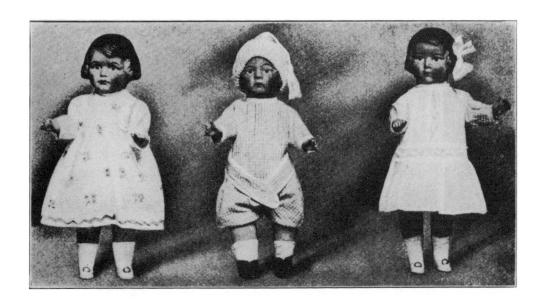

1086	109T	1107
SCHOOL GIRL	BILLY BOY	BETTY BOUNCE

These numbers are made in both of our standard sizes, retailing at **65c.** and **$1.25** each.

1129	1089½	106½
AUNT DINAH	**BABY SNOWBALL**	**UNCLE MOSE**

1102	1158	1008HO
PAJAMA BABY	**BOBBY**	**BABY DAINTY**

These numbers are made in both of our standard sizes retailing at **65c.** and **$1.25** each.

1012	1092	1009
NAUGHTY MARIETTA	**BRICK BODKINS**	**BABY DAINTY**
$1.75	**$1.75**	**$1.75**

1011	1018	1010
BABY ETHEL	**KUTIE**	**BABY BLANCHE**
$2.25	**$2.25**	**$2.25**

These dolls have composition legs and painted shoes and stockings.

INFANT DOLLS

1008 O	230	1008
$1.25	**75**c.	**$1.25**

No. 230 is a large doll and an excellent value at the price. The $1.25 numbers have composition hands and the dresses and caps are nicely trimmed with lace and ribbon.

No. 1008 is also made in the **65c.** size.

INFANT DOLLS

1000	1031	1000/0
$1.50	**$2.50**	**$1.50**

Here are three more wonderful infant dolls. No. 1031 is beautifully dressed, has diaper and booties and Nos. 1000 and 1000/0 have knitted hoods and sacques.

With mamma voice the prices are 25c. higher.

OUR BABY

1111 Infant—This number can also be had dressed as a baby as shown on front cover. A beautiful doll and one of our leaders.   Price **$3.50.**   With mamma voice **$3.75.**

16

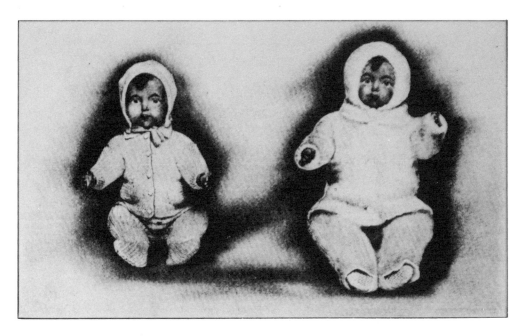

1094—$5.00   **1087—$7.50**

No. 1087 is a chubby life size baby dressed in lamb's wool brush suit. No. 1094 is made in 5 sizes ranging in price from $2.00 to $10.00 each.

1098—$5.50   **1069—$7.50**

No. 1069 has glass eyes and is tastefully dressed in expensive lace-trimmed lingerie clothes. No. 1098 has curly mohair wig, booties and elaborate French lawn dress.

213	214	212
SOLDIER	**JUMBO GIRL**	**JUMBO BOY**
75c.	**75c.**	**75c.**

221-A	222	221-B	222	221-C

Tiny Tads. Cute little dollies at **35c.** each.

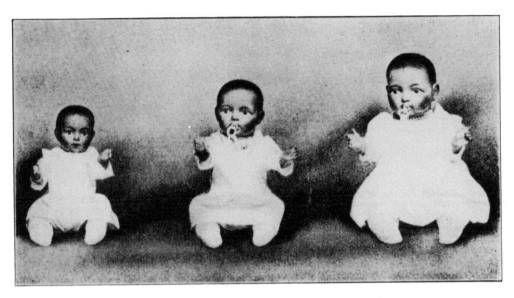

1161-2	1161-4	1161-6
65c.	**$1.25**	**$1.75**

Semi-dressed baby dolls. Some with knitted booties and some with stockings.

1114-2	1114-4	1114-6
$1.00	**$1.50**	**$2.50**

Semi-dressed dolls with mohair wigs; Stockings - Booties.

1180	1018 SC	1190-4
BABY DARLING	**BABY BOBBINS**	**IMPERIAL BABY**
$3.00	**$2.75**	**$3.50**

The Imperial Baby is made in 5 sizes, retailing from $2.25 up.

1179	1145	1121 H
$1.25	**$1.25**	**$1.25**

These dolls are of original design and tastefully dressed.

CYCLE BOY	WIGGLE WAGGLE	DIXIE FLYER
$1.25	**TOYS**	**$1.25**

These wonderful toys are exceptionally well made and are propelled by the dolls in a truly life-like manner.

The EFFANBEE Teddy Bears and stuffed toys are made in sizes and qualities retailing as low as **35c.** each. Some of them growl, others squeak, some have electric eyes, and all are true to life in every particular.

A CORNER OF OUR SAMPLE ROOM

OPERATING ROOM

DRESSMAKING DEPARTMENT

PAINTING AND SPRAYING DEPARTMENT

EFFANBEE DOLLS ARE SOLD BY PROMINENT DEALERS THROUGHOUT THE CIVILIZED WORLD. IF YOUR DEALER CANNOT SUPPLY YOU, SEND US HIS NAME AND WE WILL SEE THAT YOU GET THE DOLL YOU DESIRE. :: ::

FLEISCHAKER & BAUM

Builders of Toys - Creators of Novelties

45 East 17th Street, - New York

THE FORMATIVE YEARS
1910 to 1920

Some of Effanbee's earliest advertising in June 1912 was for *Johnny-Tu-Face, Miss Coquette,* (inspired by a German Heubach bisque girl), and *Baby Dainty,* an infant. It is possible *Baby Dainty* signified a **line** of baby dolls and not just one model, as did *Our Baby* line.

Some of the *Coquettes* had stump hands and cloth legs while others had composition legs and could stand on their own feet without any other support. Prices ranged from 50¢ to $3.50. It seems highly likely that there were two grades of quality of the same doll for different markets. A fine quality *Miss Coquette* observed in a national doll competition with composition legs and hands and the most beautifully preserved head drew universal admiration. (Not all *Coquette*-types are Effanbee.)

Johnny-Tu-Face came dressed in a three-piece knit suit with a tag across the chest reading: "To Have Me Cry, Just Turn My Head," second line, partially undecipherable: "I Laugh, When You," and below that: "Johnny Tu Face."

In June 1914 *Playthings* advertised "The Hit of Hits 'Effanbee' Baby Grumpy and her brother. Baby Grumpy is The Character Doll of The Season. We brought her out in February, but at this time we had no idea how good she was; she was just one of our line. Then she began to make friends here, there everywhere. Houses we never sold before went wild about her and today Baby Grumpy is The One Big Doll Sensation of the Season.

"Baby Grumpy's Face is a Wonderful Reproduction of a charming Baby in a Passing Moment of Petulancy. The artist has caught the Transcendent Mood in a Manner Truly Remarkable. Every Mother Will See Her Child in 'Baby Grumpy.' "

A premium advertisement for *Baby Grumpy* in *The American Woman* Magazine for December 1918 refers to the heads as "unbreakable bisque, with features permanently stamped." The inspiration for this doll was a superb German bisque doll by Gebrüder Heubach.

The first Hard-to-Break type cold press *Baby Grumpy* dolls were made as late as 1920 and for sale in the Montgomery Ward & Co. fall and winter catalog of 1921. She was the featured star of all the early Effanbee models. *Grumpy* came wearing an Effanbee Bluebird (of happiness) pin.

The *War Nurse* dolls were first shown in *Playthings,* November 1917. The uniforms reached to the ankle. By July 1918 a special news insert in the trade magazine read: "Much has been printed about the nurses' units which have gone to France, and everybody is interested in these wonderful women. Their counterparts in doll land never fail to attract attention. F. W. Trumpore, of Fleischaker & Baum, superintends a whole bevy of bright and pretty doll nurses at the Union Square Base Hospital. These nurses are up-to-date in every particular, the costume being an exact replica, according to Mr. Trumpore, of a well-known costume worn on the battlefields of Europe. Every girl must have a soldier doll, and of course the soldier doll may get wounded, so that every girl really must have a nurse doll to take care of such an emergency." By 1919 Montgomery Ward & Co. was featuring *Our Nurse Doll, Our Soldier Boy* and *Our Sailor Lad,* all by Effanbee. They appear to be three different presentations of a basic mold. The author has not had the good fortune to discover any of these intact as yet. Surely a few have survived.

We were delighted to learn a California doll club member owned a *Salvation Army Lass* with only a wig change since 1921. The blue straw bonnet, uniform and cape were original and we were able to borrow her to photograph. She seems to be a reissue of the doll *Margie* with a molded hair side part, new in 1921. We have located none of these to date.

In November 1920 Effanbee printed a full page photograph of child actress Lucille Rickson, star of the Goldwyn Picture Corporation, playing with six dolls. One appears to be a *Baby Catherine,* one is a painted eyes, long curl girl doll, two others are bent-legged cloth body babies with mohair wigs, and two are smaller and larger *Mary Janes.* A large "100% American" motif is printed on the photograph. The caption states: "The Moving Picture Companies evidently use the finest and best dolls for their productions."

One wonders if Mr. Fleischaker had a beloved black Mammy in his childhood days in Kentucky. The February/March 1918 *Playthings* devotes a page to introducing a painting of a white *Dolly Dumpling* in the arms of a proud and beaming black nursemaid. The 1915 catalog offered three black dolls, one a version of *Baby Grumpy.*

Dolly Dumpling was advertised in 1921 as a premium doll. She was a departure in 1918 from the earlier *Fairy Brand Character Dolls.* "She's a real old-fashioned, sweet-faced baby doll, the kind all little girls love to dress and undress, to spank when naughty, and to put to bed when darkness falls," declared the *Needlecraft* advertisement. A miniature storybook with four pages of illustrations in color came with the doll. The doll came in a gingham dress and bonnet, romper or long and short lingerie dresses.

As we worked more and more with the early dolls, we realized many of them had a model number on the back of the head. (A few models have no numbers and could have been earlier. Others are marked "DECO" or "F & B//DECO//NY.")

The following is a list of those located to date. We would be pleased to hear of any others.

106 (printed in reverse)........................ *Brick Bodkins* — white boy
106 (printed in reverse)........................ *Aunt Dinah* — black lady
106 (printed in reverse)........................ *Uncle Mose* — black man
108 Smiling *Grumpy*-type .... *Our Baby* — white baby
116 Sober *Grumpy*-type .... *Billy Boy* — white boy
No number Whistling *Grumpy*-type .... *Whistling Jim* — white boy
24 (Possibly intended to be 124).............. *Baby Huggims* — baby or boy or girl
144 Also marked DECO .... *Bright Eyes* — baby or boy or girl
162 One version of .... *Pouting Bess* — white girl
164 (not located) presumed .... *Pouting Bess* — white girl
166 Another version .... *Pouting Bess* — white girl
172 Very side-glancing eyes .... *Baby Grumpy* — white baby boy or girl
172 Very side-glancing eyes .... *Baby Snowball* — Black baby boy or girl
174 Eyes not quite as side-glancing .... *Baby Grumpy* — white baby boy or girl
176 Eyes look upward .... *Baby Grumpy* — white baby boy or girl
334 Some with wigs .... *Katie Kroose* — boy or girl
462 Also marked DECO .... *Miss Coquette*
   (some *Coquettes* unmarked) .... *Naughty Marietta* — same doll, different costume

The "Great American Dream" to capture the doll market from Germany was begun with these character models. Advertising for *Baby Grumpy* mentions "improved American formulas far superior to those used abroad." The circular tag spoke of "the most durable and expensive material." In 1917 *Needlecraft* magazine, in speaking of *Baby Grumpy*, said, "but the best part of it is that it is absolutely waterproof and unbreakable. You may drop her on a hardwood floor without doing her any damage." Bisque dolls were still plentiful and many a child knew the tragedy of a broken doll.

There is no consistency in the marking or body type on these early examples. A few have torsos completely stuffed with excelsior and pin and disk jointing, but within a short time all had inside joints (all metal disks **beneath** the cloth). It may have been the crude little bodies on some models that caused the company to say their earliest dolls were "long on strength but rather short in other respects."

Illustration 23. Full page advertisement by Fleischaker & Baum showing *Baby Dainty, Johnny-Tu-Face* and *Miss Coquette. Playthings,* June 1912.

"JOHNNY TU FACE"   "MISS COQUETTE"

Illustration 24. *Johnny-Tu-Face* and *Miss Coquette,* called "SURE WINNERS" in a full page ad by Fleischaker and Baum. *Playthings,* June 1912.

Illustration 26. Close-up showing profiles of both heads on *Johnny-Tu-Face. Sandy Rankow Collection.*

Illustration 25. 16in (40.6cm) *Johnny-Tu-Face;* composition head, arms and legs, cloth body; blonde painted hair; blue painted eyes, brown painted eyebrows; open/closed crying mouth with four teeth and a smiling mouth, not open; redressed in velvet and lace; marked: "F&B" on shoulder plate. Molded tear in doll's left eye. 1912. *Sandy Rankow Collection.*

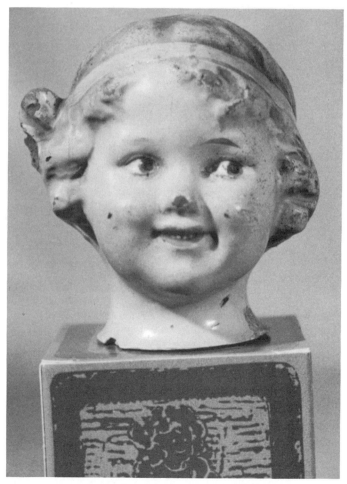

Illustration 27. *Miss Coquette* head. The ribbon bow is partially chipped and the head is unmarked. 1912. *Sherryl Shirran Collection.*

Illustration 28. 10in (25.4cm) *Tiny Tad/Coquette;* made by the Denivelle method by Effanbee; Hard-to-Break composition head, cloth body of correct size and period appears to be a replacement, composition hands to the wrist, cloth legs; brown painted hair; blue painted eyes with no eyelashes; wears a soft blue cotton dress which is not original; ribbon in hair is blue; marked on neck:

1915. *Ursula Mertz Collection.*

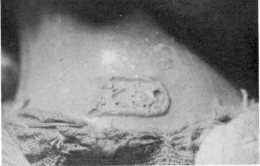

Illustration 29. Mark on neck of *Tiny Tad/Coquette,* shown in *Illustration 28. Ursula Mertz Collection.*

Illustration 30. *Coquette*-type shown in a review article on old toys in *TOYS AND NOVELTIES*. She has mitten hands, cloth legs and sewn-on shoes.

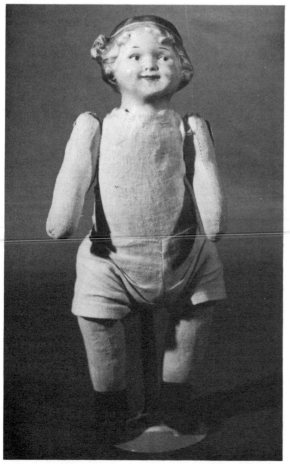

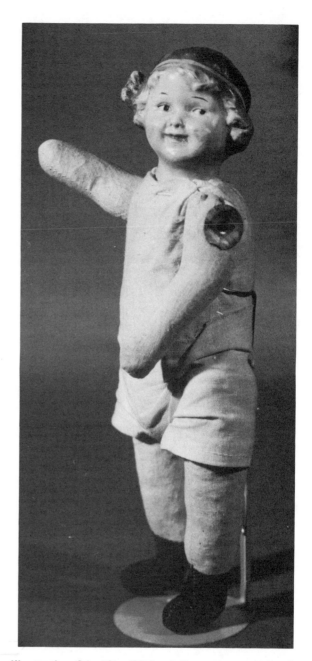

Illustration 31. 12in (30.5cm) *Coquette;* made by the Denivelle method by Effanbee; composition head, white cloth body with excelsior stuffing, pink cloth arms, pink cloth legs with black sewn-on shoes; light brown painted hair with light blue ribbon and bow molded in; blue painted eyes, brown painted eyebrows; open/closed mouth with two teeth painted in; marked on the back of the head: "[co] 462." The metal disk on the arm is on one side only. The wire goes through the other side. 1915. *Francine P. Klug Collection.*

Illustration 32. Full view of 12in (30.5cm) *Coquette* shown in *Illustration 31. Francine P. Klug Collection.*

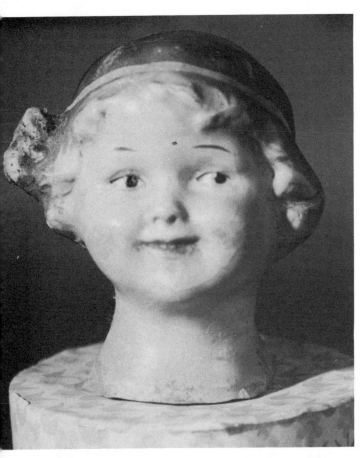

Illustration 33. Close-up of the 12in (30.5cm) *Coquette* shown in *Illustrations 31 and 32. Francine P. Klug Collection.*

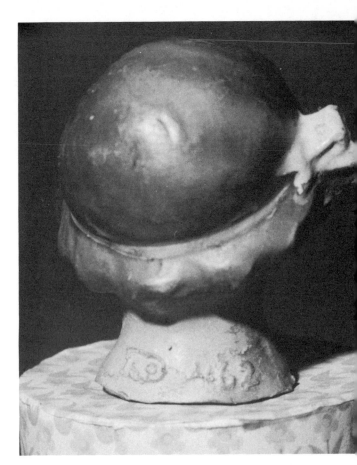

Illustration 34. Close-up of back of 12in (30.5cm) *Coquette*, seen in *Illustrations 31, 32 and 33*, showing the marking on the back of her neck: "Ⓣ©⦿ 462." The " co " is for Deco and you will note that the "4" did not mold very well. *Francine P. Klug Collection.*

Illustration 35. 12in (30.5cm) *Coquette* shown in *Illustrations 31, 32, 33 and 34*. She is wearing an outfit of pink and white checked cotton with a blue cotton bodice and sleeve cuffs, lace at the neck, panties in two pieces with the seamed center front pant leg turned up once and stitched. The exact doll and clothing appear in *Playthings* magazine. This is an economy version of *Coquette* with mitten hands rather than composition. Note that this appears to be the same doll shown in *Illustration 30. Francine P. Klug Collection.*

Illustration 36. 12in (30.5cm) infant doll shown in 1915 Effanbee catalog; composition head, flesh-colored cloth body, cloth arms, black sewn-on shoes; brown painted hair; blue painted eyes; closed mouth; wears muslin baby dress with coarse lace, lace-trimmed panties; left sleeve tag reads: "EFFANBEE//TRADE MARK" in blue-green printing on white. Could this possibly be *Little Walter* (a portrait of Walter Fleischaker)? The painted sleeping *Babyette* of the World War II era could be the same child awake. (*Babyette* is said to be of Walter Fleischaker.) *Rhoda Shoemaker Collection.*

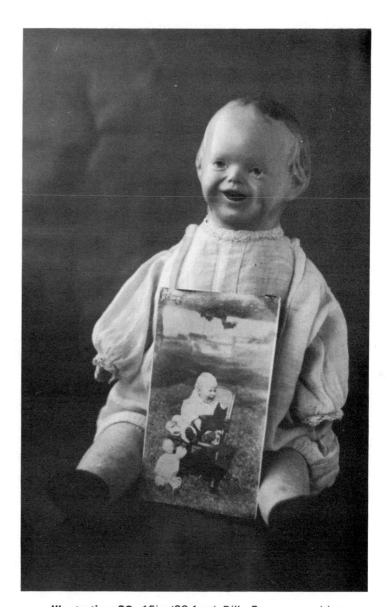

Illustration 38. 15in (38.1cm) *Billy Boy;* composition head, cloth body, composition arms to above the wrist, cloth legs with black sewn-on shoes; brown hair; blue eyes; open/closed mouth with painted-in teeth; wears original white cotton romper with lace at the neck and cuffs; embossed in raised letters: "F + B N.Y." 1913. This doll was given to the original owner at the age of one year in 1913. The photograph in front of the doll shows the original owner with her birthday doll. Her own children later played with the doll and he is still cherished. *Marjorie Bell Kurtz Collection.*

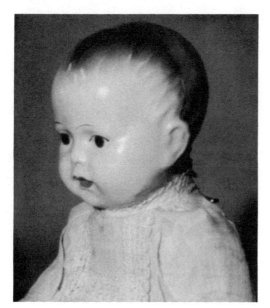

Illustration 37. Close-up of the doll shown in *Illustration 36.* Note the well modeled character head, indented temples and the modeling under the eyes. *Rhoda Shoemaker Collection.*

Illustration 39. 15in (38.1cm) *Pouting Bess;* composition head, replacement body (should be standing and stuffed with ground cork); blue eyes; marked on the back of head: ''166.'' 1915. *Pearl Morley Collection. Photograph by Richard Merrill.*

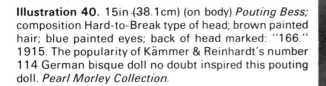

Illustration 40. 15in (38.1cm) (on body) *Pouting Bess;* composition Hard-to-Break type of head; brown painted hair; blue painted eyes; back of head marked: ''166.'' 1915. The popularity of Kämmer & Reinhardt's number 114 German bisque doll no doubt inspired this pouting doll. *Pearl Morley Collection.*

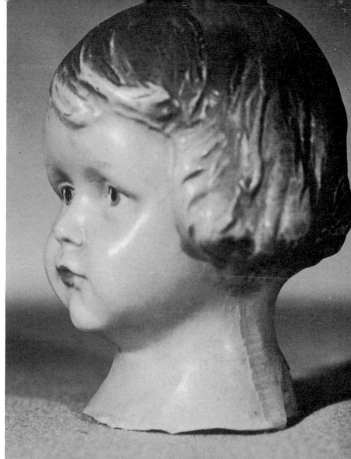

Illustration 41. Side view of *Pouting Bess* shown in *Illustration 40. Pearl Morley Collection.*

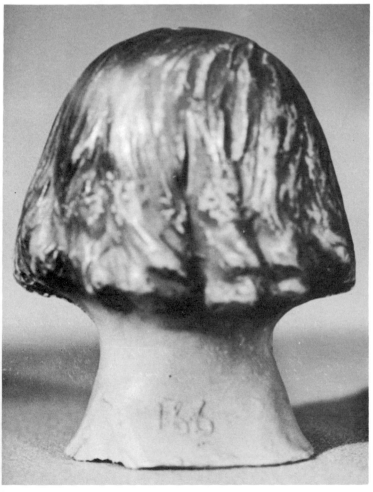

Illustration 42. Back view of *Pouting Bess* shown in *Illustrations 40 and 41. Pearl Morley Collection.*

Illustration 43. 10in (25.4cm) *Pouting Bess;* made by the Denivelle method by Effanbee; composition head, cloth body, composition arms to above the wrist, cloth legs of a calico print; brown hair; blue eyes with dark pupils, brown eyebrows; wears a cotton calico print dress which is not original, black sewn-on shoes; marked on back of head: "162." She is slightly different in molding from model 166. Model 164 has not yet been located. 1915. *Sherryl Shirran Collection.*

Illustration 44. Close-up showing the mark on the neck of the 10in (25.4cm) *Pouting Bess* as seen in *Illustration 43. Sheryl Shirran Collection.*

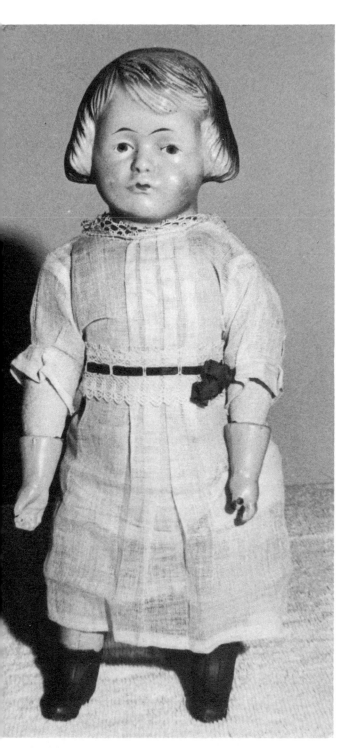

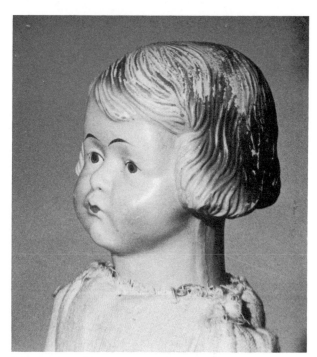

Illustration 46. Close-up of *Pouting Bess* shown in *Illustration 45*.

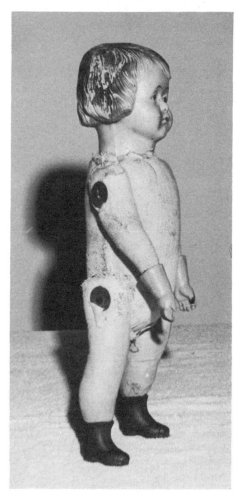

Illustration 45. 15in (38.1cm) *Pouting Bess;* composition head, cloth body, composition arms, cloth legs, composition feet; brown hair; blue eyes, brown eyebrows; closed mouth; wearing original coarse cambric chemise with lace at neck and waist, insertion for red ribbon. Circa 1914.

Illustration 47. 15in (38.1cm) *Pouting Bess* seen in *Illustrations 45 and 46,* undressed showing body construction.

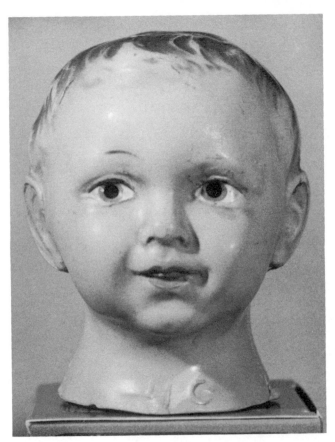

Illustration 49. Close-up of the head of the 15in (38.1cm) character boy shown in *Illustration 48*. The mark on the front of the neck appears to be "4G," but its significance is unknown at this time.

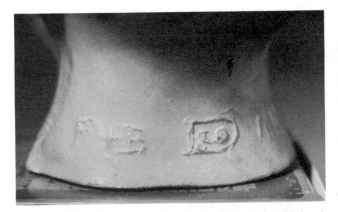

Illustration 50. Back of the head of the 15in (38.1cm) character boy seen in *Illustrations 48 and 49* showing the marking: "F + B [ICO] NY" which stands for Fleischaker & Baum, Deco, New York. *Sherryl Shirran Collection.*

Illustration 48. 15in (38.1cm) character boy, *Soldier* or *Jumbo Boy* according to costume (*Jumbo Girl* has not yet been located); composition head, cloth body, composition arms to above the wrists, cloth legs; pin and disk jointed; brown painted hair; blue painted eyes, brown painted eyebrows; closed mouth; wears replaced plaid shirt and blue trousers; marked on back of neck: "F + B [ICO] NY." 1915. *Sherryl Shirran Collection.*

Illustration 51. 15in (38.1cm) *Boy/Katie Kroose;* composition head, excelsior stuffed cloth body, composition arms up past the wrists, cloth legs with sewn-on shoes; metal disk jointing at hips and shoulders; brown painted hair; brown painted eyes; closed mouth; wears old but not original brown cotton romper; marked on the back of the neck: ''334.'' In *Effanbee — The Dolls With The Golden Hearts* by M. Kelly Ellenburg, the original company catalog is included in the book for 1918 and shows *Baby Blanche* with a wig and *Katie Kroose Boy/Girl* in peasant costumes, inspired by the Käthe Kruse German dolls. 1916.

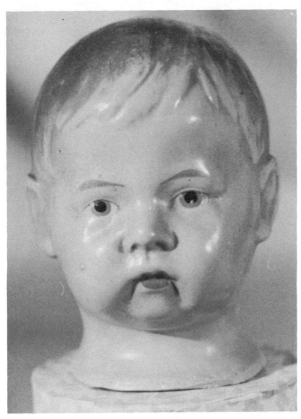

Illustration 52. Close-up of the head of the 15in (38.1cm) *Boy/Katie Kroose* shown in *Illustration 51.*

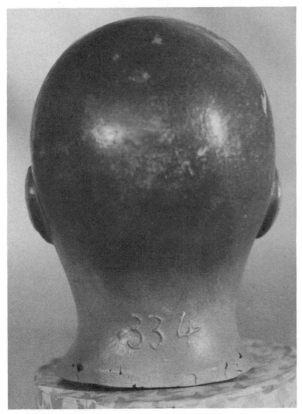

Illustration 53. Back of the head of the 15in (38.1cm) *Boy/Katie Kroose* shown in *Illustrations 51 and 52* indicating the marking on the neck.

Illustration 54. 15½in (39.4cm) *Bright Eyes;* made by the Denivelle method by Effanbee; composition head, cloth body, composition arms to above the wrists, cloth legs with inside joints; brown hair; side-glancing blue eyes with molded eyelids and creases under the eyes, brown eyebrows; closed mouth; wears clothing of brown felt which is not original but the original clothing was the same as the checked romper or dress worn by *Baby Grumpy;* marking embossed on the back of the neck: "DECO//144." This doll has a very smooth head and was shown in the 1916 Effanbee catalog. (*Baby Bright Eyes, Jr.,* was 11in (27.9cm) tall.) Some versions had bent baby legs, 1916. *Jean Hess Collection.*

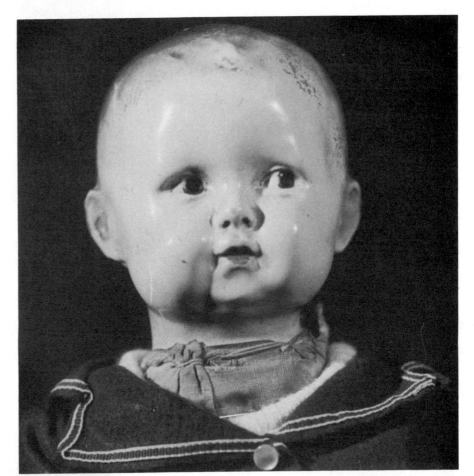

Illustration 55. Close-up of 15½in (39.4cm) *Bright Eyes* shown in *Illustration 54. Jean Hess Collection.*

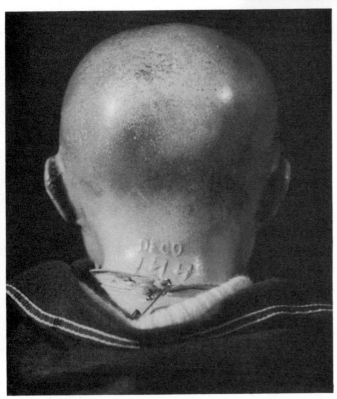

Illustration 56. Back of the head of 15½in (39.4cm) *Bright Eyes* shown in *Illustrations 54 and 55* indicating the marking. *Jean Hess Collection.*

Illustration 57. This catalog advertisement specifically mentions the maker of this doll as F. & B. (for Fleischaker & Baum). She appears to be an early girl *Baby Dainty* and is shown wearing her lace-trimmed lawn dress with white guimpe. Butler Brothers catalog, 1917.

F7876—F. & B., 2 styles, 15¾ in., lace trim flowered lawn dress. solid color guimpe: asstd. figured lawn dresses, lace trim apron, white socks, colored slippers, each in box. Asstd. ⅙ doz. in pkg.........Doz. **$8.75**

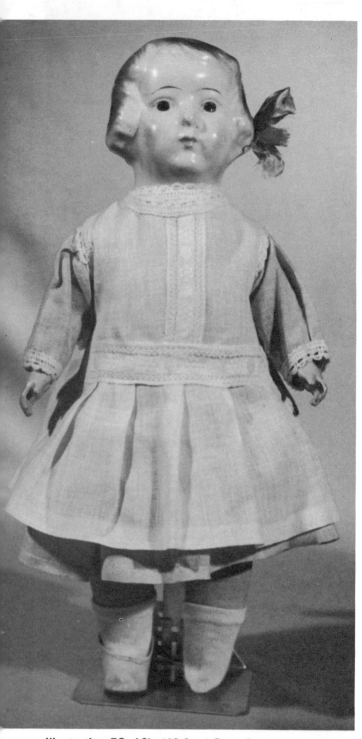

Illustration 58. 16in (40.6cm) *Betty Bounce,* made by the Denivelle method by Effanbee; Hard-to-Break composition head with a wire loop in the head for the ribbon, cloth body, composition hands, cloth legs; brown painted hair; blue painted eyes, brown eyebrows; closed mouth; all-original clothes include a pink cotton dress, white cotton pinafore with embroidered trim, one shoe is missing, original silk ribbon in hair; marked on neck: "DECO;" label at waist back reads: "Effanbee//TRADE MARK." 1915. *Ursula Mertz Collection.*

Illustration 59. Profile of 16in (40.6cm) *Betty Bounce* shown in *Illustration 58. Ursula Mertz Collection.*

Illustration 60. Close-up of 16in (40.6cm) *Betty Bounce* shown in *Illustrations 58 and 59. Ursula Mertz Collection.*

Illustration 61. Back of 16in (40.6cm) *Betty Bounce* seen in *Illustrations 58, 59 and 60,* showing marking on neck. *Ursula Mertz Collection.*

Illustration 62. Back view of 16in (40.6cm) *Betty Bounce* seen in *Illustrations 58, 59, 60 and 61,* showing the label at the waist which reads: "Effanbee//TRADE MARK." *Ursula Mertz Collection.*

99c

Dressed for School

Off to School, with silk ribbon in hair. Dress of good grade material, body stuffed with cork. Composition head and hands. Ht., 14 in. Ship. wt., 1¼ lbs.

48D2761........99c

Illustration 63. An advertisement for a 14in (35.6cm) *Betty Bounce.* Montgomery Ward & Co. catalog, 1919.

Illustration 64. 16in (40.6cm) *Betty Bounce* and 10in (25.4cm) *Tiny Tad/Betty Bounce,* both made by the Denivelle method by Effanbee; composition heads. *Betty Bounce* has a wire loop for her ribbon and wears her original dress. *Tiny Tad/Betty Bounce* also wears her original cotton dress with a red design, has black sewn-on shoes and a molded loop for her ribbon. Circa 1915. *Ursula Mertz Collection.*

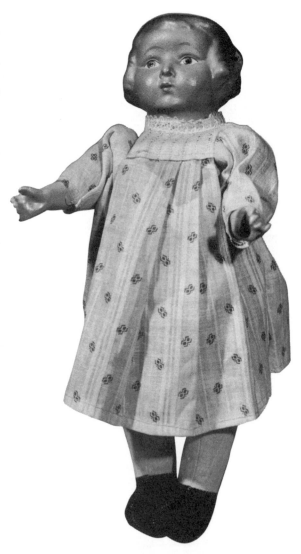

Illustration 65. 10in (25.4cm) *Tiny Tad/Betty Bounce;* composition head, cloth body, composition hands to above the wrists cloth legs with sewn-on black cloth shoes; brown painted hair; blue painted eyes, brown eyebrows; closed mouth; wears original cotton dress with a red design. 1915.

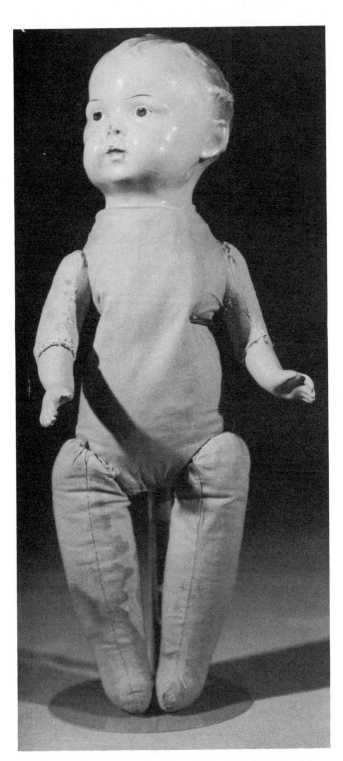

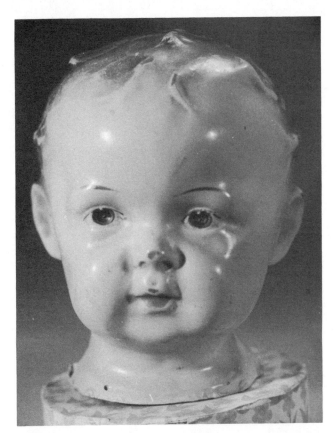

Illustration 67. Close-up of 15in (38.1cm) *Baby Huggims* head shown in *Illustration 66. Hank Levin Collection.*

Illustration 66. 15in (38.1cm) *Baby Huggims;* Hard-to-Break composition head, cloth body, composition hands to above the wrists, arms jointed inside at the shoulder, cloth legs; brown painted hair; brown painted incised eyes with white highlights, brown eyebrows; closed mouth; marked on the back of the head: "24." 1915. This doll is said to be *Baby Grumpy* in a good humor although he is not one of the various *Grumpy* versions. *Hank Levin Collection.*

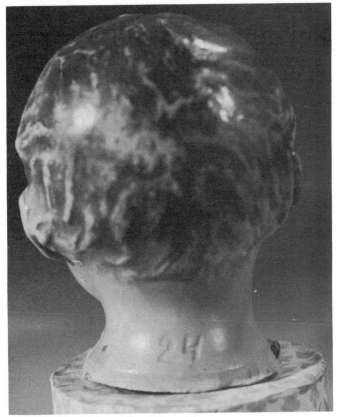

Illustration 68. Back of 15in (38.1cm) *Baby Huggims* head seen in *Illustrations 66 and 67* showing the marking. *Hank Levin Collection.*

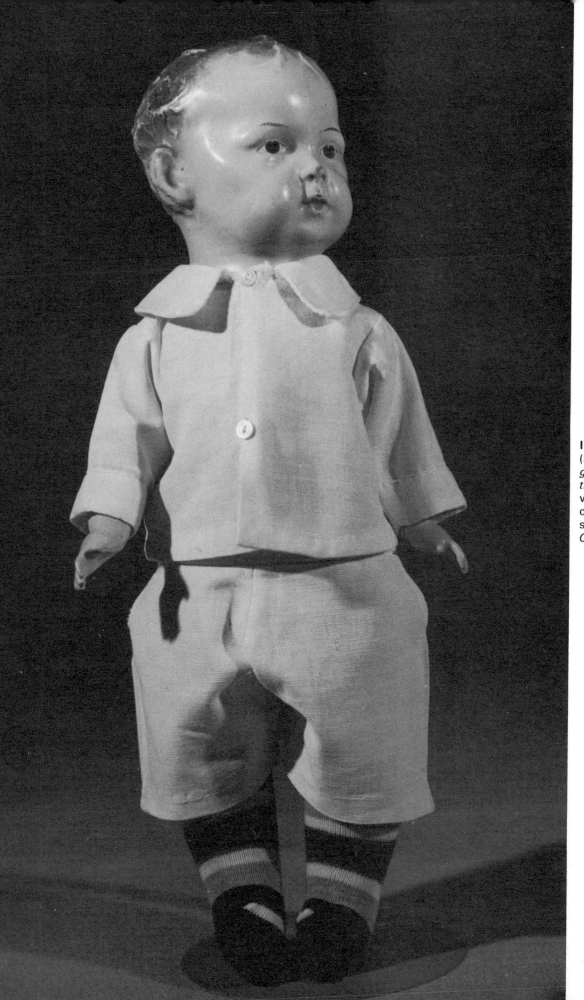

Illustration 69. 15in (38.1cm) *Baby Huggims* shown in *Illustrations 66, 67 and 68* wearing a white heavy cotton suit, striped socks. *Hank Levin Collection.*

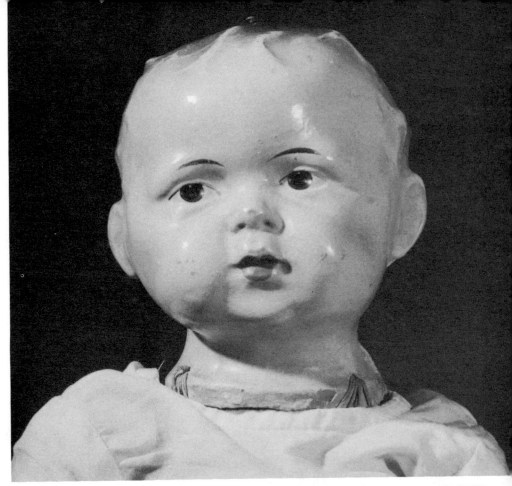

Illustration 70. 14in (35.6cm) *Baby Huggims;* Hard-to-Break composition head, cloth body, composition hands to the wrists, cloth legs; marked on the back of the head: "24" (possibly intended to be "124"). The 1915 Effanbee catalog calls this model "*Baby Grumpy* in a good humor." *Louise Kopfer Collection.*

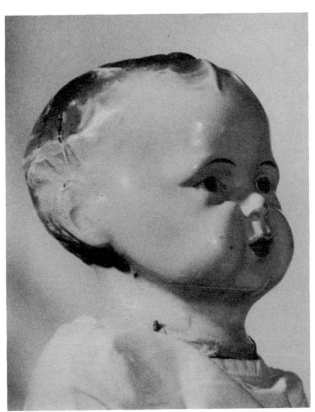

Illustration 71. Side view of 14in (35.6cm) *Baby Huggims* shown in *Illustration 70. Louise Kopfer Collection.*

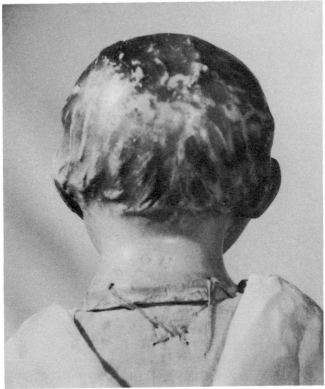

Illustration 72. Back view of 14in (35.6cm) *Baby Huggims* seen in *Illustrations 70 and 71* showing the mark "24" (possibly intended to be "124"). *Louise Kopfer Collection.*

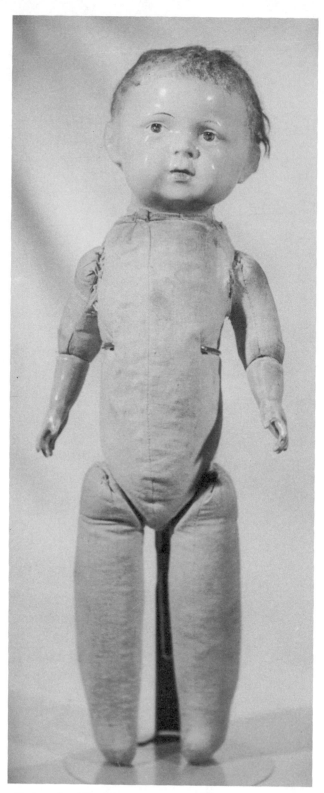

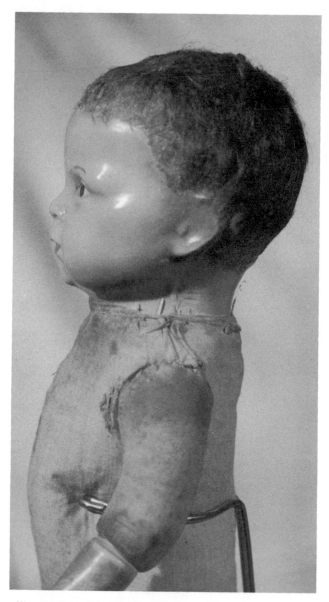

Illustration 73. 15in (38.1cm) *Baby Huggims;* composition head, cork-stuffed cloth body, composition arms to the elbows, cloth legs; brown mohair, mostly worn away; brown eyes, brown eyebrows; closed mouth. 1915. *Katherine Kuchens Collection.*

Illustration 74. Profile of the 15in (38.1cm) *Baby Huggims* shown in *Illustration 73. Katherine Kuchens Collection.*

Baby Grumpy Hard-to-Break type

Look for the Effanbee Tag

It is your Guarantee of getting a doll made under thoroughly sanitary conditions—according to improved American formulas which are actually far superior to those used abroad.

Cute Baby Grumpy
(illustrated above — 65c and up)

Couldn't you just love Baby Grumpy with the petulant little frown caught from life by our artist? This is just one of many baby-mood expressions which characterize Effanbee Dolls. All are made of only the very best materials; they cannot break; faces will never crack or peel fast, delicate tints. Will stand any amount of hard usage.

You can't go wrong—guaranteed to give perfect satisfaction. Remember—look for the tag on each doll.

Sold by good dealers
everywhere

Send for our interesting Doll History
and Illustrated Catalog—FREE

Fleischaker & Baum
45 East 17th St.
Dept. A,   New York
*Manufacturers of Effanbee
Guaranteed Dolls*

Illustration 75. Undated advertisement, circa 1915, showing the paper tag that came with the dolls along with a Bluebird Effanbee pin.

Illustration 76. Advertisement dated May 1916 for *Baby Grumpy*.

Lovable Baby Grumpy
65c and up

Effanbee Character Dolls

Stop in at the nearest Toy Shop and see Baby Grumpy in person. Inspect the extensive variety of Effanbee Guaranteed Dolls—dolls with the sweetest faces and in the cutest poses imaginable. A joy to every child.

Sanitary fast colors—faces will not crack or peel and will stand the roughest usage. All materials the best. The guarantee tag distinguishes the genuine Effanbee. Sold by dealers everywhere.

Send for our interesting Doll History and illustrated Catalog—FREE

FLEISCHAKER & BAUM
45 East 17th St. Dept. A New York
Manufacturers of Effanbee Guaranteed Dolls.

Illustration 77. Advertisements for *Grumpy* found in *The American Woman* magazine. The advertisement on the left appeared in December 1918 and the one on the right appeared in 1919. Note that in the description it is stated that the head is made of "unbreakable bisque."

Grumpy
*Given for **Eight** Subscriptions*

No. 6173. It is that winsome little frown that gives Grumpy her charming personality.

Baby Grumpy stands 14 inches high and is fully jointed; she will sit down and place her hands in any position. She comes fully dressed as shown in the picture; her clothes may be taken off and put on, and additional dresses may be made as desired. Her dress is white pique, lace-trimmed around neck, and with hem, sleeves, and yoke edged with pink-and-white trimming. White stockings, white pique hat with pink cord and balls, held in place by an elastic under chin. Pink cheeks, mouth red, eyes blue, and light hair.

Grumpy's head is made of unbreakable bisque; her features are permanently stamped.

Grumpy
*Given for **Eight** Subscriptions*

No. 1600. It is that winsome little frown that gives Grumpy her charming personality.

Baby Grumpy stands 14 inches high and is fully jointed; she will sit down and place her hands in any position. She comes fully dressed as shown in the picture; her clothes may be taken off and put on, and additional dresses may be made as desired. Her dress is white pique, lace-trimmed around neck, and with hem, sleeves, and yoke edged with pink-and-white trimming. White stockings, white pique hat with pink cord and balls, held in place by an elastic under chin. Pink cheeks, mouth red, eyes blue, and light hair.

Grumpy's head is made of unbreakable bisque, her features are permanently stamped.

Baby Grumpy

Premium No. B 1600

Given for Four Subscriptions

Made in America

BABY GRUMPY is the doll sensation of the year. Her face is a wonderful reproduction of a charming baby in a passing moment of petulancy. Every mother will see her child in Baby Grumpy. The complexion is truly wonderful, but the best part of it is that it is absolutely waterproof and unbreakable. You may drop her on a hardwood floor without doing any damage. Baby Grumpy stands 14 inches high and is fully jointed, so that she will sit down and place her hands in any position desired. She comes fully dressed just as shown in the picture; her clothes may be taken off and put on and additional dresses may be made as desired. Her dress is fancy white pique, lace-trimmed around neck, and with hem, sleeves, and yoke edged with pink - and - white trimming. She wears white stockings and white pique hat with pink cord and balls, held in place by an elastic under chin. Baby's cheeks are pink, her mouth red, eyes blue, and hair light.

SPECIAL BARGAIN OFFER. If you will send us a club of **four** new subscriptions to The American Woman at our regular subscription price of **25 cents** each, we will send each subscriber this paper one year, and we will send you **Baby Grumpy (Premium No. B 1600).**

Made in America

Grumpy

Every Child's Favorite Doll

*Given for **Twelve** Subscriptions*

No. 6173. Baby Grumpy is the doll sensation of the year. Her face is a wonderful reproduction of a charming baby in a passing moment of petulancy. Every mother will see her child in Baby Grumpy. The complexion is truly wonderful, but the best part of it is that it is absolutely waterproof and unbreakable. You may drop her on a hardwood floor without doing any damage. Baby Grumpy stands 14 inches high and is fully jointed, so that she will sit down and place her hands in any position desired. She comes fully dressed as shown in the picture; her clothes may be taken off and put on and additional dresses may be made as desired. Her dress is fancy white pique, lace-trimmed around neck, and with hem, sleeves, and yoke edged with pink-and-white trimming. She wears white stockings and white-pique hat with pink cord and balls, held in place by an elastic under chin. Baby's cheeks are pink, her mouth red, eyes blue and hair light.

LEFT: Illustration 78. Advertisements for a 14in (35.6cm) *Baby Grumpy* given as a premium offer for subscriptions obtained to *The American Woman* magazine. Note that the offer on the left is for four new subscriptions while the offer on the right took 12 new subscriptions. Note the original hat shown in the ads.

Baby Grumpy

Height, 14¼ Inches

Cork stuffed body jointed at shoulders and hips. Composition head and hands. Painted hair. Pink linene dress and bonnet. Shipping weight, 2 pounds.
49 E 2522—
.... **$1.49**

Illustration 79. Advertisement for 14½in (36.9cm) *Baby Grumpy*. This is probably the last of the cold press *Grumpy* dolls. Montgomery Ward & Co. Fall and Winter catalog, 1921.

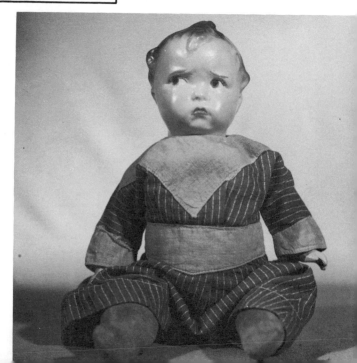

Illustration 80. 11½in (29.2cm) *Baby Grumpy, Jr.*, composition head, cloth body, composition arms to above the wrists, cloth legs; brown painted hair; blue painted eyes, brown painted eyebrows; painted closed mouth; dressed in old blue romper; incised on back of head: "172." 1915 on.

Illustration 81. 11½in (29.2cm) *Baby Grumpy, Jr.*, and 14in (35.6cm) *Baby Grumpy.* Both have composition head and arms to up past the wrists, cloth bodies and legs; brown painted hair and blue painted eyes. *Baby Grumpy, Jr.* is incised on the back of the head: "172" while *Baby Grumpy* is incised: "174." 1915 on.

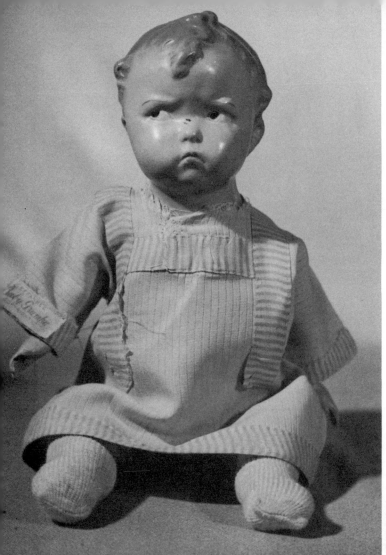

Illustration 82. 14in (35.6cm) *Baby Grumpy;* brown painted hair; blue painted eyes with a white highlight looking upward, brown painted eyebrows; wearing pink and white striped cotton pique dress; mark embossed on head: "176;" label on sleeve reads: "EFFANBEE//Baby Grumpy//COPYRIGHTED." 1915 on. *Jeanette Gustin Collection.*

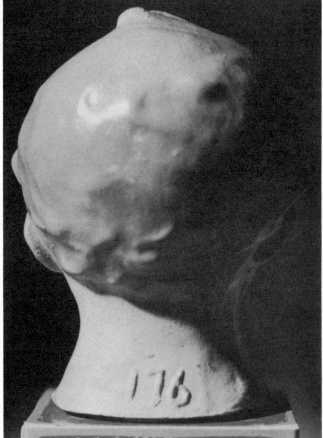

Illustration 83. The back of 14in (35.6cm) *Baby Grumpy's* head seen in *Illustration 82* showing the embossed marking "176." *Jeanette Gustin Collection.*

Illustration 84. 14in (35.6cm) *Baby Grumpy* dolls from three similar but slightly different molds; composition heads and hands to above the wrists, ground cork-stuffed muslin bodies and legs; brown painted hair, blue painted eyes, brown eyebrows. The doll on the left is dressed in a blue and white checked gingham outfit and is marked: "174." The doll in the center is wearing an old handmade embroidered dress and is marked: "DECO." The doll on the right is wearing an outfit of blue and white striped percale on corded pique and is marked: "176." Center doll. *Frances James Collection.* Doll on right, *John Axe Collection.*

Illustration 85. 14in (35.6cm) *Baby Grumpy* dolls. The doll on the left is marked: "174." The doll on the right is marked: "176" and the eyes seem to be a bit more side-glancing. The label on the sleeve reads: "EFFANBEE//Baby Grumpy //COPYRIGHTED." Doll on right, *John Axe Collection.*

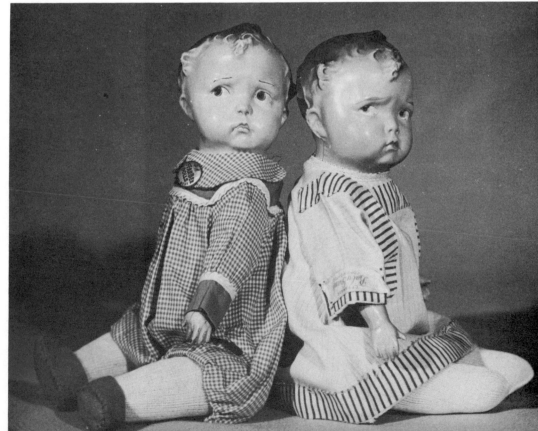

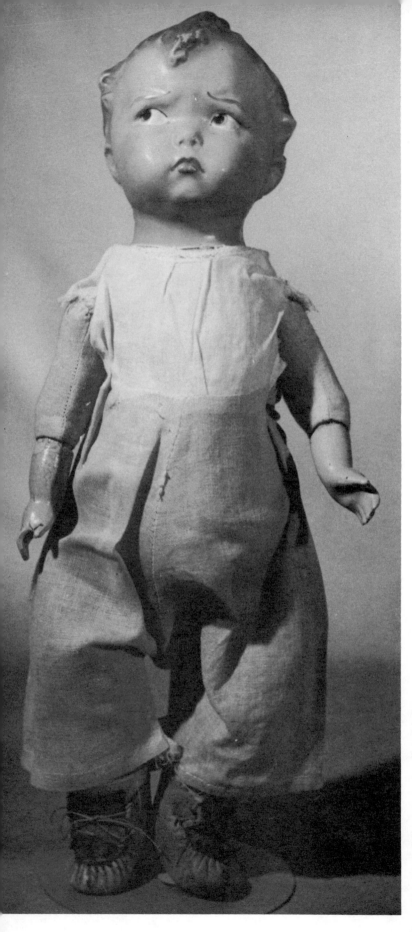

Illustration 86. 15in (38.1cm) *Baby Grumpy;* Hard-to-Break composition head and arms up past wrists cork-stuffed cloth body and legs; brown painted hair; blue painted incised eyes, brown eyebrows; pouty mouth; wears original beige trousers but the top is missing; marked in embossed lettering: "176." Mint original paint. 1915. *Sherryl Shirran Collection.*

Illustration 87. Close-up of 15in (38.1cm) *Baby Grumpy* seen in Illustration 86. Note the incised eyes, the eye highlights, the dark lines at the top of the eyes, the red dots at the corners and the downturned mouth. The mint paint on this doll should serve as an aid for restoring *Baby Grumpy* dolls correctly. *Sherryl Shirran Collection.*

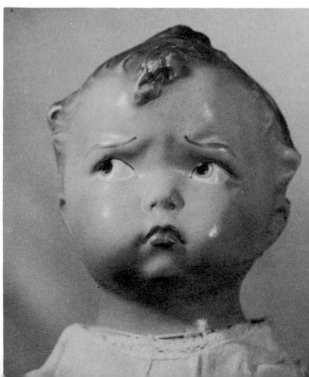

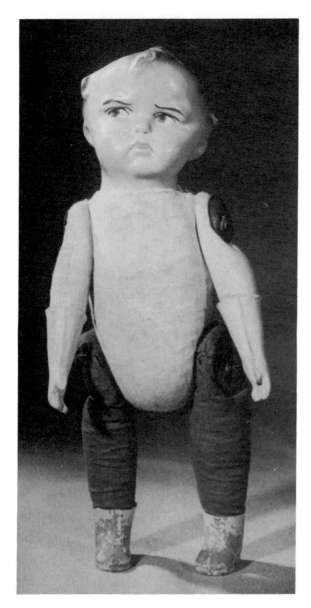

Illustration 89. 14in (35.6cm) *Baby Grumpy* seen in *Illustration 88* showing the different hand and wrist, this is the true gauntlet hand as opposed to the wired-on type. Note the pin and disk jointing at the arms and hips and the unusual composition shoes. *Hank Levin Collection.*

Illustration 88. 14in (35.6cm) *Baby Grumpy;* made by Denivelle method by Effanbee; composition head, ground cork-stuffed cloth body, composition arms to the elbows, cloth legs with composition shoes; brown painted hair; blue two-tone eyes, dark brown eyebrows; closed mouth; marked: "172" on back of neck. This is evidently an early version as it does not have the inside jointing. The arm slips over the cloth top. Circa 1915. *Hank Levin Collection.*

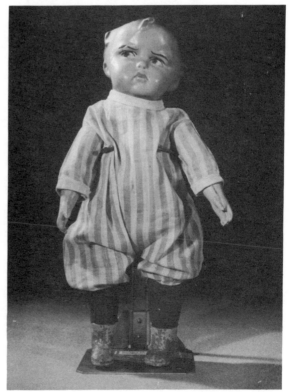

Illustration 90. 14in (35.6cm) *Baby Grumpy* seen in *Illustrations 88 and 89* shown wearing his original blue and white striped cotton romper. *Hank Levin Collection.*

Illustration 91. *Baby Grumpy, Jr.,* head incised: "172" and *Baby Grumpy* head embossed: "DECO//172." Both are Hard-to-Break composition. The head marked "DECO//172" appears to be a size in between *Baby Grumpy* and *Baby Grumpy, Jr.* The paint on the *Baby Grumpy, Jr.,* head has been restored. The *Baby Grumpy* head has its original paint and has a slight ridge at the bottom of the neck which has been eliminated on the smaller model. Head on the right, *Barbara Mongelluzzi Collection.*

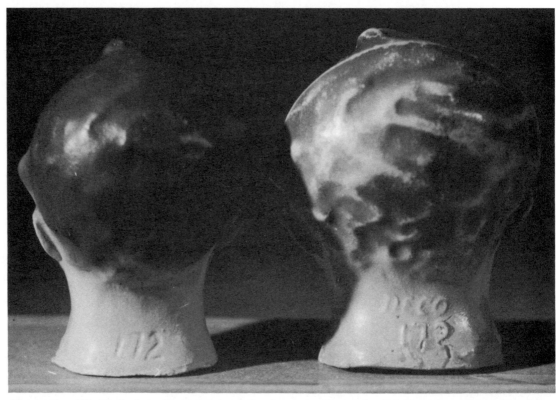

Illustration 92. Back of the heads of the dolls shown in *Illustration 91.* Note the markings and the variation in size. Head on the right, *Barbara Mongelluzzi Collection.*

Illustration 93. 21in (53.3cm) *Our Baby,* a smiling version of *Baby Grumpy* but not sold under that name; Hard-to-Break composition head and hands to above the wrists, ground cork-stuffed white muslin body and pink legs; brown painted hair; blue painted eyes deeply incised with white highlight, brown eyebrows; open /closed mouth with two teeth; satin and velvet clothes are not original but some came in christening clothes or short baby dresses; marked on the head: ''108.'' Head measures a full 14in (35.6cm) circumference and the paint is rubbed off the tip of the nose. This version also came as a standing boy in the 1915 catalog. Very, very few are found this large from this era. 1915. *Madalaine Selfridge Collection.*

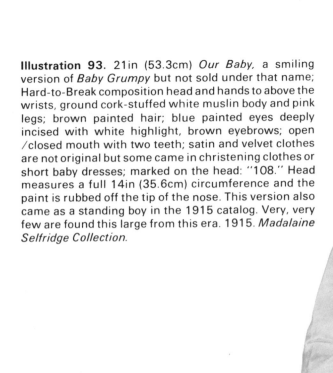

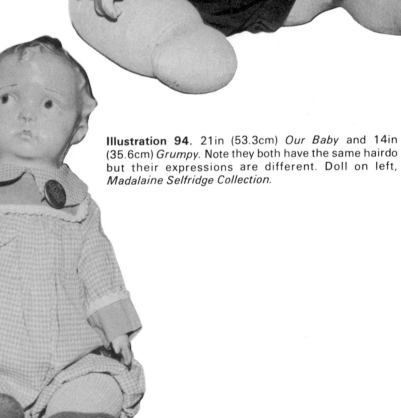

Illustration 94. 21in (53.3cm) *Our Baby* and 14in (35.6cm) *Grumpy.* Note they both have the same hairdo but their expressions are different. Doll on left, *Madalaine Selfridge Collection.*

Illustration 95. 10in (25.4cm) *Dutch Boy;* manufactured by Effanbee; purchased by Madame Hendren undressed, and issued as her own line, a common practice; composition head, cloth body, arms with mitt hands and legs; brown hair; blue eyes, brown eyebrows; closed mouth; wears all felt green suit with beige belt and collar; marked on neck: "172." Not all Madame Hendren *Dutch Boys* are *Grumpy* dolls. *Louise Kopfer Collection.*

Illustration 96. The back of the 10in (25.4cm) *Dutch Boy* seen in *Illustration 95* showing the marking on the back of its neck. *Louise Kopfer Collection.*

Baby Grumpy—2 styles, 14½ in., pouting expression, white pique Dutch suit, colored chambray apron, white pique dress with contrasting chambray trim, white socks
F7882—Asstd. ⅙ doz. in box.
Doz. **$9.00**

Baby Grumpy—11½ in., girls and boys, pouting expression, blue and pink checkered gingham rompers and dress, solid color trim, matched sunbonnets, white socks.
F7854—Asstd. ⅓ doz. in box.
Doz. **$4.75**

Illustration 97. Two ads showing different versions of *Baby Grumpy.* Two styles of 14½in (36.9cm) *Baby Grumpy* are shown on the left while a boy and a girl, both 11½in (29.2cm) are shown on the right. Butler Brothers catalog, 1918.

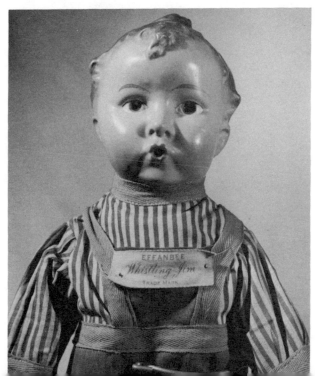

Illustration 100. 16½in (41.9cm) *Whistling Jim* shown in *Illustrations 98 and 99.* Note body construction: legs are slightly curved but not as much as those of a baby doll; slight indentation in mid torso shows whistling device which still works. *Henrietta Ameiss Collection.*

Illustration 98. 16½in (41.9cm) *Whistling Jim;* Hard-to-Break composition head, ground cork-stuffed cloth body, composition hands to the wrist, black cloth sewn-on shoes; highly colored red-brown painted hair; blue painted intaglio eyes, brown eyebrows; perforated mouth; dressed in red and white striped shirt, blue trousers trimmed with faded red tape; no number incised on back of the head; label on front of clothes reads: "EFFANBEE//Whistling Jim//TRADE MARK." This is a whistling version of *Grumpy* but renamed *Whistling Jim.* Whistle mechanism in the torso still works faintly. 1916. *Henrietta Ameiss Collection.*

Illustration 99. Close-up of 16½in (41.9cm) *Whistling Jim* shown in *Illustration 98. Henrietta Ameiss Collection.*

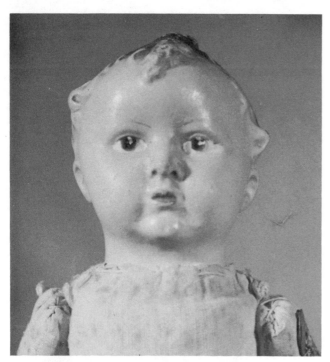

Illustration 101. 15in (38.1cm) *Billy Boy,* a sober version of *Baby Grumpy;* Hard-to-Break composition head, ground cork-stuffed cloth body, composition hands, cloth legs, disk jointed arms; brown painted hair; blue eyes; closed mouth; marked on back of head: "116." 1915. *Bea De Armond Collection. White House Doll and Toy Museum.*

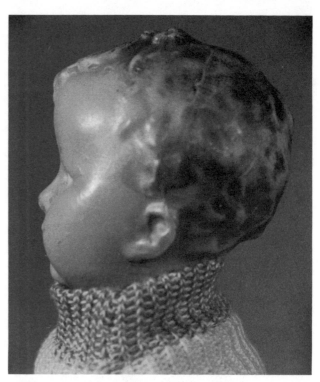

Illustration 102. Side view of 15in (38.1cm) *Billy Boy* shown in *Illustration 101.* Note head contour. *Bea De Armond Collection. White House Doll and Toy Museum.*

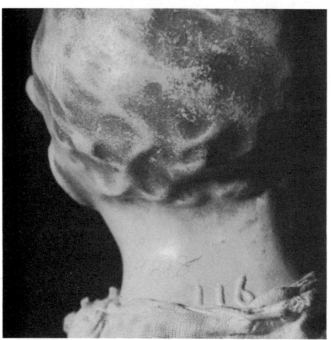

Illustration 103. Back view of 15in (38.1cm) *Billy Boy* shown in *Illustrations 101 and 102.* Note marking on neck. *Bea De Armond Collection. White House Doll and Toy Museum.*

Illustration 104. 14½in (36.9cm) *Baby Snowball;* composition head and arms to above the wrists, cloth body and legs; black painted hair, eyes and eyebrows; no original clothes. Circa 1915. Paint has been restored.

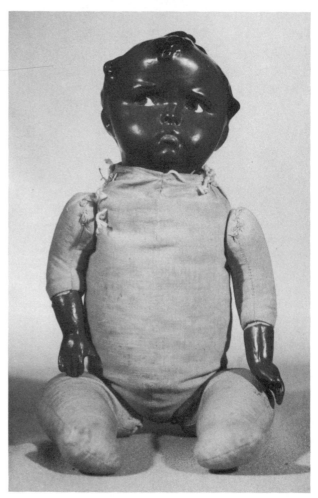

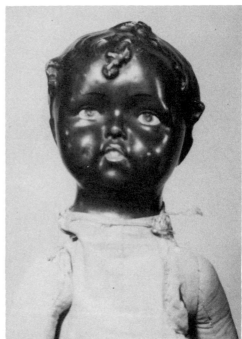

Illustration 106. Close-up of 15in (38.1cm) *Aunt Dinah* shown in *Illustration 105. Pearl Morley Collection. Photograph by Richard Merrill.*

Illustration 105. 15in (38.1cm) *Aunt Dinah,* a smiling adult version of *Grumpy;* composition head, cloth body, composition hands to above the wrists, cloth legs; black painted hair, brown incised eyes with dark pupils, black eyebrows; open/closed mouth with two teeth; wears old red calico dress but missing apron and head kerchief; marked on the neck with a reversed "106." *Pearl Morley Collection.*

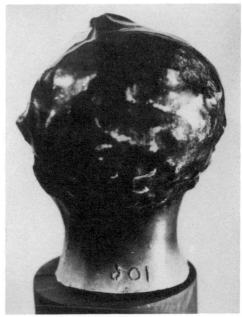

Illustration 107. Mark on the back of 15in (38.1cm) *Aunt Dinah* seen in *Illustrations 105 and 106* showing the "106" reversed. *Pearl Morley Collection. Photograph by Richard Merrill.*

Illustration 108. 15in (38.1cm) black *Grumpy*-type as a boy; a smiling *Baby Snowball;* composition head, muslin body, composition arms to above the wrists, blue and white striped cloth legs with molded composition feet; black hair, brown incised eyes, black eyebrows; open /closed mouth with two teeth; wears original tan trousers and a handmade red jacket; marked with a reversed "106." Circa 1915. This is the same mold as *Aunt Dinah.* A white boy of the same mold is called *Black Bodkins. Fredi Chevrier Colection.*

Illustration 110. Child model uses *Baby Grumpy* in posing. This one is wearing the 1915 striped outfit and has a big bow tied around its neck. The advertising was for "Ansco Cameras and Speedex Film." The ad copy stated: "Your children's appealing and playful poses change so rapidly that to catch them your camera must be able to *jump into action." The Ladies' Home Journal,* May 1916.

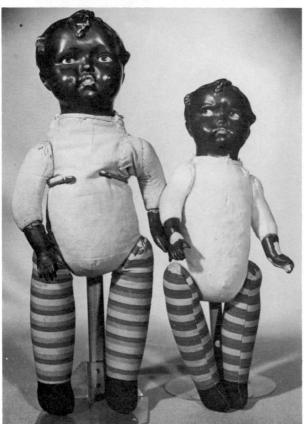

Illustration 109. 15in (38.1cm) *Aunt Dinah* and 12in (30.5cm) black *Grumpy,* called *Baby Snowball.* Both have composition heads, ground cork-stuffed muslin bodies, composition hands to above the wrists and tan, red and green striped material simulating socks for legs with sewn-on black shoes; black hair; brown incised eyes with black eyebrows; open/closed mouths (*Aunt Dinah* has two painted teeth). The back of *Aunt Dinah*'s neck is marked with a reversed "106," and *Baby Snowball* is marked: "172." The 1915 catalog shows *Aunt Dinah* as a woman and *Baby Snowball* (a black *Grumpy*) as a baby or young child. The same mold or doll (106) was made up as a boy (white). The clothing made the difference. Doll on left, *Pearl Morley Collection.*

Mary Jane and Others

Mary Jane was the "star" of the Effanbee players of her type in her era. The other versions of girl dolls in the same period may have had names as well but if they did we have no record of them. The company was very serious, indeed, about advertising and its powers. They may have named only one doll they wished to feature the most and thus create a demand for *Mary Jane* dolls.

The very first version may have been the bisque example by Lenox Potteries, of Trenton, New Jersey. According to *The Collector's Encyclopedia of Dolls* by the Colemans the Lenox company was formed in 1906. Their sculptor and ceramist was Issac Broome, a native of Canada, who trained at the Pennsylvania Academy of Fine Arts. World War I cut off the supply of

Illustration 111. 20in (50.8cm) Effanbee doll manufactured by Lenox Potteries, Trenton, New Jersey; bisque head, composition body, wooden arms and legs; wears a pink georgette dress trimmed in lace net; fancy weave socks with leather shoes; has Bluebird Effanbee pin on dress; marked on back of head: "Lenox//Effanbee;" circa 1920. A gift from Effanbee to the Newark Museum, Newark, New Jersey. *Collection of the Newark Newark Museum (Acc. No. 20, 1157). Photograph by Armen.*

Illustration 112. 20in (50.8cm) Effanbee doll manufactured by Lenox Potteries, Trenton, New Jersey; bisque head, compositon body, wooden arms and legs; wears pink georgette dress with lace and net rosettes at hem bottom; hat has white satin crown and blue chiffon brim; marked on the back of the head: "Lenox//Effanbee." A gift from Effanbee to the Newark Museum, Newark, New Jersey. *Collection of the Newark Museum (Acc. No. 20, 1158). Photograph by Armen.*

imported German dolls. During the tremendous effort by American manufacturers to take over the doll business in this country, the original thinking was simply to duplicate a typical European doll. *Mary Jane* is an example of this early effort. Two bisque head models were given by Effanbee to the Newark Museum in New Jersey. The Colemans date the costume styles at about 1920 but the heads could have been cast a bit earlier. These dolls were never retailed so are rare indeed. We are so appreciative of being allowed permission to include their photographs in this volume.

We feel the bisque *Mary Jane* may have come first since she was **not** put on the market and the idea abandoned to substitute instead a composition model, but have no proof of our theory. We have never seen an example of a composition *Mary Jane* which was survived in original condition, as have the two bisque models. However, they are perfectly restorable by informed doll repairers; paint tended to craze on the wood pulp head, fingers were subject to breakage. Examples rarely have their original clothes; some were sold in 1919, in simply a short chemise. Fortunately old catalogs yield good material on how to properly dress these dolls.

For doll hospital specialists who have a doll that must be repainted to be acceptable in a collection we have some information taken from a crazed but original painted doll. There are 18 brown lash strokes above the blue-gray metal eye and 18 below with a red dot at each eye corner. The brown brows are multi-stroked and extend well beyond the outer eye corner. The cheeks are rosy; there are two red dots in the nostrils, and a pinkish-red cupid's bow mouth. There are four upper teeth which appear to be celluloid with felt behind them.

The first wig apparently was short mohair in a "real fluffy" style according to 1917 advertising. Oddly enough Effanbee called her another sweet-faced character doll like *Baby Grumpy*. Actually *Mary Jane* was what collectors today refer to as a dolly-faced doll with a bland expression. Yet she must have been very popular as she shows up in the catalogs over a period of years. Any child with a vivid imagination could create the smiles and tears of her doll in her own mind, according to her own mood. This very fact may have been comforting and non-threatening to a sensitive child as opposed to a doll which pouted constantly.

One 1920 Sears, Roebuck and Co. catalog refers to the *Mary Jane* doll thus: "entire doll of the strong composition which looks like bisque," so the intent to complete with German bisque dolls is very evident (Even the Germans did not make their ball-jointed dolls entirely of bisque!)

Several models of good quality composition shoulder or breastplate heads on kid bodies were manufactured as well. The wooden arms were strung through a tube in the body and the hips were jointed so the dolls could sit nicely. Lower limbs were molded composition. Some of these have survived rather well considering their age and type.

The third girl type was the ground cork-stuffed cloth body. These were light in weight for their size and can now be properly costumed from old catalog illustrations. Low necks were emphasized in the 1920 Sears, Roebuck and Co. catalog. (Before the breastplate head, when the cut-off cold press Hard-to-Breaks were used, necklines had to be right under the chin.)

Due to war times, nurse dolls were on the market in 1917 and later soldiers and sailors. None of these have surfaced, all original, except in advertising. They may be unrecognized when found without original clothing.

Illustration 113. Advertisement for *Mary Jane. Ladies' Home Journal,* December 1917.

Illustration 114. Advertisements for *Mary Jane* from *Ladies' Home Journal.* The one on the left appeared in November 1919 while the one on the right was in the December 1919 issue.

$5.48

Doll With Real

Hair Wig

With Sleeping Eyes

Girls, this doll's hair can be combed and dressed in 'most any fashion. She has sleeping eyes with real hair lashes. She wears a pretty lace-trimmed dress and lawn combination. Head and fully jointed body made of composition. About 20 in. high. Ship. wt., 3½ lbs.

48D2829—Price.....$5.48

Illustration 115. Advertisement showing *Mary Jane.* Montgomery Ward & Co. catalog, 1919.

Effanbee

100% AMERICAN

THIS IS OUR WAY OF ADDING TO

OUR COUNTRY'S PRODUCTS

THE TOY MANUFACTURERS OF THE U.S.A.

ARE SPENDING $65,000 TO ADVERTISE

AMERICAN TOYS

YOU CAN HELP

IF YOU LINK UP WITH THE CAMPAIGN

FLEISCHAKER & BAUM

GEN. OFFICE
45 Greene St.
Cable Address
EFFANBEE

SALES DEP'T.
45 East 17 St.
NEW YORK

FACTORIES
42-44 Wooster St.
47-49 Greene St.

Illustration 116. A full page advertisement from *Playthings,* October 1919 by Fleischaker & Baum showing the symbol the Toy Manufacturers of the U.S.A., depicting Uncle Sam's hat filled to brimming with **American** dolls and toys. German toys were heavily imported prior to World War I.

Illustration 118. 24in (61cm) *Mary Jane;* composition head and body, wooden arms, composition legs; dark brown human hair wig; blue-gray metal eyes, brown painted eyebrows, brown painted upper and lower eyelashes; open mouth with six teeth and a molded tongue; marked on the back of the head and on the torso: "Effanbee." This doll was given to the owner when found in the attic of an old home that was to be razed. Circa 1918. *Catherine Foutz Collection. Photograph by Catherine Foutz.*

Illustration 119. Back view of the 24in (61cm) *Mary Jane* seen in *Illustration 118.* Note the marking visible on her back. *Catherine Foutz Collection. Photograph by Catherine Foutz.*

Illustration 117. 15in (38.1cm) *Mary Jane;* composition head and body, wooden arms with composition hands, composition legs; brown mohair wig; blue-gray metal eyes, brown eyebrows, painted upper and lower eyelashes; open mouth with four teeth and felt tongue; marked on head and torso: "Effanbee." This is a rare small size. Sears, Roebuck and Co. in Philadelphia, Pennsylvania, listed *Mary Jane* at 16in (40.6cm), 18in (45.7cm), 20in (50.8cm) and 24in (61cm). The 15in (38.1cm) size was $4.95 as opposed to some other dolls selling at $1.25 and $1.89. Circa 1918. *Idama Keeton Collection.*

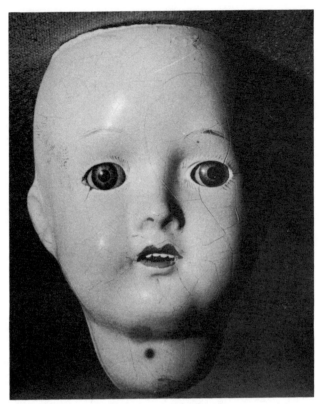

Illustration 120. *Mary Jane* composition head; blue-gray metal eyes with solid pupils, painted upper and lower eyelashes; open mouth with four teeth and a felt tongue; marked on the back of the head: "Effanbee." 1917. *Edell Lashley Collection.*

Low Prices on Very Fine Dolls

Dressed Handsomely.

"Mary Jane" Jointed Dolls

	Height, Abt., In.	Shipping Wt., Lbs.	General Catalog Price	Sale Price
18P2992	24	6	$11.75	$10.25
18P2996	20	4	9.25	7.98
18P3000	18	3½	7.85	6.79
18P3004	16	2½	6.95	5.75

We recommend these dolls as being among the finest in America. Completely dressed in fine quality lace and ribbon trimmed dress. Entire doll of the strong composition which looks like bisque. Lifelike moving eyes. Beautiful wig of real hair in long curls, easily redressed. Jointed at neck, shoulders, elbows, wrists, knees and hips. High grade dolls of extra value at our prices.

Illustration 122. Advertisement for *Mary Jane.* Sears, Roebuck and Co., Chicago, Illinois, catalog. 1920.

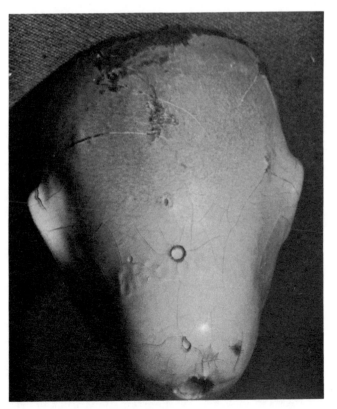

Illustration 121. The back of the *Mary Jane* head seen in *Illustration 120* showing the marking: "Effanbee." *Edell Lashley Collection.*

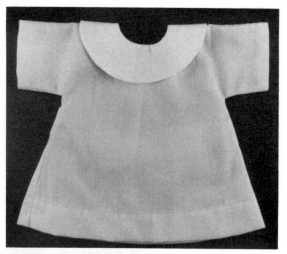

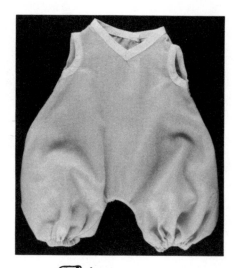

Illustration 123. Original drawing (what is left of it) from the cover for the pattern showing the dress for a 12in (30.5cm) Mary Jane. Note the Bluebird pin on the dress. Circa 1920. Next to the drawing is a reproduction of the original dress made by Sandy Williams from the original pattern.

Illustration 124. Original drawing from the cover for the pattern of the undergarments for a 12in (30.5cm) Mary Jane. Circa 1920. Also shown is a reproduction of the original undergarments made by Sandy Williams from the original pattern.

MARY JANE PATTERN
Redrawn by Sandy Williams

Doll dresses of this period were quickly sewn and had no extra finishing touches. Usually the seams and hems were left raw — no turned-in seams or hand-sewing. Tiny gold safety pins closed the garments. Dresses were made up in plaids or pale colors of maize, pink or blue. Bloomers usually matched the dress. Dress collars either matched the dress or were white (either a broadcloth or an organdy). The patterns presented here are meant as a guide. First, measure your doll against the bloomers; make the bloomers up and then measure the doll against the dress pattern pieces before making the dress up.

Materials needed: 1/3yd (.30m) of fabric for dress and bloomers, thread to match, white thread, 1/4yd (.23m) of white fabric for collar, package of 1/4in (.65cm) white elastic for bloomers, four small gold safety pins, tailors chalk, package of white narrow double fold bias tape, tiny snap or button, yarn or embroidery thread (optional — for trimming dress).

Bloomers: Usually bloomers of this period can be seen peeking out from under the short dresses, made out of the same fabric as the dress. The neckline and the armhole seams were sewn with white narrow double fold bias tape covering their raw edges. You may wish instead to sew the bloomers as sketched — with an eyelet ruffle at the neckline and at the leg seams; turn the armhole edges in and hem (use a bleached cotton muslin, batiste or broadcloth fabric). On the original bloomers of this period, the seam allowance on the leg opening was only turned up once and the elastic was sewn on top of this unfinished seam allowance. The elastic manufactured today for home sewing use does not have this stretch — no matter how hard you pull the elastic you just cannot pull it hard enough. This is one change that is necessary to make — you must make a casing to pull the elastic through.

Sew the center back of bloomers together from dot to crotch edge; narrowly hem raw edges of center back opening; press left back on fold line. Sew front bloomer to back bloomer at shoulders; press seams toward back. Sew white narrow double fold bias tape to neck and armhole areas; take a tiny dart in bias tape at center front of neck so the tape will lie flat; press. Sew front and back bloomers sides together; press. Sew front leg/crotch area to back leg/crotch area (you may need to ease back crotch area on front crotch area). Sew leg crotch area again; trim and press. Turn leg seam allowance up to form a casing in which to pull the elastic through; sew close to edge of casing leaving a small opening in which to pull the elastic through. Wrap the elastic around the doll's mid thigh, pull snug, mark sewing line with tailors chalk, leave a 1/4in (.65cm) seam allowance on each end of the elastic. Pull elastic through casing using a tiny gold safety pin. Overlap the 1/4 (.65cm) seams together so they lie flat; stitch together; sew casing opening closed. Place bloomers on doll and close back opening with two tiny gold safety pins.

Dress: Slit back dress opening and narrowly hem. Sew front to back dress at shoulders. Press shoulder seams to back. Staystitch around dress neckline. Cut collar out of white fabric or out of matching dress fabric. Narrowly hem edge of collar. With right side of collar against wrong side of dress, sew dress and collar together at neckline; using a narrow seam allowance, sew edges of collar to center back dress opening; trim neckline seam. Flip collar right side out and press. Turn sleeve hem up and stitch.

Cut two belt pattern pieces out. Fold one belt piece lengthwise (with right sides together); stitch around belt on two sides leaving open where marked; clip corners; turn right side out and press. Repeat with other belt piece. Stitch belt ties between dots on each side of back dress (fold of belt tie faces up).

Sew front dress to back dress at side seams and underarms in one continuous seam; trim and clip underarm seams. Press side seams to back of dress. Turn up hem; evenly easing in fullness and topstitch. At this point you may wish to embroider the collar, sleeve and hem edges as illlustrated or leave them plain.

Place dress on doll and close center back opening with two tiny gold safety pins. Cross belt ties at center back of dress; mark center back and sew tiny snap or button to belt ties to close.

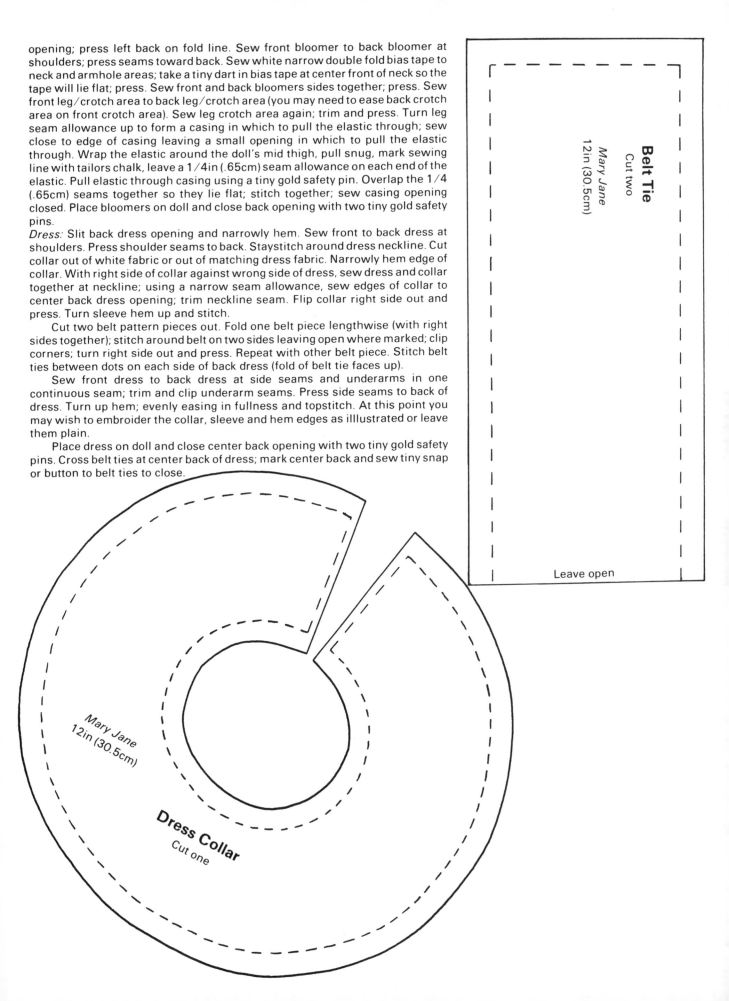

Belt Tie
Cut two

Mary Jane
12in (30.5cm)

Leave open

Dress Collar
Cut one

Mary Jane
12in (30.5cm)

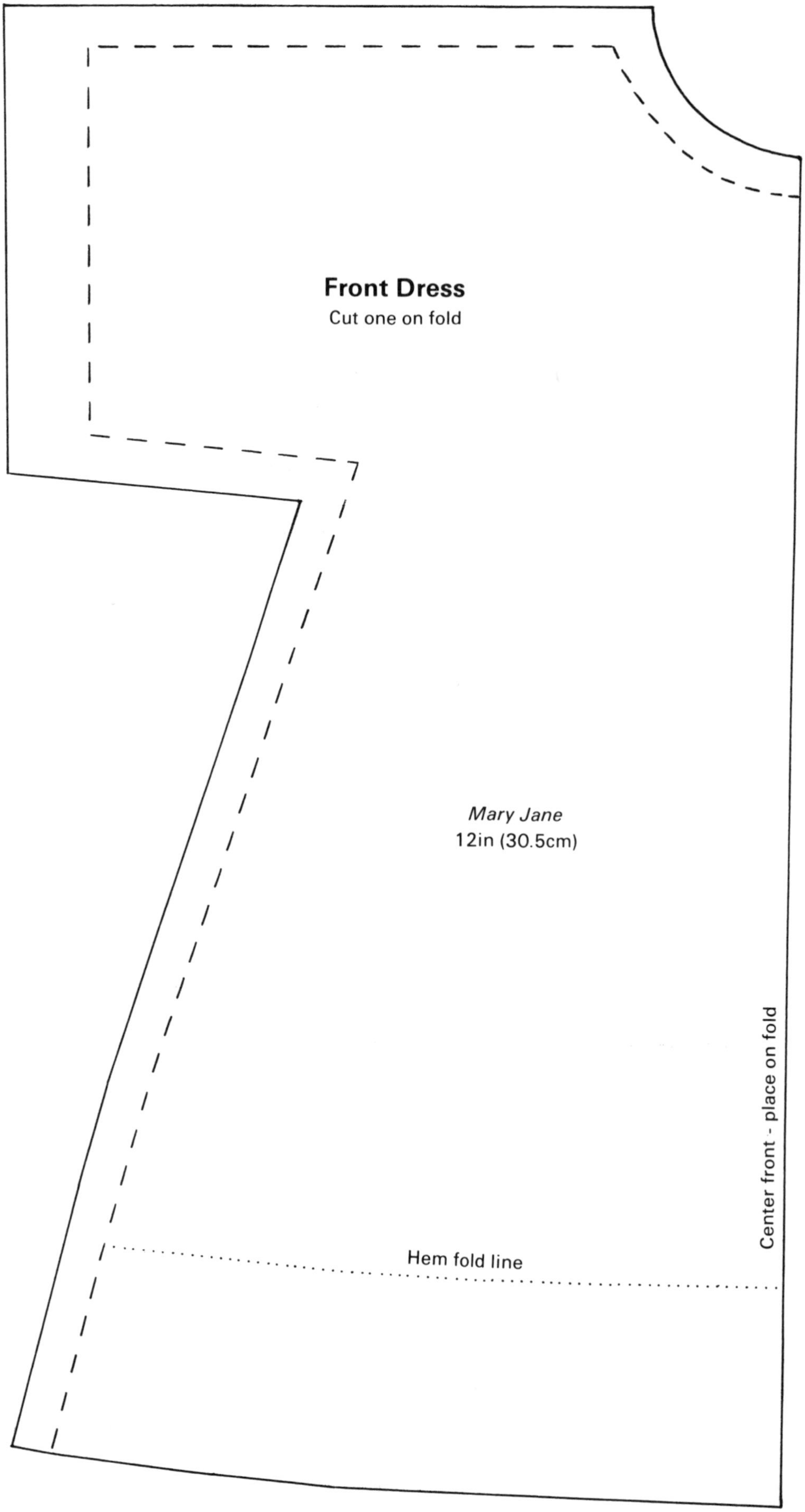

Front Dress
Cut one on fold

Mary Jane
12in (30.5cm)

Center front - place on fold

Hem fold line

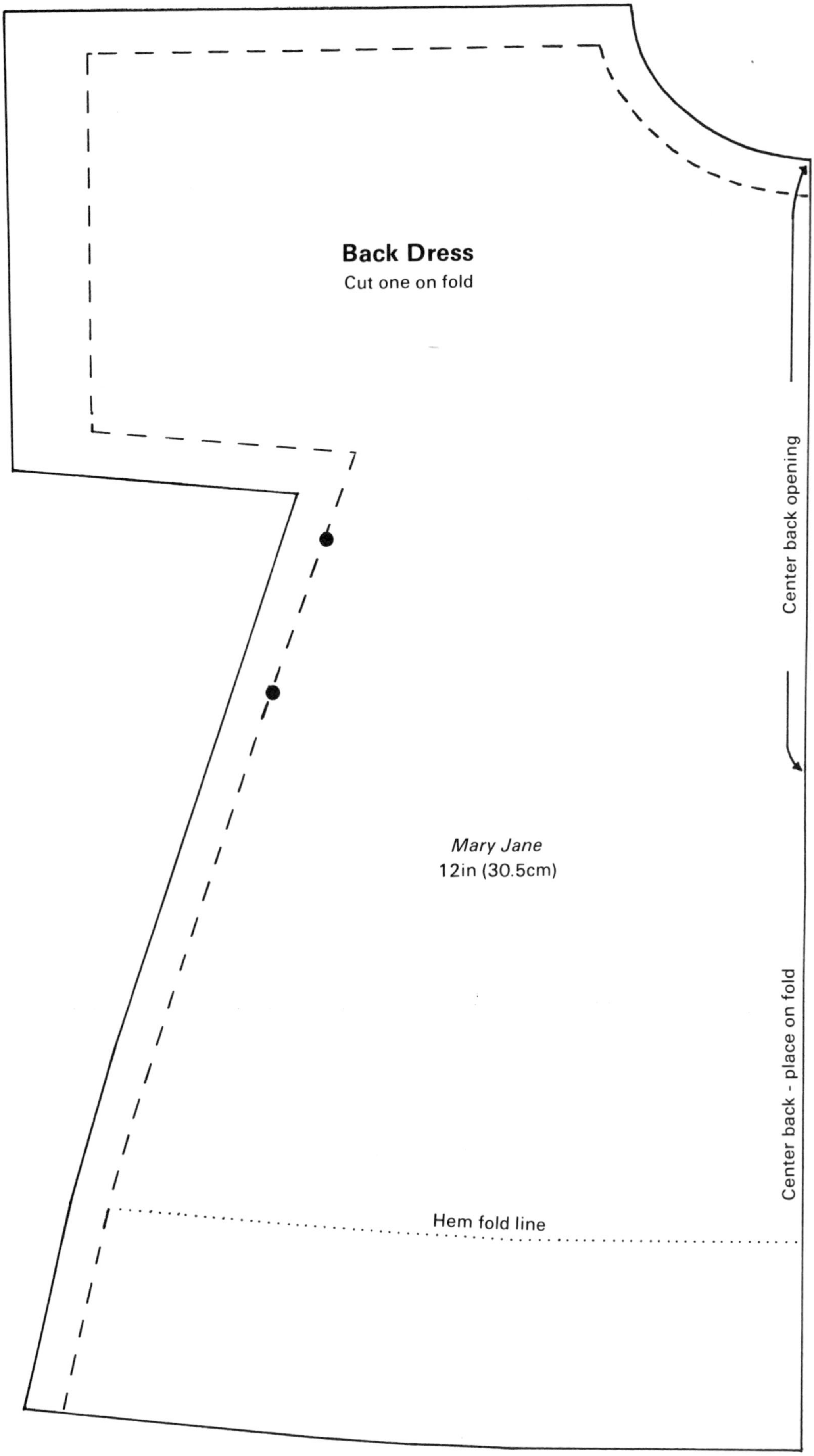

Back Dress
Cut one on fold

Mary Jane
12in (30.5cm)

Center back opening

Center back - place on fold

Hem fold line

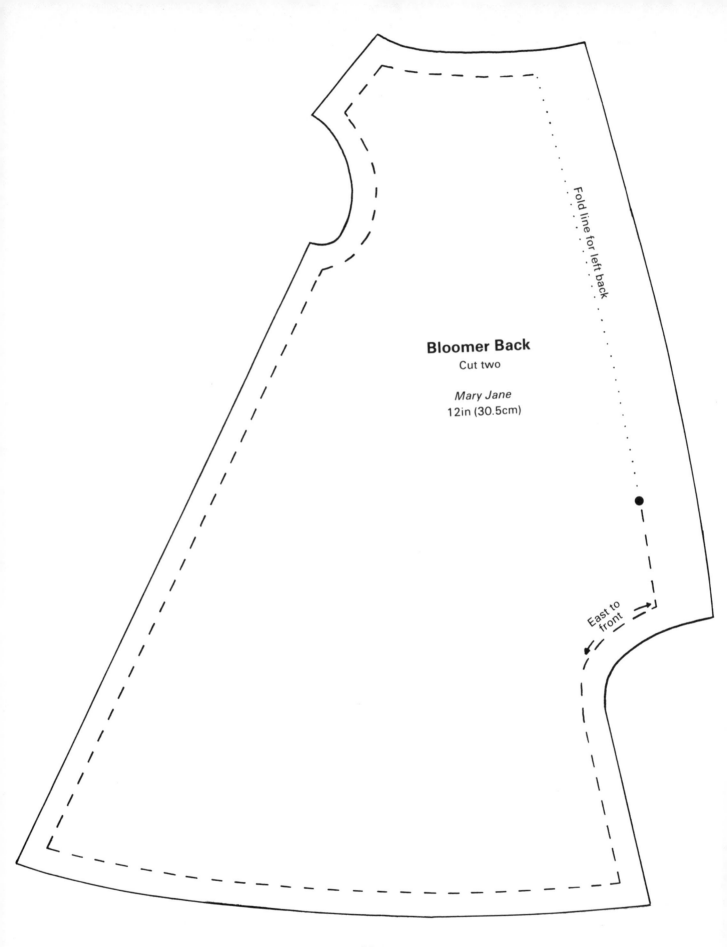

Bloomer Back
Cut two

Mary Jane
12in (30.5cm)

Fold line for left back

East to front

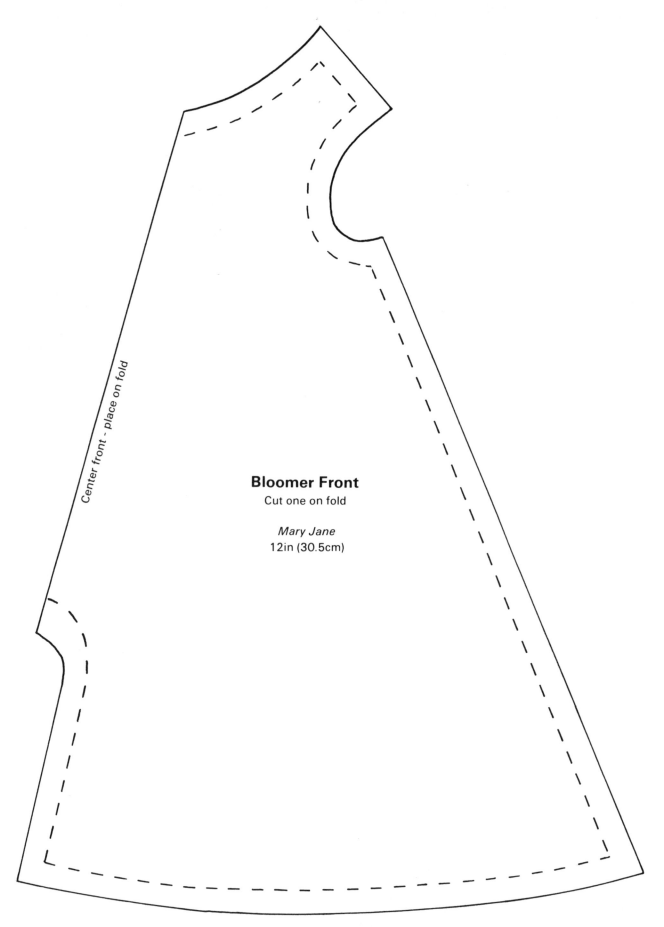

Center front - place on fold

Bloomer Front
Cut one on fold

Mary Jane
12in (30.5cm)

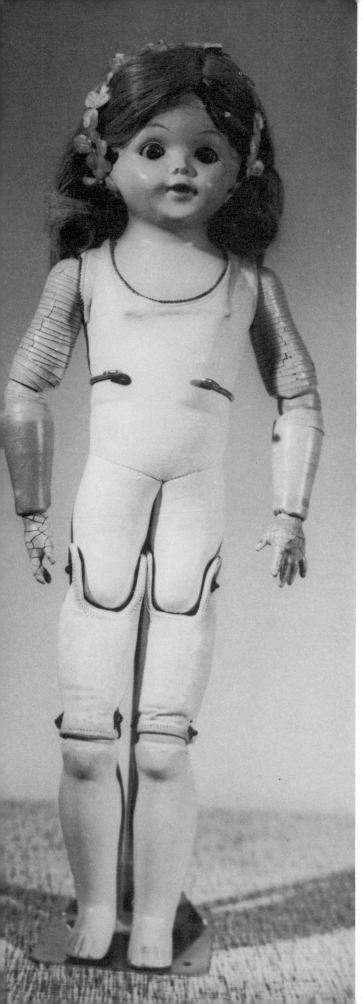

Illustration 125. 20in (50.8cm) kid-bodied doll; composition head, wooden arms with composition hands, composition legs; pin and disk joints at hips and knees to enable doll to sit nicely, elastic goes through tube in body for stringing; medium blonde human hair wig; blue-gray metal eyes, brown painted eyebrows, painted upper eyelashes; open/closed mouth; marked on back: "Effanbee." *Sara Barrett Collection.*

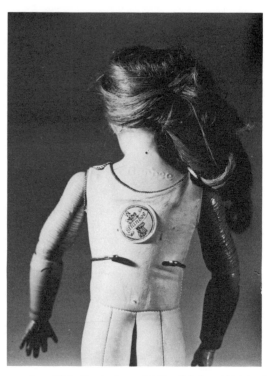

Illustration 126. Back view of 20in (50.8cm) kid-bodied doll seen in *Illustration 125* showing the marking on the back. Note the label also on the back which is shown in detail in *Illustration 127. Sara Barrett Collection.*

Illustration 127. Enlargement of the rare label on the back of the 20in (50.8cm) kid-bodied doll. This was drawn from the full page advertisement appearing in *Playthings* shown in *Illustration 156. Sara Barrett Collection.*

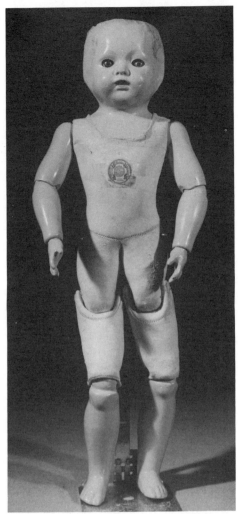

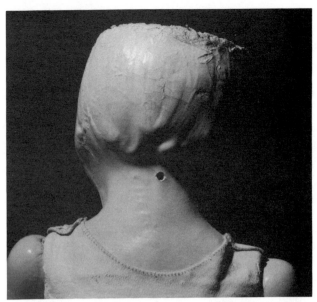

Illustration 130. Back view of the 20in (50.8cm) kid-bodied doll seen in *Illustration 128* showing the stylized mark "Effanbee" running vertically just to the left of the hole for tying the eyes in the box. By tying them, the eyes were held in place when the doll was being shipped, making it less likely for them to be jarred loose. 1920. *Judy Johnson Collection.*

Illustration 128. 20in (50.8cm) kid-bodied doll; composition shoulder head, wooden arms, composition lower legs; arms are jointed by elastic which passes through the torso, legs are pin and disk jointed at hips and knees; blue-gray metal eyes; light brown painted eyebrows, painted eyelashes; open/closed mouth, two teeth; dimples. 1920. *Judy Johnson Collection.*

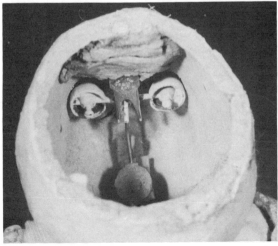

Illustration 129. Head sliced away on the 20in (50.8cm) kid-bodied doll shown in *Illustration 128* so that eyes could be inserted. Eyes were fastened in with a wad of cement-like material. *Judy Johnson Collection.*

Illustration 131. 20in (50.8cm) kid-bodied doll seen in *Illustrations 128, 129 and 130* shown with her wig of dark long curls; wears old madras blouse with woven design, very fine pink and white checked cotton pleated skirt on bodice with ribbon sash around the collar. 1920. *Judy Johnson Collection.*

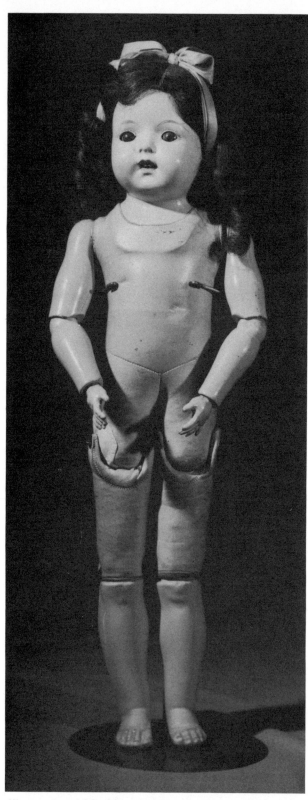

Illustration 132. 24in (61cm) kid-bodied doll; composition head, wooden arms with composition hands, composition legs; wooden ball-jointed arms which are strung on elastic which passes through a tube in the body, hips and knees are pin and disk jointed so doll sits easily; dark human hair wig; blue-gray metal eyes, brown painted eyebrows, painted upper and lower eyelashes; open mouth, two molded upper teeth. 1919. *Edell Lashley Collection.*

Illustration 133. 24in (61cm) kid-bodied doll shown in *Illustration 132,* wearing an old soft batiste dress with hand smocking at the neck and hem top, original leather shoes; marked on the back of head: ''Effanbee.'' 1919. *Edell Lashley Collection.*

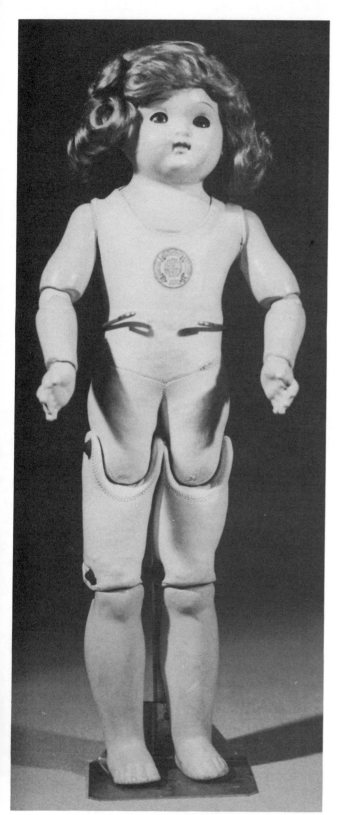

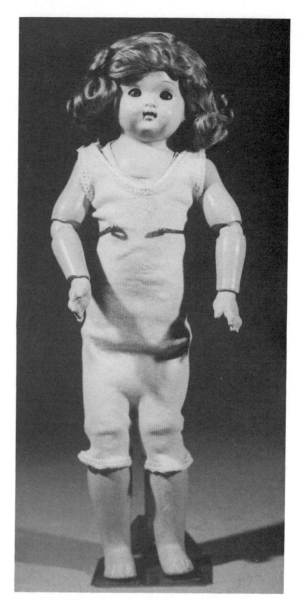

Illustration 135. 18in (45.7cm) kid-bodied doll seen in *Illustration 134,* shown in her original underwear suit. 1920. *Judy Johnson Collection.*

Illustration 134. 18in (45.7cm) kid-bodied doll; composition head, wooden arms, composition legs; elastic strung through the arms, pin and disk jointed legs at hips and knees; brown mohair wig; blue-gray metal eyes, brown painted eyebrows, painted upper and lower eyelashes; closed mouth. 1920. This doll is shown undressed in the January 1920 *Playthings. Judy Johnson Collection.*

Illustration 136. Enlargement of the label on the 18in (45.7cm) kid-bodied doll seen in *Illustrations 134 and 135* reading: ''Effanbee//GENUINE//KID BODY// 100% AMERICAN//CORK STUFFED.'' *Judy Johnson Collection.*

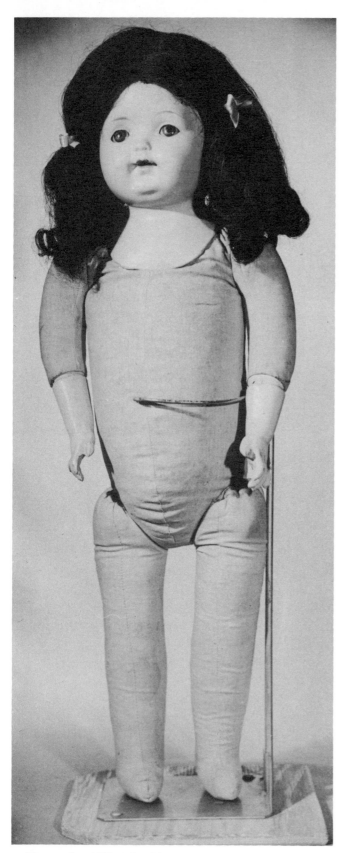

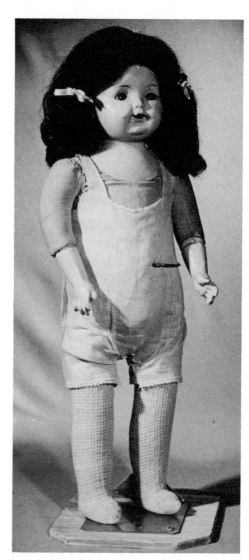

Illustration 138. 24in (61cm) standing *Baby Catherine* shown in *Illustration 137* wearing her original underwear with lace at the edge of her original stockings. *Judy Johnson Collection.*

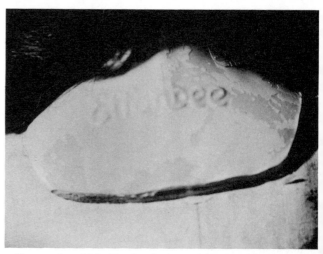

Illustration 137. 24in (61cm) standing *Baby Catherine;* composition head, cork-stuffed cloth body, composition arms, cloth legs; dark human hair wig; blue-gray metal eyes, brown painted eyebrows, painted upper and lower eyelashes; open mouth. 1919. *Judy Johnson Collection.*

Illustration 139. The back of the 24in (61cm) standing *Baby Catherine* see in *Illustrations 137 and 138,* showing the mark on the back of the shoulder plate: "Effanbee." *Judy Johnson Collection.*

$1.79
High-Grade Dressed Doll with Real Hair

An exceptionally **pretty** dressed doll. Body stuffed with cork. Head and hands made of composition. Jointed hips and shoulders. Dress made of crepe. Underwear of good quality material. Complete with shoes and stockings.

Article No.	About Ht. In.	Ship. Wt., Lbs.	Price
43D2798	12½	1¼	$1.79
43D2799	15½	1¾	2.49
48D2800	18½	2½	3.49
48D2809	25	6	5.55

LEFT: Illustration 140. Advertisement showing a standing *Baby Catherine* in proper original dress. The material is a form of crepe. 1919. Montgomery Ward & Co. catalog.

RIGHT: Illustration 141. An advertisement for a cork-stuffed doll showing the proper costume. The dress is said to be made of fine quality voile trimmed with dainty lace. Because of the more elaborate clothes, this doll was considerably more expensive than the one shown in *Illustration 140*. Sears, Roebuck and Co. catalog, Chicago, Illinois, 1920.

Real Hair
Especially Recommended

	Ht. About Ins.	Shpg. Wt., Lbs	General Catalog Price	Sale Price
18P3123	24	4¾	$9.95	$8.95
18P3129	20	3¼	7.98	6.95
18P3139	18	2½	6.65	5.98
18P3143	16	2	4.98	4.35
18P3147	14	1½	3.89	3.25

This is our wonderful new line of fine dressed dolls, and we wish all our friends might see them, for they are much lovelier than any line sold in our previous catalogs. First of all, the dolls have well formed, strong cloth covered bodies, stuffed plump, and jointed at hips and shoulders. The heads are beautifully modeled of light weight composition, almost unbreakable, and have pretty, low necks. Fitted with eyes which open and shut. The lovely wig is of real hair which can easily be recurled, and has a wide ribbon bow. Then there is the gorgeous dress, made of fine quality voile and trimmed with dainty lace. It is a charming style and nicely finished throughout. Excellent underwear, socks and shoes. Each of the five sizes is like the picture, and is a remarkable value at our price.

OUR LATEST NOVELTY

War Nurses. To retail at all prices from One Dollar up

LEFT: Illustration 142. *War Nurses* of various sizes; shoulder heads with cloth bodies, composition arms to below the elbows, cloth legs; wearing headdresses and apron bibs with a red cross symbol on each. *Playthings,* November 1917.

"CUNNING BABY" DRESSED DOLL
With Moving Eyes

"Effanbee" quality. Composition head and hands, painted features, bobbed mohair wig.

MOVING EYES

F7538—15½ in., white organdie dress, lace inserted yoke and skirt, lace trim, lace edge jacket effect, ribbon rosette, lace trim underwear ribbon rosette on lace straw hat, white socks, colored slippers. ½ doz. in box. Doz. **$24.00**

LEFT: Illustration 143. Advertisement for *Cunning Baby*. Butler Brothers catalog, 1918.

BELOW: Illustration 145. Advertisements for *French Baby*. The name *French Baby* alludes to the costuming of the doll, said to be copied from a Paris, France, style. Butler Brothers catalog, 1918.

FRENCH BABY DRESSED DOLL
With Moving Eyes

"Effanbee" quality, composition head and hands, painted features, bobbed mohair wig. Extra value at this price.

MOVING EYES

F7539—15½ in., flowered lace stripe material, solid color lawn cross-over collar with tie strings forming sash. French bonnet to match costume, lawn underwear, white socks, colored slippers. ½ doz. in box. Doz. **$21.00**

F7539

French Baby

15½ in., "Effanbee" quality, bobbed mohair wig, flowered dress, solid color trim, French bonnet, lawn underwear, white socks, colored slippers.
F7539— ½ dz. bx. Doz. **$21.00**

$2.80
Fashionably Dressed Doll
With Sleeping Eyes

This plump little dolly has an extremely pretty face, sleeping eyes and mohair wig. Her dress is stylishly made of flowered voile with large bow in back. Hat to match dress. Composition head and hands, which will not break easily. Cork stuffed body. Size about 15 in. Shipping weight, 2 pounds.
48D2825—Price.....**$2.80**

Illustration 146. Advertisement for *French Baby* which appears to be a different mold from the *French Baby* of 1918, shown in *Illustration 145*. Montgomery Ward & Co. catalog, 1919.

Illustration 144. Shown here are *Our Sailor Lad, Our Nurse Doll* and *Our Soldier Boy,* sold by Montgomery Ward & Co. These dolls each have a shoulder head, cloth body, composition arms to above the wrists and cloth legs, they are of various sizes. *Playthings* shows *War Nurse's* headdress coming just to the doll's shoulder. In this illustration it reaches to the doll's waist which may be an artist's conception. Montgomery Ward & Co., calls her *Our Nurse Doll.* She would have the same marks as the *Salvation Army Lass. War Nurses* were advertised in *Playthings,* November 1917. The price mentioned was from $1.00 up so there may be one smaller size than is offered here. Montgomery Ward & Co. catalog, 1919.

Our Sailor Lad

Surely this little Jackie will find a warm and hearty welcome in every American home. 15 in. high. Good quality uniform. Head and hands made of composition. Ship. wt., 2 lbs.
48D2828—
Price.............. **$1.89**

Our Nurse Doll

Mohair wig, composition head and hands, cork stuffed body. Dressed throughout with good material.

Article No.	Ht.,In.	Ship. Wt.,lbs.	Price
48D2795	12	1½	$1.52
48D2796	14½	1¾	2.42
48D2797	18½	2	2.99

Our Soldier Boy

Every American child would be proud to own this little Sammy in fine khaki uniform with spiral puttees. 15 in. high. Composition head and hands. Ship. wt., 2 lbs.
48D2827—Price **$1.89**

Illustration 147. Advertisement showing the *Salvation Army Lass* dolls. *Playthings,* August 1921.

THE SENSATIONAL NOVELTY OF THE YEAR

SALVATION ARMY LASSIES

Effanbee *Dolls*

Illustration 148. 15in (38.1cm) *Salvation Army Lass;* composition head, ground cork-stuffed cloth body, composition arms, cloth legs; replaced wig (original was blonde with bangs); blue eyes, brown eyebrows; open/closed mouth; paint has been retouched wears original navy cotton dress with beige bodice, replaced shoes; marked: "Effanbee." 1921. Appears to be the doll *Margie* in a new presentation. Produced by arrangement with the Salvation Army. Shown on the cover of *Playthings* in July 1921. *Elfriede Morris Collection.*

Illustration 149. 15in (38.1cm) *Salvation Army Lass* seen in *Illustration 148,* shown in her original blue straw bonnet, red sateen cape and regulation uniform. The ribbon saying "The Salvation Army Lass" is missing from the bonnet. *Elfriede Morris Collection.*

Illustration 150. 15in (38.1cm) *Margie;* composition head, cloth body, composition arms, cloth legs; molded blonde painted hair; blue painted eyes, brown painted eyebrows. Doll is wearing the Bluebird Effanbee pin. 1921. An actual doll has never been located to photograph. *Playthings,* June 1921.

Mohair Wig

With arms outstretched, this little doll is all ready to be embraced by some fortunate little girl. Her dress is white with lace and ribbon trimming. White underwear, and removable shoes. Well stuffed body, jointed at shoulders and hips. Composition hard-to-break head arms and breast plate. Painted features mohair wig. Height, 14¾ inches. Shipping weight, 18 ounces.
49 E 2517 .... 94c

Illustration 152. This doll appears to be *Margie* with the addition of a wig. Montgomery Ward & Co. Fall - Winter catalog, 1921.

Dolls that were made to love

Baby Grumpy
Height, 14¼ Inches

Cork Stuffed Body
Jointed at shoulders and hips. Composition head, hands and breast plate. Pink organdie dress. Shipping weight, 2¼ pounds.
49 E 2523 .. $1.85

Cork stuffed body jointed at shoulders and hips. Composition head and hands. Painted hair. Pink linene dress and bonnet. Shipping weight, 2 pounds.
49 E 2522— $1.49

Height, 14½ In.
Cork stuffed body, jointed at shoulders and hips. Composition head and hands. Flowered voile dress and cap. Shipping weight, 1½ pounds.
49 E 2518-$1.19

Height, 14½ In.
Cork stuffed body, jointed at shoulders and hips. Composition head and hands. Pink organdie dress. Removable shoes and stockings. Satin sash. Shipping weight, 18 ounces.
49 E 2519-$1.19

ABOVE: Illustration 151. These dolls, with the exception of *Baby Grumpy*, appear to be *Margie* as advertised in *Playthings*. They each have a shoulder head of composition as well a composition hands to above the wrists. Montgomery Ward & Co. Fall - Winter catalog, 1921.

Height, 15½ Inches

Well stuffed body with hip and shoulder joints. Hard-to-break composition head, hands and shoes. Painted features; mohair wig. Plaid gingham plaited dress. Light blue knitted mercerized cap. Shipping weight, 2 pounds.
49 E 2520 .... $1.29

RIGHT: Illustration 154. The exact name of this doll is unknown but the advertisement notes her head, hands and shoes are Hard-to-Break composition. Montgomery Ward & Co. Fall - Winter catalog, 1921.

Attractive birthday doll that any little girl would like to have. Pink figured organdie dress; pink and white pleated hat. Body, head, arms and legs are made of composition and are hard to break. Features and hair are painted. Jointed at shoulders and hips. Removable shoes and stockings. Shipping weight 2 pounds. $1.49
49 E 2521 ....

Height, 14½ Inches

Illustration 153. This doll appears to be *Margie* and has composition legs as well as arms. Montgomery Ward & Co. Fall - Winter catalog, 1921.

45c EACH

18F3458   18F3470   18F3466   18F3486

Special Stuffed Character Dolls. "Hard to Break."
Strong cloth covered bodies. Durable composition hands and head with painted hair and features. They will stand a lot of rough handling. Costumes of medium quality cotton materials. Jointed at hips and shoulders. Height, about 11½ inches. Shipping weight, 1¼ pounds. **Order by number.**

SEARS, ROEBUCK AND CO.

Illustration 155. These appear to be the last of the Hard-to-Break dolls. They were made for the economy buyer. Possibly a few have survived. They each have a composition head, cloth body, composition arms and cloth legs; painted hair; painted eyes, painted eyebrows; and a painted mouth. Sears, Roebuck and Co. catalog, 1921.

EARLY BABIES

Effanbee manufactured baby dolls from the very beginning years of the company. A *Baby Dainty* model was available as early as 1912. (Since we have arranged the *Baby Dainty* dolls into a separate chapter, you will find those elsewhere.) *Playthings* magazine, May 1914, pictured a *Baby Dainty* with a pacifier, in a long christening dress. *Christening Babies* in six sizes were prominently advertised in the trade magazine in April 1919. The May 1919 issue illustrated six sizes of blonde mohair wigged, sleep-eyed sitting infants. The full dresses are flared up behind them and appear to be beautifully trimmed in rows of lace or braid. We know of none of these that have survived intact.

The dolls of this period were cold press composition or Hard-to-Break with cork-stuffed bodies (for lightness). Most of the baby dolls were dolly-faced, but *Baby*

Catherine was an exception. She had dimples and the lively expression of a real child. The outstanding all-compositon baby (no original advertising) with turning wrists is a character face version as well.

Dolly Dumpling, 1918, was quite heavily advertised over a period of time. She was a dolly-faced baby, yet evidently quite popular.

Baby Bud followed the *Kewpie,* and was classified as a "Novelty Art Doll." Of course, he (or she) was definitely a character doll with the impish smile. No doubt many of them were bought by adults for adults. *Baby Bud* was issued in many forms, and is a joy to add to an Effanbee collection. This doll was almost surely inspired by the German bisque *Baby Bud.* Japan made its version too.

Illustration 156. Full page advertisement appearing in *Playthings* showing the child and dolls which were used in a drawing on the label for the kid-bodied dolls. Copyrighted 1919 by Fleischaker & Baum. The doll on the floor is a shoulder head baby with a cloth torso. The girl holds a *Mary Jane* and a bent-leg baby in her right arm and a shoulder head baby and a shoulder head girl with cloth legs in her left arm.

"OUR BABY" DOLLS
In Short Slips

Composition heads, painted features and hair, composition forearms, cork stuffed bodies, asstd. pink & blue ribbon trim.

F7905—F. & B., 14 in., white lawn slip, lace trim yoke, neck and sleeves, w h i t e socks, lace edge panties, lace trim lawn cap, ribbon bows and strings. ½ doz. in box. **Doz. $8.75**

F7906—20½ in., white lawn slip, lace trim yoke, ribbon and lace trim cap, lawn strings, crocheted bootees, cork stuffed body. 1 in box. **Each. $1.25**

Illustration 157. This advertisement shows two attractive examples of the proper costume for cork-stuffed baby dolls. Butler Brothers catalog, 1917.

"OUR BABY" DOLLS—In Short Slips
Excellent values—"Effanbee" quality. Well modeled composition heads and hands, painted features and hair unless specified, well stuffed bodies, hip and shoulder joints. There will be a large demand for these.

F7905—14 in., white lawn slip, lace trim yoke, neck and sleeves, white socks, lace edge panties, lace trim lawn cap, ribbon bows and strings. ½ doz. in box.... **Doz. $8.90**

F7906—20½ in., white lawn slip, lace trim yoke, neck and sleeves, ribbon and lace trim cap, lawn strings, panties, crocheted bootees. ½ doz. in box. **Doz. $16.50**

F7907—20 in., mohair wig, white lawn dress, lace trim underskirt, lace edge panties, lace trim lawn cap, ribbon bows and strings, open mouth with pacifier, **crocheted bootees.** ½ doz. in box. **Doz. $28.00**

Illustration 158. Advertisement for *Our Baby*. Butler Brothers catalog, 1918.

Illustration 159. Effanbee baby dolls in elaborate christening gowns. Redrawn by Sandy Williams from the reverse side of the original Effanbee pattern for a 12in (30.5cm) *Mary Jane*.

"HARD-TO-BREAK" BABIES
With Long Slips

Composition heads and hands, painted features and hair, shoulder and hip joints.

F7912—F. & B., 14 in., lace trim lawn slip, underskirt and stork effect panties, lace trim pink flannelette jacket, composition head and hands, painted features and hair, open mouth, pacifier on ribbon. 1/12 dz. bx. Doz. **$10.50**

F7892—17 in., embroidery trim long white lawn slip, lace trim neck and sleeves, cap to match, lace trim underskirt and panties. 1 in box..............Each, **98c**

Illustration 160. Advertisement showing Hard-to-Break baby dolls. Note that actual names of the dolls are not used but "F. & B." is listed. Butler Brothers catalog, 1917.

HIGH GRADE BABIES
Worsted Sweater

Unbreakable composition heads and hands, painted features, asstd. blonde and brunette mohair wigs, moving eyes, cork stuffed bodies, concealed joints, white worsted sweater suits and caps, asstd. pink and blue ribbon trims, white stockings, kid shoes, pacifiers on ribbon. Each in box.

F7533—11¾ in...Each,	**$1.90**	
F7534—13½ " .. "	**2.50**	
F7535—16½ " .. "	**3.65**	
F7536—20½ " .. "	**4.90**	
F7537—32 " .. "	**6.00**	

Illustration 161. Advertisement for a baby doll in five different sizes. Butler Brothers catalog, 1917.

NEW "BUY ME" DOLLS
Hard to Break

Composition heads and hands, painted features, sleeping eyes, asstd. blonde and tosca mohair wigs, concealed hip and shoulder joints, flesh color legs, lace trim lawn slips, ribbon rosettes and strings on caps, stork effect panties. 1 in box.

F7907 — 20 in., concealed joints, open mouth with pacifier, mohair wig, white lawn dress, lace trim yoke and bottom, lawn cap, ribbon bows and strings, underskirt, lace edge panties, crocheted bootees. 1 in box. Each, **$2.40**

F7908—12 in., white socks. Each, **$1.20**
F7909—14½ in., white socks. Ea., **$1.60**

F7910—18 in., crocheted bootees............Each, **$2.25**
F7911—20 in., crocheted bootees............Each, **$2.85**

LEFT: Illustration 162. Advertisement for baby dolls. Butler Brothers catalog, 1917.

Illustration 163. 22in (55.9cm) *Baby Catherine;* composition shoulder head, cloth cork-stuffed body, composition arms to the elbows, cloth legs; brown mohair wig; blue-gray metal sleep eyes, brown painted eyebrows, painted upper and lower eyelashes; open mouth for pacifier.

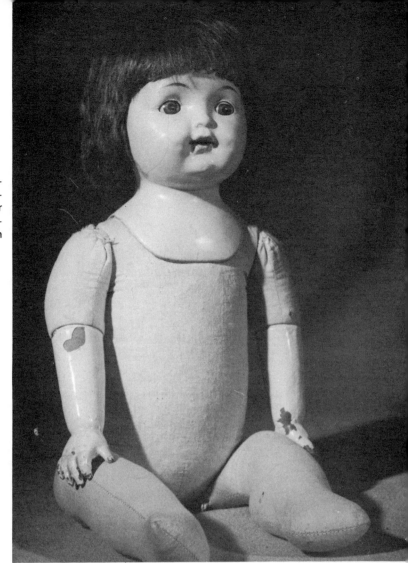

Illustration 164. Close-up of 22in (55.9cm) *Baby Catherine* shown in *Illustration 163.* Note the dimples.

Illustration 165. Close-up of 22in (55.9cm) *Baby Catherine* seen in *Illustrations 163 and 164,* showing the open mouth for the pacifier.

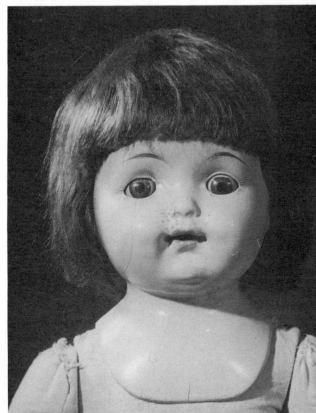

$1.37

Character Dolls to be Dressed

Do you notice the expression in this doll's face? Doesn't it look life-like? This beautiful doll has a heavy mohair wig. Composition head and hands. Body stuffed with cork and covered with flesh color cloth. White socks.

Article No.	Ht. In.	Ship. Wt., lbs.	Price
48D2785	11½	1	$1.37
48D2786	14½	1½	1.77
48D2787	17	2	2.79
48D2788	20½	3½	3.80

Illustration 168. Advertisement for *Baby Catherine.* Montgomery Ward & Co. catalog, 1919.

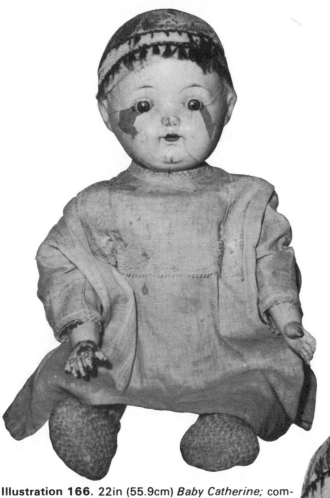

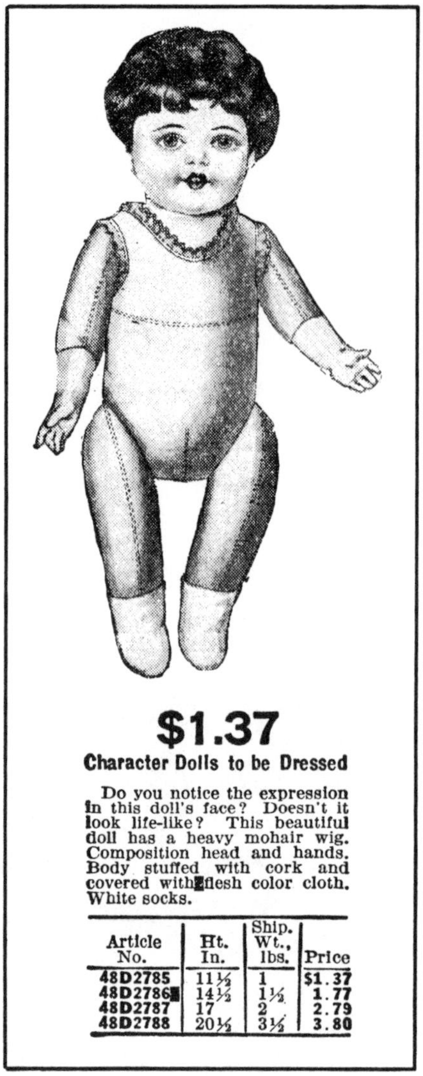

Illustration 166. 22in (55.9cm) *Baby Catherine;* composition head, ground cork-stuffed cloth body, composition arms to below the elbows, cloth legs; brown mohair wig; blue-gray metal eyes, brown painted eyebrows, painted upper and lower eyelashes; open/closed mouth; wears original booties and chemise with coarse lace at the neck, sleeves and bodice, ribbons on the bodice; marked on the back of the shoulder plate: "Effanbee." Shown as found in an attic in the 1950s, damaged by dampness. The body is well preserved. Note the remnants of the early wig which was made on strips in the European style.

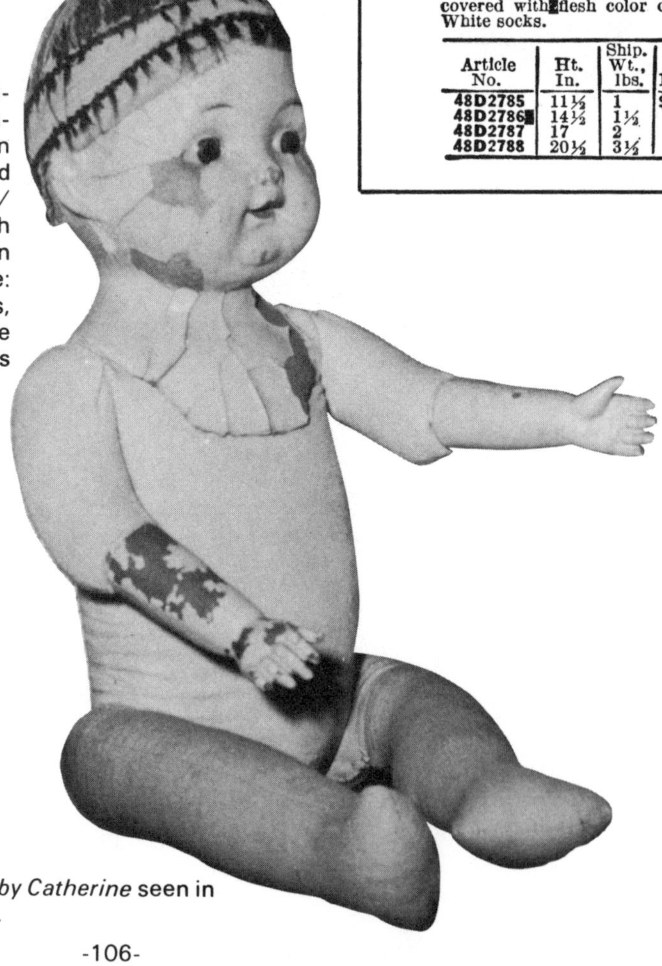

Illustration 167. 22in (55.9cm) *Baby Catherine* seen in *Illustration 166,* shown undressed.

HIGH GRADE DRESSED BABY DOLLS

Composition heads and hands, mohair wigs, moving eyes, cork stuffed bodies, concealed joints, long fine white lawn slips, lace and ribbon run embroidery yoke and belt, lace and insertion panel front, ribbon bow trim, ruffle bottom and sleeves, lace trim underwear, lace trim cap, ribbon bows and tie strings, open mouth with pacifier. **Elaborately dressed.** No finer dolls on the market at these reasonable prices, 1 in box.

F7872—18 in., white socks.......Doz. **$57.00**
F7873—20 in., crocheted bootees.. " **72.00**
F7874—24 in., crocheted bootees.. " **90.00**

Illustration 169. Advertisement for baby dolls in elaborate christening gowns. At least some of the *Christening Babies* were *Baby Catherine* models. Butler Brothers catalog, 1918.

"BABY CATHERINE"—With Moving Eyes

MOVING EYES

Bobbed mohair wig, **moving eyes.** Elaborately dressed. A style that will appeal to "little mothers."

Composition heads and hands, excellent flesh finish painted features, short **mohair wigs,** moving eyes, well modeled cork stuffed bodies, hip and shoulder joints, white organdie short baby dress, lace and rosette trim, lace trim petticoat and panties, fancy bonnet, white socks, pink or blue **leatherette bootees,** pacifier on ribbon. ½ doz. in box.

F7563—13 in.	Doz.	**$22.50**
F7564—14½ in.	Doz.	**$32.00**
F7565—18 in.	Doz.	**$42.00**
F7566—21 in.	Doz.	**$60.00**

Illustration 170. Two views of *Baby Catherine* shown in original clothes. Butler Brothers catalog, 1918.

"Baby Catherine"

Short **mohair wigs,** moving eyes, white organdie short baby dress, lace and rosette trim, lace trim petticoat and panties, fancy bonnet, white socks, pink or blue **leatherette bootees,** pacifier on ribbon. ½ doz. in box.

	Doz.
F7563—13 in	**$22.50**
F7564—14½ "	**32.00**
F7565—18 "	**42.00**
F7566—21 "	**60.00**

Illustration 171. The brushed wool outfit on this 22in (55.9cm) doll was called a "teddy bear suit." This is similar to one in the 1915 Effanbee catalog. The name of the company, "F. & B." (for Fleischaker & Baum) was included in the advertisement and the doll wholesaled for $5.00, about half of the retail price. The description here mentions a mohair wig but the doll shown appears to be a painted hair model, possibly form the previous year. Butler Brothers catalog, 1917.

"DE LUXE" BABY BUNTING
Made in U. S. A.
A doll of high quality. Clothing may be taken off.

F7949—F. & B. 22 in., "hard-to-break" composition head fine bisque finish, painted features, mohair wig, composition forearms, cork stuffed bodies, position limbs, concealed hip and shoulder joints, knit worsted teddy bear suit, brush finish, pearl buttons, buttonholes, crotcheted bootees, pacifier with ribbon. 1 in box.

Each, **$5.00**

The Eskimo Baby

I am dressed in an all-wool suit. My body is stuffed with cork, making me light in weight. Jointed at shoulders and hips. Head made of composition with beautiful mohair wig. Length of doll, 22 in. Ship. wt. 3 lbs.

48D2716—Price.....................$9.25

Illustration 172. Advertisement for 22in (55.9cm) *Eskimo Baby*. In the 1915 Effanbee catalog this doll was called merely a "Chubby life-size baby" so *Eskimo Baby* is the name given to it by Montgomery Ward & Co., Montgomery Ward & Co. catalog, 1919.

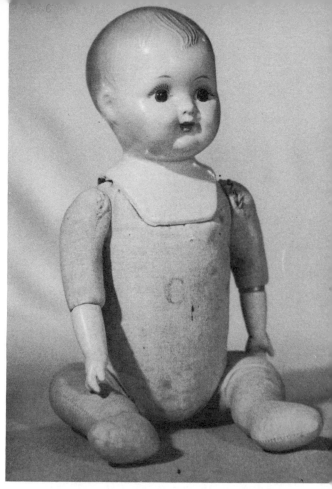

Illustration 175. 15in (38.1cm) *Dolly Dumpling;* wood pulp composition breastplate head, ground cork-stuffed muslin, body, composition arms to below the elbows, cloth legs; golden painted hair; blue painted eyes, tan eyebrows, dark eyelashes; closed mouth; wore a gingham or print dress or romper; marked on back of head: "Effanbee." Advertised in *Playthings,* January 1918.

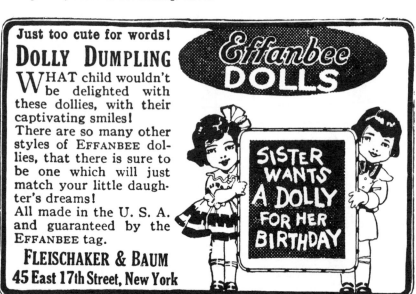

Just too cute for words!

DOLLY DUMPLING

WHAT child wouldn't be delighted with these dollies, with their captivating smiles! There are so many other styles of EFFANBEE dollies, that there is sure to be one which will just match your little daughter's dreams! All made in the U.S.A. and guaranteed by the EFFANBEE tag.

FLEISCHAKER & BAUM
45 East 17th Street, New York

Effanbee DOLLS

SISTER WANTS A DOLLY FOR HER BIRTHDAY

Illustration 173. Early advertising for *Dolly Dumpling*. The doll was said to wear the Effanbee "guarantee" tag. The actual doll was often not shown. Source unknown, 1919.

Illustration 174. *Dolly Dumpling,* re-drawn from an original advertisement by Sandy Williams.

Illustration 176. Close-up of 15in (38.1cm) *Dolly Dumpling* shown in *Illustration 175.*

BELOW: Illustration 178. Advertisement for *Dolly Dumpling* to be given as a premium for eight subscriptions to *Needlecraft* magazine. *Needlecraft,* June 1921.

Dolly Dumpling
Given for **Eight** *Subscriptions*

No. 6481. Dolly Dumpling is not a character-doll nor an ornamental novelty doll. She is a real oldfashioned, sweet-faced baby doll, the kind all little girls love to dress and undress, to read to, to spank when naughty, and to put to bed when darkness falls. Everyone will love Dolly Dumpling at sight and will want to hug her and talk to her. For the latter purpose she brings a miniature story-book, with a really-truly fairy-tale hand-somely printed and illustrated with four page-illustrations in colors. Dolly Dumpling is **14** inches tall, and wears a lovely baby-dress of white lawn with lace edging and a bonnet to match. The illustration does not show full length of dress which is over half a yard long. She is everything that one could desire, with unbreakable, American-style head and a jointed, stuffed body. Do not fail to invite Dolly Dumpling into your family. We pay all her traveling-expenses, and she will stay with you forever.

"EFFANBEE" DOLLY DUMPLINGS

F7757—2 styles, "Romper Babies," solid color linene and flowered novelty rompers, bias trim square neck and sleeves, 1 with belt and elastic knees, turnback bonnets to match costumes, white socks. ⅙ doz. in pkg.

Doz. **$12.00**

F7758—Baby, white lawn dress, full skirt, insertion headed lace edge flounce, square lace neck and trim sleeves, lace trim white lawn bonnet with ribbon strings, lace trim panties, white socks. ½ doz. in box.

Doz. **$12.00**

F7757

F7758

The latest new comer in the doll world— "Effanbee" creation. 14½ in., modeled composition breast plate, heads and composition hands, painted features and hair, cork stuffed chubby bodies, position limbs, concealed hip and shoulder joints. Each in fancy box with "Dolly Dumpling" illustrated litho booklet.

F7756—3 styles, "Little Girl," colored lawn, flowered novelty voile and checked gingham dresses, short waists, full plaited skirt, lace trim or bias bound square necks and sleeves, French bonnets to match costumes, lace trim panties, white socks. ¼ doz. in pkg.

Doz. **$12.00**

F7756

Illustration 177. Advertisements for *Dolly Dumpling*. Butler Brothers catalog, 1918.

LIGHT AND DURABLE

Illustration 179. *Baby Catherine* from the reverse side of the pattern for a dress for a 12in (30.5cm) *Mary Jane,* redrawn from the original by Sandy Williams.

Highest Quality Full Composition
Made in America

Illustration 180. An advertisement showing an all-composition Effanbee doll with a mohair wig and eyes which appear to be painted. She is wearing a simple chemise with lace trim at the neck, sleeves and hem. She is shown with the first paper tag used by Effanbee on dolls and toys. The tag reads: "IF IT IS EFFANBEE IT'S GUARANTEED (In a banner)//WHEN//BUYING A//DOLL OR ANY//STUFFED TOY,//LOOK FOR THE//EFFANBEE//LABEL" on one side and on the other side: "GUARANTEE//THIS TOY//IS MADE UNDER//SANITARY CONDITIONS OF//THE MOST DURABLE AND//EXPENSIVE MATERIALS AND//BY THE MOST MODERN MA-//CHINERY.//IT IS GUARANTEED TO//GIVE SATISFACTORY//WEAR.//EFFANBEE." This doll represents an attempt to make a doll similar to a German bisque doll. *Playthings,* 1916.

LIGHT AND DURABLE

Illustration 181. An advertisement showing an all-composition Effanbee doll with a curly mohair bob wig, sleep eyes and painted eyebrows. She is wearing a basic lace-trimmed chemise. Note that this doll is wearing the first paper tag which is also shown. *Playthings,* July 1916.

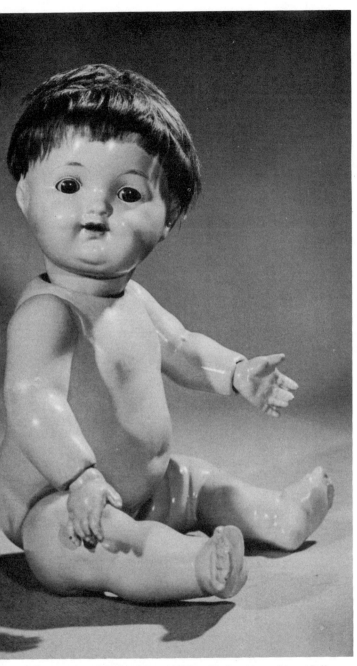

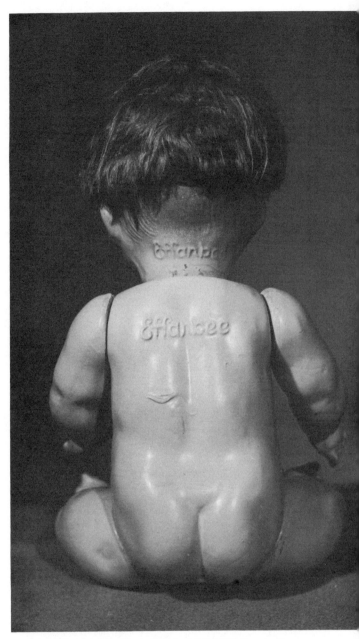

Illustration 182. 16in (40.6cm) all-composition doll; brown mohair wig; gray celluloid-on-tin sleep eyes, brown eyebrows, painted upper and lower eyelashes; mouth is open for pacifier; turning or jointed wrists; marked on back and on neck: "Effanbee." 1918. This doll does not show up in any Effanbee advertising. Such a doll with turning wrists is shown in catalogs for Colonial Doll Co. It also came in a 12in (30.5cm) size. *Ernestine Howard Collection.*

Illustration 183. Back view of 16in (40.6cm) all-composition doll seen in *Illustration 182,* showing the marking on the neck and the back. *Ernestine Howard Collection.*

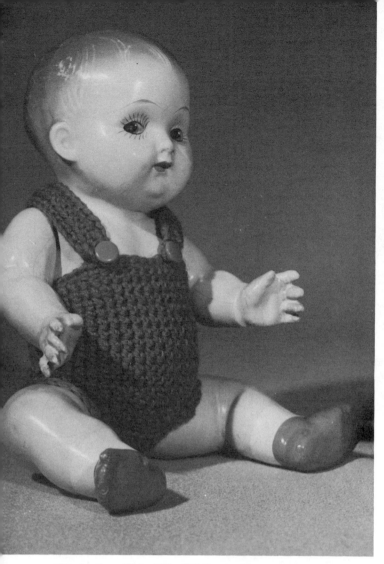

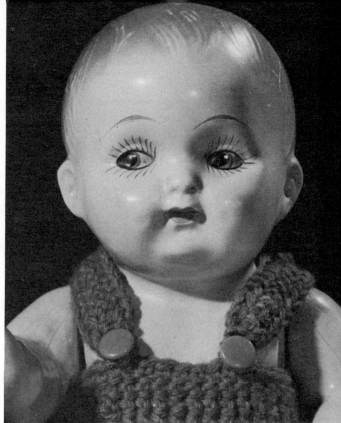

Illustration 185. Close-up of the 12in (30.5cm) all-composition baby shown in *Illustration 184*.

Illustration 184. 12in (30.5cm) all-composition baby; brown painted hair; blue painted eyes, brown painted eyebrows, exaggerated painted eyelashes; closed mouth; old but not original blue crocheted outfit; marked on back: "Effanbee." Seems to be a second version of *Dolly Dumpling* and followed a version with separate turning hands. Note the hand-painted blue shoes painted right over the feet just like *Baby Bud's* and the white painted socks. (Also came as a black baby.) 1919.

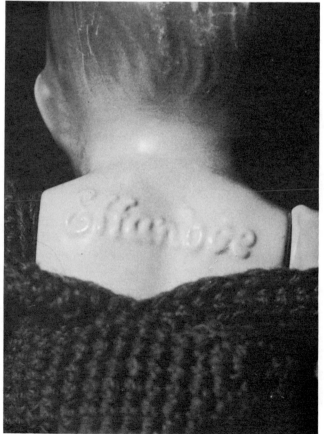

Illustration 186. Back view of 12in (30.5cm) all-composition baby seen in *Illustrations 184 and 185,* showing the marking on the back.

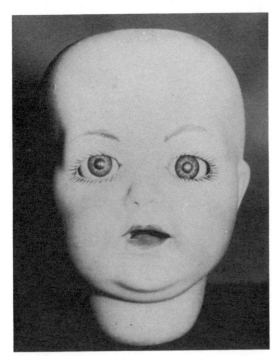

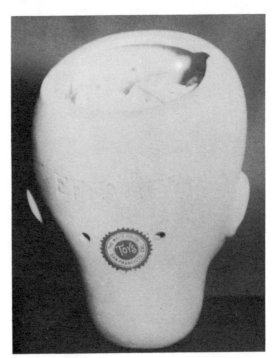

Illustration 187. 5in (12.7cm) character baby head; metal sleep eyes, painted eyebrows and eyelashes; missing teeth; marked on the back of the head: "EFF-ANBEE." The marking of the capital letters is different from that on the bisque *Mary Jane*. The bisque is not the quality of the German version but represents an effort during World War I. It is unknown if these babies were made by Lenox Potteries or another firm. *Naomi Klitgaard Collection.*

Illustration 188. The back of the 5in (12.7cm) character baby head seen in *Illustration 187*, showing the mark incised on the back of the head just above the ears: "EFFANBEE," and the paper label which reads: "THE WHITE HOUSE//TOYS//SAN FRANCISCO, CAL." The White House Firm, often mentioned in *Playthings* magazine, won many awards for outstanding window displays. *Naomi Klitgaard Collection.*

Baby Bud and Early Babies

Illustration 189. 6in (15.2cm) *Baby Bud;* all-composition; brown painted hair; brown painted eyes, painted eyebrows; open/closed mouth; molded shirt; finger on his left hand goes to the mouth. 1918. This is Effanbee's version of *Baby Bud*, a German bisque doll.

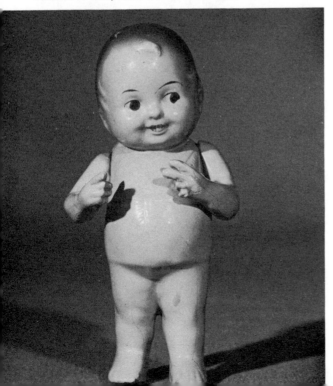

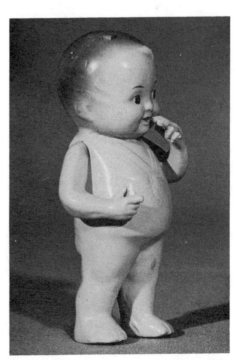

Illustration 190. Side view of 6in (15.2cm) *Baby Bud* seen in *Illustration 189,* showing the finger going to the mouth.

Illustration 191. Advertisement showing *Bathing Bud,* said by Effanbee to be for ornamental and decorative purposes; shown here with the silk bathing suit and hand kerchief. The stylized marking is shown below the doll. *Playthings,* June 1918.

Illustration 192. Advertisement for *Bathing Bud.* This is an example of how a catalog changes or omits the company name of a doll. *Bathing Bud* is here in simply titled "Ready for a Swim." Montgomery Ward & Co. catalog, 1919.

97c

Ready for a Swim

This dolly has a pretty new silk bathing suit and is anxious to go to the beach with some little girl. She wears a bandanna on her head. Jointed at shoulders. Height about 6 in. Ship. wt., ¾ lbs.
48D2831—Price....**97c**

Effanbee

Illustration 193. *Baby Bud Kewpie*-type; all-composition; human hair dark brown wig; black painted side-glancing eyes, plucked eyebrow dot, exaggerated painted eyelashes; closed mouth; a molded shirt, hand-painted "bathing beach" shoes; marked on back: "Effanbee." This model came dressed as *Riding Hood Bud.* The hands have been redesigned to be more *Kewpie*-like. 1919. *Georgia Cannon Colleciton.*

RIDING HOOD BUD
Cotton Cloth Costume
with Basket

Illustration 194. *Riding Hood Bud.* Note hand-painted shoes over bare feet. *Playthings,* October 1919.

VALENTINE BUD
Crepe Paper Costume with Parasol
Pastel Colors

Illustration 195. *Valentine Bud.* Note the *Kewpie*-type plucked eyebrows and the exaggerated eyelashes. *Playthings,* 1919.

Illustration 196. 6in (15.2cm) *Hawaiian Bud;* all-composition; black mohair wig; brown painted eyes, black painted eyebrows; closed mouth; wears a paper lei and grass skirt; marked on back: "Effanbee." 1918 or later. These dolls were made to special order and dressed in Hawaii. *Yvonne Green Collection.*

Illustration 197. 6in (15.2cm) *Hawaiian Baby Bud;* all-composition; marked: "Effanbee." The wig is missing on this doll and it has much lighter paint. A few were dressed in Oriental trouser suits with a blouse top.

Baby Effanbee/Baby Dainty

The German bisque *Bye-Lo* Baby designed by Grace Storey Putnam created a sensation in the doll world that no manufacturer could ignore. In January 1925, *Playthings* magazine introduced a *Bye-Lo* type, *Baby Effanbee,* said to be a ':'Heavenly Infant Doll.''

''Born on a cloud, 'EFFANBEE BABY' comes hurtling through space to be taken into a good home. Eager little arms stretch out to greet her and to tuck her away warmly and securely. 'EFFANBEE BABY' portrays the irresistible charm of a newborn infant. You just want to hug and squeeze her to your heart's content.'' The models of said dolls were on display at the New York, New York, salesroom.

In the out-of-print book *Effanbee The Dolls With The Golden Hearts* by M. Kelly Ellenburg, actual Effanbee company catalog pages are shown with *Bye-Lo*-type twins, No. 3835, and a single *Baby Effanbee* No. 3971, in christening dress and blanket, with bib embroidered ''Baby Effanbee'' in script. (Mr. Morris Lutz of Effanbee had loaned the author this and other source material.)

Most examples of this doll the author has collected appear to be veterans of many happy hours of play with some little girl. A mother would not have to caution her daughter to be so very careful with this composition *Bye-Lo*-type as she would with the bisque version.

By March 1925 the *Baby Effanbee* identity has been dropped. The same doll is now photographed in a wicker bassinet and rechristened *Baby Dainty,* a name which had been used earlier for a girl doll! *Playthings* magazine headlines, ''They're so human.'' *Baby Dainty* was one of the many styles of Effanbee baby dolls, with the Effanbee label at the neck front of the dress, and wrapped in either a pink or blue eiderdown blanket.

By August 1925 *Baby Dainty* is advertised in *Playthings* as *Pat-o-Pat* with patent applied for. Her dress has been shortened to above her shoe tops and she is presented in a high chair, a slightly older version of *Baby Dainty* but having the same head. A metal mechanism has been inserted into the arms and torso which caused the doll to clap her hands when pressed on the chest. The copy reads: ''A new baby doll with added play value. *Pat-o-Pat* claps her chubby hands in a manner so lifelike, so realistic that she appears almost human. Sales can be further increased if you will take advantage of our demonstration proposition.'' Whether the company offered a live demonstrator or had an electrical device to cause the doll to clap is not explained.

A doll is usually not generally well distributed when first heralded in *Playthings* trade magazine. Butler Brothers wholesale catalog for December 1925 offered the original *Baby Effanbee/Baby Dainty* models, advertising them simply as ''Effanbee'' Infant and Baby Dolls. The name of the prestigious company was considered more important than the name of the doll. It was emphasized that each doll came with trademark label and Bluebird Effanbee button. There were two sizes:

12½in (31.8cm) and 15in (38.1cm), not including long dresses or blankets, Twins in flannelette nightgowns on a dimity and flannelette covered pillow trimmed in ribbon rosettes, came in a box. Imagine the joy of the receiving child! Dolls with painted eyes were $2.75 a pair wholesale and with sleep eyes, $3.75 a pair.

A Seattle newspaper advertisement for The Bon Marche department store, December 1925, offered the newer *Pat-o-Pat* for $2.45 retail. By contrast the doll shown just above was a German ball-jointed girl doll in chemise with sleep eyes and sewn mohair wig for $1.65.

The Chicago Mail Order Company catalog of 1926 /1927 offers ''Genuine Bye-lo [sic] Babies'' at $2.79 for the 16in (40.6cm) size and on the same page ''Pat-a-Pat Baby [sic], makes Pattycakes,'' 20in (50.8cm) size, including a long dress, for $1.98 retail. This was the painted-eye version which was more economical.

As of September 1926, *Baby Effanbee/Baby Dainty* was available as a premium doll in the *Junior Home* children's magazine. For two subscriptions to the publication, one would receive a 13in (33cm) doll with painted eyes, all bundled up in an eiderdown blanket over a long dress. A Bluebird Effanbee button is affixed to the ribbon on the blanket. ''This is a genuine Effanbee Doll which name signifies high quality, made in America, under sanitary conditions'' the offer reads in part.

Other Babies

At this period of time, there were also some little economy-type dolls available, yet still high quality compared to many other brands. An all-composition baby came in sizes 9½in (24.2cm) and 12in (30.5cm) sizes and sold for 49¢ in the smaller size. The 1926 Montgomery Ward & Co. catalog mentions the smaller dolls not being finished as well as some Effanbees, yet an example has been found with very high quality finish so they must have been done in both grades.

A different small doll with a continuous composition yoke similar to *Bubbles,* with arms strung on a metal spring, is offered in 1926 in both the *National Cloak and Suit Company* catalog of New York, New York, and Montgomery Ward & Co. catalog. The former price was 75¢ and the latter 79¢. The *National Cloak and Suit Company* catalog description calls this baby a ''little Crumpy [sic] (misprint, no doubt meant to say *Grumpy)* Character Doll'' so possibly this doll was advertised in early Effanbee catalogs as a pleasant version of *Grumpy,* but we found no other mention of it anywhere else. Possibly one will be discovered with the original paper tag someday. So much information can be reconstructed by studying the trade magazines, the advertisements in ladies' magazines and other sources, yet mysteries remain which keep the hobby fascinating as each new bit of ''lost'' information is rediscovered and revealed.

Famous Effanbee Dolls
Dear Little White and Colored Babies

For those who want Baby Dolls of the very best quality throughout and yet do not wish to pay much for them we are offering these genuine Effanbee Dolls. They have dainty lifelike features with eyes hair, cheeks, mouth and general expression painted by the expert Effanbee artists. The heads and arms are carefully moulded of almost unbreakable composition and the natural shaped bodies are stuffed with best quality cotton. These dolls are supposed to be babies about 2 months old and they have excellent crying voices.

Each is wrapped up in a dainty blanket with ribbon to match and wears a long white lawn dress. Both the colored and the white baby are very natural looking and any little girl is sure to like them. Each is about 12 inches tall not including dress.

| 49 E 2537— White Baby...... **$2.19** Postage, 10¢ extra | 49 E 2536— Colored Baby...... **$2.19** Postage, 10¢ extra |

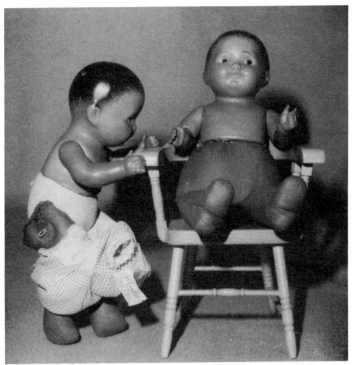

Illustration 198. Advertisement showing 12in (30.5cm) *Baby Dainty* dolls in white and black; composition heads, cloth bodies, composition hands, cloth legs. Montgomery Ward & Co. catalog, 1926.

Illustration 200. 10½in (26.7cm) and 11in (27.9cm) black baby dolls; compositon heads, continuous composition shoulders, cloth bodies, compositon arms, cloth legs; black painted hair; brown painted eyes with dark brown pupils, black eyebrows; closed mouths. The romper on the doll on the left is pulled down to reveal the pin and disk jointing of the earlier version. The simplified version has the legs cut as part of the torso and then stuffed and stitched across for the joint. 1926. Doll on left, *Edell Lashely Collection.*

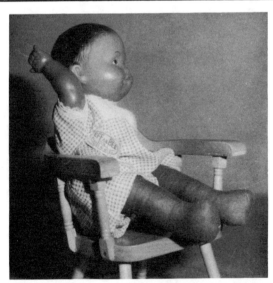

Illustration 199. 10½in (26.7cm) black baby doll; composition head, continuous compositon shoulder, white cloth body, composition arms, brown cloth legs; black painted hair; brown painted eyes with dark brown pupils, black eyebrows; closed mouth; wears red and white checked cotton romper with a white yoke and coarse lace at the neck and sleeve. The arm is raised to show the original label at the waist which reads: "EFF-ᴀɴBEE//DOLL//FINEST & BEST" in the oval and "MADE IN//USA" beneath the oval on a cloth tag. Marked in script on the back of the shoulder: "Effanbee." 1926, although some models could be earlier. *Edell Lashley Collection.*

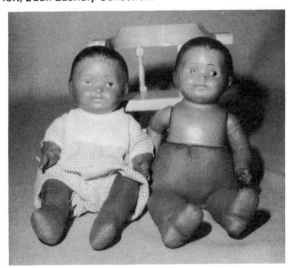

Illustration 201. 10½in (26.7cm) and 11in (27.9cm) black baby dolls shown in Illustration 200. Note the rounded foot on one and the longer, shaped foot on the other. Both dolls have a continuous composition yoke marked on the back: "Effanbee." Doll on the left, *Edell Lashley Collection.*

Genuine EFFANBEE Baby Doll

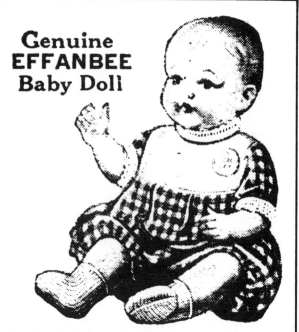

Effanbee Dolly with chubby, full length composition arms, jointed at the shoulders, and bent baby legs that move easily from the hips. Full length arms and head are of almost unbreakable composition and the stuffed body is very durable. Her dainty checked gingham rompers trimmed with a white yoke and lace. Removable socks. 10¼ inches tall.

49 E 2661.......... **79¢**

Postage, 6¢ extra

Illustration 202. Advertisement for the white baby doll. Montgomery Ward & Co. catalog, 1926.

75¢

36B921—Baby will adore this pretty→ little Crumpy Character Doll which costs only 75 cents. It has unbreakable composition head with pretty painted face and painted hair; stuffed body and legs with white socks; composition arms and hands; jointed at the shoulders. Dressed in pretty check Rompers. About 9 in. tall. Postage 8¢ extra. **75¢**

Illustration 203. Advertisement for 9in (22.9cm) *Crumpy* [sic] (should be *Grumpy*) character doll; continuous compositon breastplate. This is not the typical *Grumpy* known to collectors. National Cloak & Suit Co. catalog, New York, New York, Fall and Winter, 1926.

Illustration 204. Advertisement for 9½in (24.2cm) and 12in (30.5cm) black and white baby dolls; all-composition; wearing simple dresses and diapers. Other versions were found with superior paint finish. Montgomery Ward & Co. catalog, 1926.

Composition Baby Dolls

White and Colored Baby Dolls made of composition with jointed legs and arms. Painted eyes, hair and features. Not so well finished as the Effanbee dolls listed above. 9½ in. tall.

49 E 2503—
White doll......... **49¢**
49 E 2502—
Colored doll........ **49¢**

Postage, each, 8¢ extra

LOOK, CHILDREN!

Here Is "BABY DAINTY"

THIS BABY DOLL IS ALL THE RAGE

A lifelike 3-day-old infant Doll wrapped in pink or blue eiderdown blanket. This is positively the cutest dolly you ever saw. Mama will be crazy about it, too. Just right to cuddle up close to you. This is a genuine Effanbee Doll which name signifies high quality, made in America, under sanitary conditions. Length in blanket, 15 inches; length of doll, 13 inches. Cries like a real baby. Given free, postpaid, for only 2 yearly subscriptions to **Junior Home**, with the $5.00 collected.

Illustration 205. Rare advertising for the painted-eye *Baby Dainty* which was originally introduced as *Baby Effanbee* which would evolve into *Pat-o-Pat*, the mechanized version. Note the Bluebird Effanbee button on the ribbon. *Junior Home* (a children's magazine), September 1926.

Illustration 206. Advertisement for *Baby Effanbee/Baby Dainty* dolls, although they are not so named in the advertising. Great emphasis is put on the Effanbee label shown on the garments. Butler Brothers catalog, December 1925.

"EFFANBEE" INFANT and BABY DOLLS

INFANT DOLLS — CRYING VOICES

The best models from the nationally advertised "EFFANBEE" line. Realistic composition heads and baby hands practically indestructible, painted features and hair, loosely jointed legs, fine cotton stuffed bodies. Each with trademark label and button.

Measurements are actual length of dolls, not including long dresses or blankets.

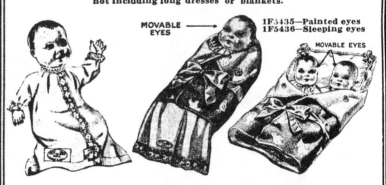

MOVABLE EYES →

1F5435—Painted eyes
1F5436—Sleeping eyes

MOVABLE EYES

Extra Long Dress—Fine quality white organdie dress, ribbon rosette and lace trim, lace trim lawn slip, flannelette diaper, ribbed stockings, **sleeping eyes.** 1 in box.

1F5425—12½ in., without cap.
Each **$1.75**

1F5426—15 in., lace and ribbon trim baby cap.
Each **$2.35**

In Blankets — Sleeping eyes, lace and ribbon trim long white organdie dress, lawn slips, pink or blue cotton blankets with white figures, wide satin ribbon bows. 1 in box.

1F5430—12½ in., without cap.
Each **$1.95**

1F5431—15 in., lace trim baby cap, ribbed stockings and flannelette diaper.
Each **$3.50**

Twins In Blanket—Flannelette nightgowns with overstitched fronts and lace and ribbon trim sleeves, gilt baby pins, each pair in pink or blue cotton blankets with white juvenile figures, wide satin ribbon bow, dimity and flannelette covered pillow with 2 ribbon rosettes, overstitched edges. 1 pair in box.

1F5435—Two 12½ in. dolls with painted eyes.
Pair **$2.75**

1F5436—Two 12½ in. dolls with sleeping eyes.
Pair **$3.75**

PAT-O-PAT

Patent Applied For

A new baby doll with added play value.

Dolly **"Pat-o-Pat" claps** her chubby hands in a manner so life-like, so realistic, that she appears almost human.

"Pat-o-Pat" will sell on sight. Sales can be further increased if you will take advantage of our demonstration proposition.

Write us for full particulars.

FLEISCHAKER & BAUM

Sales Department:
45 East 17th Street

General Office:
45 Greene Street

New York, N. Y.

EFFANBEE DOLLS
THEY WALK · THEY TALK · THEY SLEEP

Illustration 207. Full page advertisement for *Pat-o-Pat*. *Playthings,* August 1925.

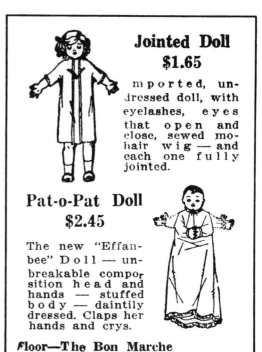

Jointed Doll $1.65

mported, undressed doll, with eyelashes, eyes that open and close, sewed mohair wig — and each one fully jointed.

Pat-o-Pat Doll $2.45

The new "Effanbee" Doll — unbreakable composition head and hands — stuffed body — daintily dressed. Claps her hands and crys.

Floor—The Bon Marche

Illustration 208. Advertisement for the Effanbee *Pat-o-Pat* doll. In recent years some writers have concluded that $2.45 was a very inexpensive price for a doll, yet here we see a German bisque doll, fully-jointed with sleep eyes, costing only $1.65 as compared to the Effanbee product. December 1, 1925.

Illustration 209. Advertisements for the *"Bye-lo"* [sic] *Baby Doll* and the *Pat-o-Pat* doll. This shows how the *Pat-o-Pat* doll was designed to give competition to the bisque *Bye-Lo* doll. The sleep-eyed version of *Pat-o-Pat* cost more. Chicago Mail Order Co. catalog, Chicago, Illinois, Fall and Winter, 1926/1927.

Illustration 210. Comparative view of, from left to right, 12½in (31.8cm), 15in (38.1cm) and 12½in (31.8cm) *Baby Effanbee/Baby Dainty* dolls. The doll on the left has gray-blue painted eyes with very dark centers and white highlights and gray eyebrows. The doll in the middle has golden blonde painted hair and gray-blue metal sleep eyes with dark centers. The doll on the right has golden blonde painted hair with molded hair lines at the front edge and gray-blue metal sleep eyes with dark centers. All have muslin bodies.

Illustration 211. 15in (38.1cm) and 13in (33cm) *Pat-o-Pat* babies (an Effanbee version of the *Bye-Lo* doll); composition heads, muslin bodies, composition wired-on hands to above the wrists, cloth legs; both arms and legs are seamed at the top centers and bottoms; metal bars run inside the arms almost to the hands; gray-blue eyes with dark blue pupils and white highlights on the eyes of the doll on the right (the eyes on the doll on the left have flaked away somewhat). These are well-played-with survivors, each with a mechanical mechanism which causes the doll to clap its hands when pressed on the chest.

-121-

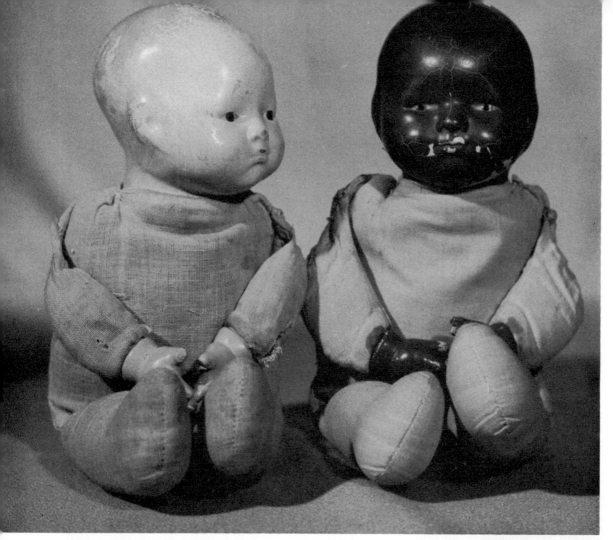

Illustration 212. 12½in (31.8cm) white and black *Baby Effanbee/Baby Dainty* dolls; composition heads, cloth bodies, composition hands to just above the wrists, cloth legs; doll on left has golden blonde painted hair with slight hair molding at the front edges, gray-blue eyes with dark blue pupils and white highlights, tan eyebrows; doll on right has black hair, brown painted eyes with very dark centers and gray eyebrows.

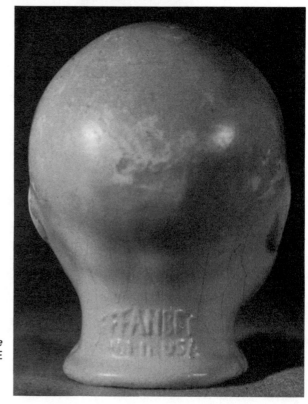

Illustration 213. Marking on the back of an *Effanbee Baby/Baby Dainty* or *Pat-o-Pat*: "EFFANBEE//MADE IN USA."

The Baby Dainty Dolls

The *Baby Dainty* dolls are a classic example of the variations on a name, within one company, over many years. The newer collector tends to believe a doll is one certain thing, one version or idea. Among creative manufacturers ever trying new concepts, company names were switched from model to model over the years. *Baby Dainty,* (then an infant), was among the earliest products of Fleischaker & Baum, proudly advertised in *Playthings* magazine in June 1912.

The name of the doll in the beginning seemed to refer to the clothing. The wide collar, sleeves and dress bottom were trimmed with Valenciennes lace, as was the the baby bonnet which was also adorned with ribbon rosettes. An infant pacifier was on a ribbon around the neck but the mouth does not appear to be open at this time. It seems probable these first models were not marked *Effanbee* as yet.

By 1917 Butler Brothers wholesale catalog offered four sizes of *Baby Dainty* infants: 14in (35.6cm), 17in (43.2cm), 19in (48.3cm) and 21in (53.3cm). The mouth was now open, a mohair wig has been added and inside joints were mentioned for the cork-stuffed body. This is the Hard-to-Break cold press composition type. The clothing consisted of a lawn slip and underwear with a lace-trimmed jacket. The buyer often made elaborate dresses with much handwork after purchasing the doll. One could also obtain the more elaborately factory-dressed dolls in the better toy stores.

By 1918 Butler Brothers advertised *Baby Dainty* infants as having a breastplate head which is more commonly known as a shoulder head doll today. The basic doll is the same as the previous year, with an open mouth and pacifier, a wig and inside joints. The sizes have been changed to: 15in (38.1cm), 18½in (47cm), 21½in (54.6cm) and 24in (61cm). Although the dolls in the catalog are illustrated with fancy bonnets and lace-trimmed dresses, the printed description on the three largest dolls lists only a lace-trimmed chemise or lawn underwear. Since fancy clothing could double the price of a doll, this was a way of offering a bigger bargain to dealers.

Baby Dainty was originally a line of dolls, not one specific doll. The girl doll may have come on the market as early as 1918 to 1920. All models found are breast-plate or shoulder head examples. One version seems to be featured in the December 1920 *Good Housekeeping* magazine. This doll has a wig as does one doll in the author's collection, but most of the *Baby Dainty* dolls had painted hair.

The earliest versions had the script *Effanbee* on the back of the shoulder plate. These are found with the first wired-on composition arms to above the wrists, and later full composition arms with hands less well delineated than a still later version would be. The earliest example had full cloth ground cork-stuffed legs with inside joints. The third type of arms could be found combined with all cloth legs which have eliminated the

inside joints and are stitched to the body. This was surely made for an economy market. The most familiarly known *Baby Dainty* is the molded hair, painted eye version which is actually marked: "Effanbee//Baby Dainty" on the back shoulder plate. The composition legs extend to above the knees and are wired onto the cloth body. She actually was a very petite mama doll with a voice in the torso. The plain hair was usually covered by a brimmed bonnet which greatly added to her charm. Since these dolls were more affordable than the larger Effanbee models, they were probably given to children to play with and the bonnets were often lost.

The company made one version of a 12in (30.5cm) *Baby Dainty* by using the same head and arm mold but longer and heavier wired-on legs to make a larger 14½in (36.9cm) doll for an economy market. Eventually a deluxe version was made with glassene sleep eyes and a mohair wig. The marking was changed from: "Effanbee//Baby Dainty". to "Effanbee//Dolls//Walk. Talk.Sleep" within an elongated oval. The larger doll measures 16in (40.6cm) to 17in (43.2cm) tall but does not seem to be advertised to be an actual *Baby Dainty.* Yet the mold is a larger version of the same doll with an added wig and sleep eyes. One catalog version calls her

"BABY DAINTY"

Illustration 214. *Baby Dainty,* termed a "sure winner...a work of art" in an advertisement by Fleischaker & Baum. *Playthings,* June 1912.

Coquette due to the flirting eyes. The flirting eye models of the marked *Rosemary* seem to begin with a size 18in (45.7cm).The dolls listed at 16in (40.6cm) or smaller turn out to be versions of the girl *Baby Dainty,* whether or not so named. The sleep eyes, open mouth and a wig could greatly change the appearance of the doll. Some versions had more elaborate party dresses as opposed to the school dress versions.

Baby Dainty was, no doubt, one of the most popular dolls of her day and one who has survived with her original clothes intact is a treasure indeed.

"BABY DAINTIES"

Composition head and hands, painted features, open mouth, full mohair wigs, cork stuffed bodies, concealed hip and shoulder joints, lace trim lawn slips and underwear. 1 in box.

F7914—14 in., white socks.
Each, **$1.25**

F7915—17 in., white socks.
Each, **$1.85**

F7916—19 in., crocheted boot-ees............Each, **$2.50**

F7917—21 in., crocheted boot-ees............Each, **$3.40**

Illustration 215. The *Baby Dainty* shown here is a baby doll, not the more well-known girl doll. There were four sizes offered: 14in (35.6cm), 17in (43.2cm), 19in (48.3cm) and 21in (53.3cm). Butler Brothers catalog. 1917.

"BABY DAINTIES"

Composition breast plate, heads and composition hands, painted features, open mouth and pacifier, full mohair wigs, cork stuffed bodies, concealed hip and shoulder joints.

F7914   F7915-17

F7914—"Effanbee," 15 in., white lawn baby dress, lace trim neck, yoke, sleeves and bottom of skirt, ribbon and lace trim cap, lace trim panties, white socks. 1 in box.
Doz. **$14.40**

"Effanbee"—Fine white lawn dress, lace trim neck, yoke, sleeves and bottom of skirt, lace and ribbon bow trim caps to match, ribbon strings, crocheted booties. 1 in box.
F7915—18½ in., lace trim chemise..........Doz. **$21.00**
F7916—21½ in., lawn underwear............." **33.00**
F7917—24 in., lawn underwear............." **43.80**

Illustration 216. Advertisement for *Baby Dainty.* Butler Brothers catalog, 1918.

LOOK FOR THIS BUTTON ON EACH DOLL

Effanbee DOLLS

FOR CHRISTMAS—
An Effanbee Doll will amuse and educate your little girl

TO a little girl, Christmas means a doll—the best plaything in the world. Effanbee Dolls do more than amuse—they educate. A little girl's first sewing is done on a dress for her doll. Unconsciously she learns about dressmaking and other things, too.

The clothes of Effanbee Dolls are created by a skilled designer and might be patterns for your little girl's clothes. Fully jointed, lite-like, American dolls. Buy one for your little girl's Christmas at an Effanbee dealer's or write us direct.

FLEISCHAKER & BAUM
45 East 17th Street,   New York City

Effanbee DOLLS

Illustration 217. Advertisement showing the Blue-bird (of happiness) pin. *Good Housekeeping,* December 1920.

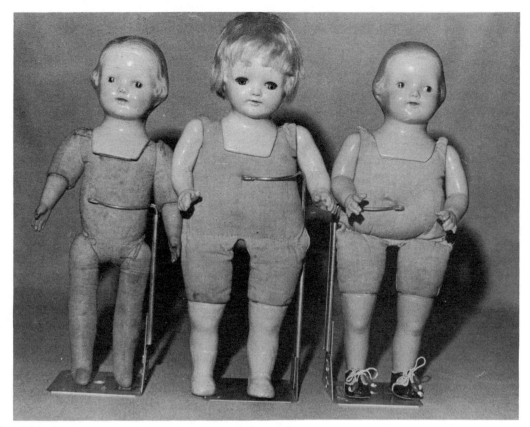

Illustration 218. A comparative view of three *Baby Dainty* dolls.

The doll on the left has a composition shoulder head, cloth body, composition arms to the elbows, cloth legs; cork-stuffed body; light brown painted hair; blue eyes, light brown eyebrows; closed mouth; marked on the back of shoulder plate: "Effanbee" in script. This doll was made before the first mama doll. *Rhoda Shoemaker Collection*.

The *Baby Dainty* in the center is a rare version. She has a composition shoulder head, cloth body, composition arms with mitten hands, composition legs to above the knees, stitched "swing" legs; blonde mohair wig; rare tin sleep eyes for this period, tan eyebrows; molded shoes and socks; marked on the back of the shoulder plate: "Effanbee" in script. The doll wore shoes and socks over her molded ones! Circa 1926.

The *Baby Dainty* on the right has a composition shoulder plate, cloth body, newer and more delicate and shapely composition arms and hands, composition legs to above the knees, stitched "swing" legs; molded blonde painted hair; blue painted eyes, light brows; closed mouth; marked on the back of the shoulder plate: "EFFANBEE//BABY DAINTY." The comb marks on this doll are more detailed than on the doll on the far left. She is later than 1926.

Illustration 219. A comparative view of the backs of the three *Baby Dainty* dolls shown in *Illustration 218*. The doll on the left is marked: "Effanbee" in script; the doll in the middle is marked: "Effanbee" in script; the doll on the right is marked: "EFFANBEE//BABY DAINTY." Doll on far left, *Rhoda Shoemaker Collection*.

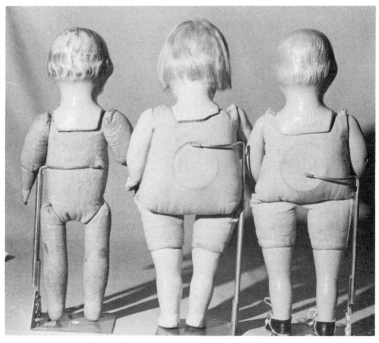

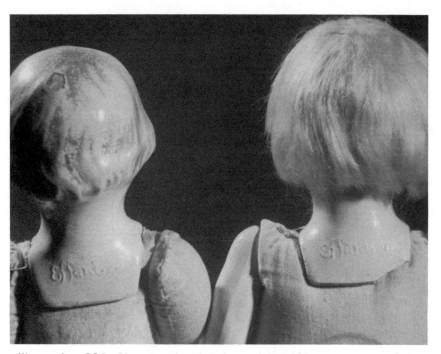

Illustration 220. Close-up showing the script marking on the two *Baby Dainty* dolls. Doll on left, *Rhoda Shoemaker Collection*.

Illustration 221. *Baby Dainty* as seen on the right in *Illustrations 218 and 219*, shown in her original dress. The label on her dress hem reads: "EFFₐNBEE//DOLL //FINEST & BEST" within an oval.

Effanbee Doll

I Go
To Sleep

I Walk

Beautiful
EFFANBEE
Dollies

12 Inches Tall

She has the expression of a five-year-old child. Head and jointed arms are best composition and she has a "Ma-Ma" voice. Painted eyes and hair. Pink crepe combination dress and bloomers, black shoes and white stockings.

49 E 2657...... $1.79
Postage, 8¢ extra

She's 14 inches tall. Sleeping eyes, real lashes and mohair wig. Head and jointed arms are composition; body is cotton stuffed. "Ma-Ma" voice. Pink lace trimmed organdie dress, petticoat and combination suit; pink trimmed straw hat; shoes and stockings.

49 E 2609...... $3.89
Postage, 14¢ extra

Illustration 222. The 12in (30.5cm) doll shown here has painted eyes, cloth legs and came with an Effanbee button on her chest. Her hands are in the second hand shape used. The 14in (35.6cm) doll has a wig and sleep eyes and costs considerably more. The *Baby Dainty* name has been omitted. Montgomery Ward & Co. catalog, 1926.

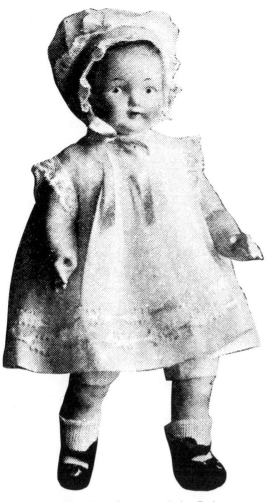

Illustration 223. 14in (35.6cm) *Baby Dainty;* composition shoulder head, cloth body, full composition arms; composition legs to above the knees; painted blonde hair; blue painted eyes, brown eyebrows; outfit came in pink, blue, green or lavender cotton with white braid trim on skirt, the same trim used on a *Bubbles* toddler doll of the same season. Price in 1927 was $2.00. *Good Housekeeping* magazine.

Illustration 225. 14in (35.6cm) *Baby Dainty;* composition shoulder head, cloth body composition arms with inside disk joints, cloth legs; blonde painted hair; blue painted eyes; closed mouth; marked: ''EFFANBEE// BABY DAINTY.'' The earlier inside joints on the legs have been eliminated and the legs are sewn to the torso. This would be a time saving device. *Rhoda Shoemaker Collection.*

Illustration 224. Close-up showing the difference in eye painting of two *Baby Dainty* dolls. The doll on the left has a bit darker shade of paint and darker brown hair.

Illustration 226. 14in (35.6cm) *Baby Dainty;* composition shoulder head, cloth body, composition arms and legs to above the knees; blonde painted hair; blue painted eyes, tan eyebrows, painted upper eyelashes; closed mouth; wearing original pink voile dress with a band of pink flowered voile at the skirt bottom, topped by lace, same lace at the neck and sleeves, shoes not original; marked on back of shoulder plate: "EFFANBEE//BABY DAINTY." 1929. *Nancy Carlson Collection. Photograph by David Carlson.*

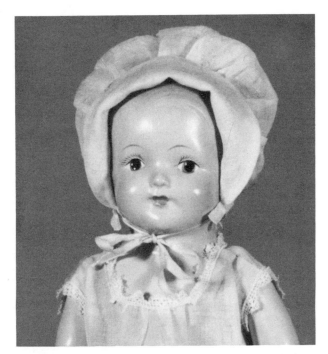

Illustration 227. Close-up of 14in (35.6cm) *Baby Dainty* seen in *Illustration 226,* showing her original puff bonnet. *Nancy Carlson Collection. Photograph by David Carlson.*

Illustration 228. Back view of 14in (35.6cm) *Baby Dainty* seen in *Illustrations 226 and 227,* showing the marking on the back of the shoulder plate: "EFFAN-BEE//BABY DAINTY." *Nancy Carlson Collection. Photograph by David Carlson.*

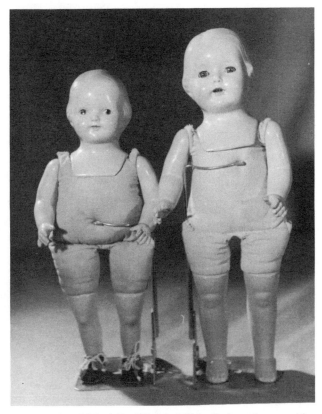

Illustration 229. 14in (35.6cm) *Baby Dainty* shown with her "big sister" version, a 16in (40.6cm) *Baby Dainty.* The larger doll has brown glassene sleep eyes and an open mouth with teeth. They are both the same basic mold and have inside jointed arms and wired-on composition legs.

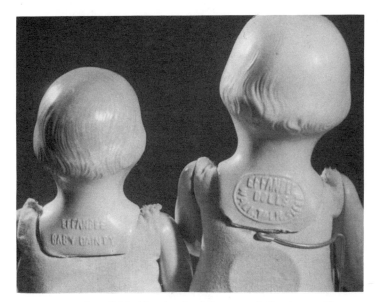

Illustration 230. The back of the two dolls shown in *Illustration 229.* The smaller doll is marked: "EFFAN-BEE//BABY DAINTY." The larger doll is marked: "EFFANBEE//DOLLS//WALK.TALK.SLEEP" in an elongated oval. The larger doll is intended to have a wig.

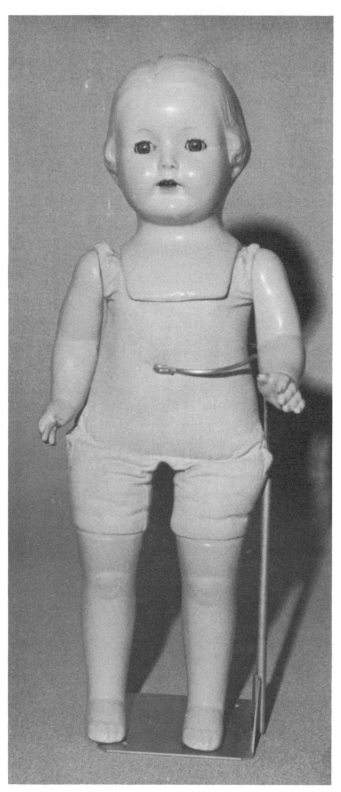

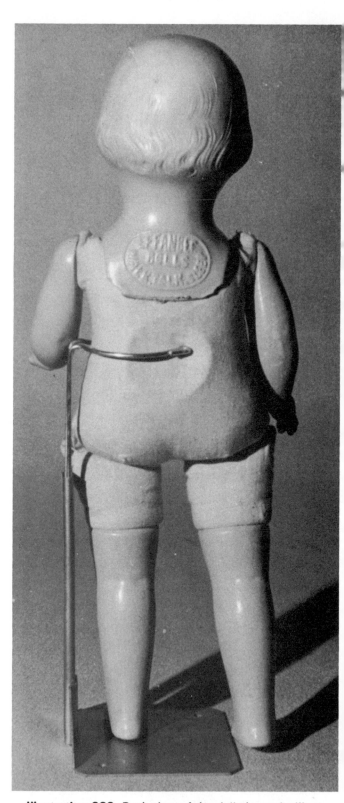

Illustration 231. 16in (40.6cm) doll by Effanbee, name unknown; composition head, cloth body, composition arms, composition legs to above the knees; missing her mohair wig; brown eyes, light brown eyebrows, hair eyelashes; open mouth with four teeth and a felt tongue.

Illustration 232. Back view of the doll shown in *Illustration 231* showing the marking: "EFFANBEE// DOLLS//WALK.TALK.SLEEP" in an elongated oval.

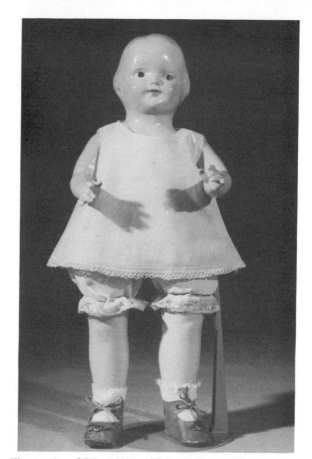

Illustration 234. 14½in (36.9cm) *Baby Dainty* shown with her original blue cotton slip trimmed with lace over her blue cotton combination suit trimmed with lace on the panties. Her shoes are also original. *Gloria Welty Collection.*

Illustration 233. 12in (30.5cm) *Baby Dainty* and 14½in (36.9cm) *Baby Dainty,* shown together for comparison purposes. They both have a composition shoulder head, cloth body, all composition arms with disk joints, wired-on composition legs to above the knees, stitched "swing" upper legs; blonde painted hair; blue eyes, light brown eyebrows; painted mouth. The doll on the right is wearing her original blue cotton combination suit. Doll on right, *Gloria Welty Collection.*

Illustration 235. 14½in (36.9cm) *Baby Dainty* shown here with her original soft blue lawn dress with woven lace at the neck and sleeves as well as two rows of braid on the skirt bottom. The original puff bonnet is missing. *Gloria Welty Collection.*

Illustration 236. 14½in (36.9cm) *Baby Dainty;* composition head, cloth body with a mama cryer, composition arms, composition legs to above the knees; blonde mohair wig over molded hair; blue tin sleep eyes, light brown eyebrows, real hair upper eyelashes and painted lower eyelashes; closed mouth; wears a yellow organdy dress over matching undergarments, matching bonnet; incised on the back of the shoulder plate: "EFFAN-BEE//BABY DAINTY." This doll has heavier arms and legs than the usual *Baby Dainty.* Her clothing is that of a more deluxe model. Circa 1924. *John Axe Collection. Photograph by John Axe.*

A Christmas Doll for Every Little Girl

Lucinda, $3.95

One of the Effanbee family--a dainty little golden haired girl in a blue voile dress and bonnet, and the cunningest blue underthings.

Illustration 237. Advertisement for *Lucinda.* There are no sizes given for *Lucinda* but she is probably one of the 16in (40.6cm) *Baby Dainty* varieties. Advertisement from a Seattle, Washington, newspaper, December 1926.

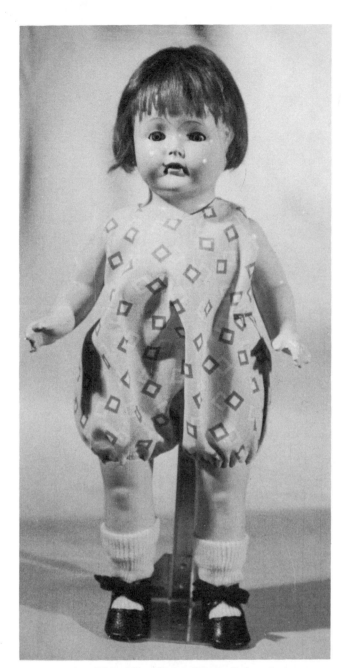

Illustration 238. 16in (40.6cm) *Baby Dainty,* but not so marked; composition shoulder head, cloth body, full composition arms with disk joints, wired-on composition legs to above the nicely modeled knees; brown mohair wig; blue metal eyes, brown eyebrows, human hair eyelashes; open mouth with two teeth and a felt tongue; molded ears; wears a combination suit of cotton print in shades of green with white, elastic gathered legs, shoes are proper but replaced; marked: "EFFANBEE//DOLLS// WALK.TALK.SLEEP" in an elongated oval. *Judy Johnson Collection.*

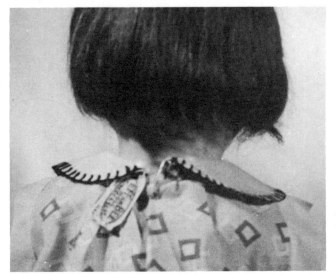

Illustration 239. Back view of the doll seen in *Illustration 238,* showing the label on her dress which reads: "EFFᴀɴBEE//DOLL//FINEST & BEST" in an elongated oval with "MADE IN USA" beneath it. *Judy Johnson Collection.*

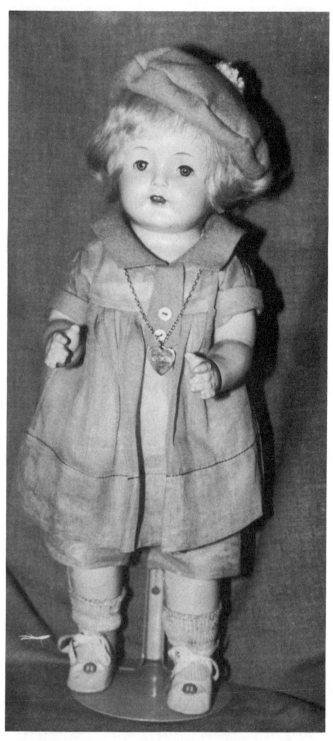

Illustration 240. 16in (40.6cm) *Baby Dainty* shown completely dressed in her original cotton print dress in shades of green with white and white organdy collar, cuffs and pocket with black cotton embroidery, black velvet bow at the neck, replacement hat. *Judy Johnson Collection.*

Illustration 241. 17in (43.2cm) *Baby Dainty;* composition shoulder head, cloth body, composition arms with disk joints, wired-on composition legs to above the knees; blonde mohair wig; blue metal eyes, real upper eyelashes, painted lower eyelashes; open mouth with two upper teeth and a felt tongue; wears a white combination suit with cuffs on legs of the pink dress material, white cotton slip, pink organdy dress with blue felt collar, cuffs and front dickey with two buttons, matching felt beret; cotton printed tag at back right yoke; locket around neck marked: "EFFANBEE." *Kerra Davis Collection. Photograph by Beth Hobbs.*

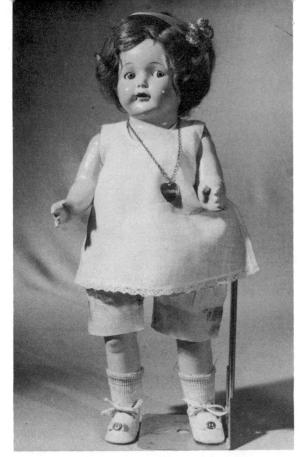

Illustration 243. 16in (40.6cm) *Coquette* shown in *Illustration 242* wearing her frock, designed by Famous Viennese Modiste, a flowered organdy dress in tones of lavender with Valenciennes lace at the neck, sleeve and hem top. See *Illustration 390* for original advertising on this doll as seen in the Montgomery Ward & Co. catalog for 1929. *Ursula Mertz Collection.*

Illustration 244. Advertisement showing some of the smaller dolls with the trademark ("EFFANBEE" in the heart) button instead of the locket. Shown here are 14½in (36.9cm) *Baby Dainty* dolls with or without a wig. Also shown are 19in (48.3cm), 20in (50.8cm), 24in (61cm) and 28in (71.1cm) dolls marked "Rosemary" but not so named here. Butler Brothers catalog, 1928.

Illustration 242. 16in (40.6cm) *Coquette;* composition shoulder head, cloth body, composition arms. composition legs to above the knees; brown mohair wig; blue flirting metal eyes, brown eyebrows, painted upper and lower eyelashes; open mouth with two teeth and a felt tongue; wearing combination suit with leg bands of material to match her dress, muslin slip with lace at hem over combination suit, original cotton socks and shoes; marked on the back: "EFFANBEE//WALK.TALK.SLEEP" in an elongated oval. 1929. *Ursula Mertz Collection.*

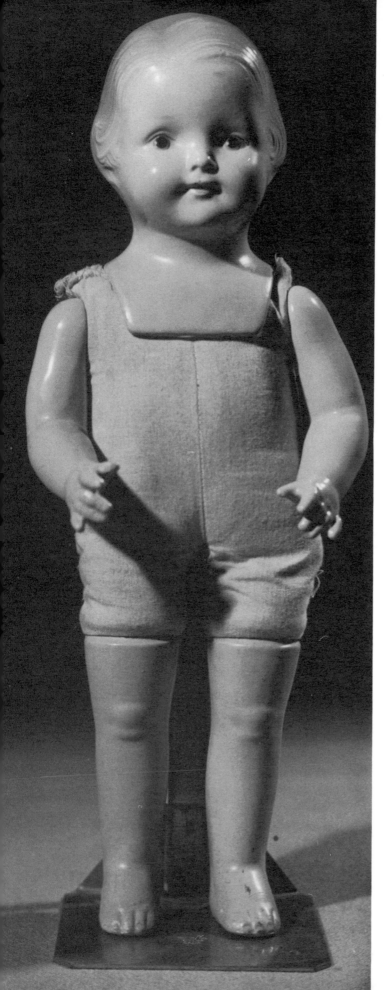

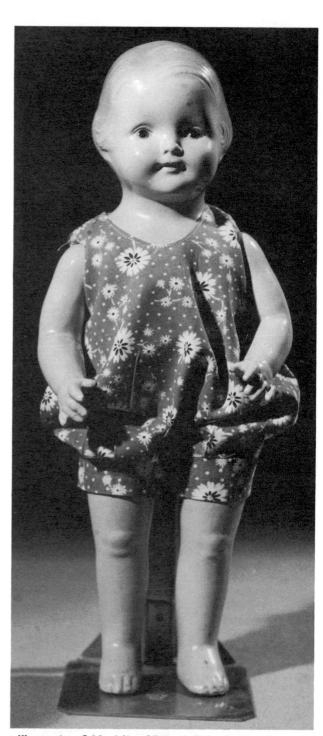

Illustration 245. 14in (35.6cm) *Baby Dainty;* composition shoulder head, cloth body, composition arms, wired-on composition legs; blonde painted hair; blue eyes, light brown eyebrows; closed mouth. This doll has a slightly different body type. The leg tops have never been stitched as in the "swing" leg version. Both legs are identical.

Illustration 246. 14in (35.6cm) *Baby Dainty* shown in *Illustration 245* wearing her combination suit of red cotton print with touches of navy and white.

Illustration 248. The back of the 14in (35.6cm) *Baby Dainty* showing the woven gold and red label sewn at the back of her dress at the yoke which reads: "EFFᴀɴBEE//DURABLE//DOLLS" within a heart and beneath the heart: "MADE IN U.S.A."

Illustration 247. 14in (35.6cm) *Baby Dainty* shown in *Illustrations 245 and 246* wearing her red flowered cotton print dress (the daisies have navy blue centers) with a white sheer collar trimmed with red bias tape, lace at the sleeves, bonnet brim and ties match the dress collar, shoes and socks are missing.

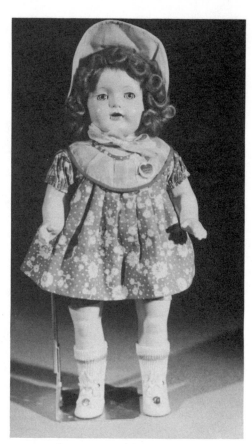

Illustration 250. Front view of the 16in (40.6cm) dressed doll shown in *Illustration 249*. Note the Effanbee trademark pin reading: "EFFᴀɴBEE//DURABLE//DOLL" on a gold heart with a white background.

Illustration 249. Comparative view of two 16in (40.6cm) Effanbee dolls, one dressed and the other undressed, names unknown, which appear to be larger versions of *Baby Dainty*. They both have a composition shoulder head, cloth body, composition arms, wired-on composition legs to above the knees; light brown eyebrows, human hair eyelashes; an open mouth. The doll on the left has a brown mohair wig in original curl and green eyes, while the doll on the right is shown without a wig and has brown eyes. The doll on the left is all original and wears a cotton print dress of bright blue with red centers in the flower design, a combination suit under the dress which is the same as the one on the doll in *Illustration 246. Judy Johnson Collection.*

Illustration 251. Back view of the 16in (40.6cm) dressed doll shown in *Illustrations 248 and 249*. Note the four sections to the bonnet and the style of the blue print dress. The mercerized socks have a blue matching stripe. The woven tag is sewn into the dress seam rather than the yoke and reads: "EFFᴀɴBEE//DURABLE//DOLLS" within a heart and beneath the heart: "MADE IN U.S.A." *Judy Johnson Collection.*

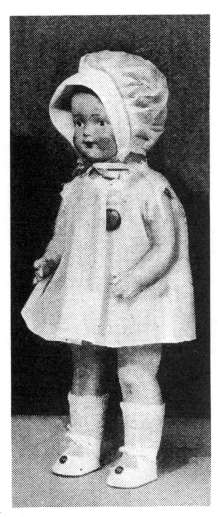

Illustration 252. *Baby Dainty* with composition shoulder head, cloth body, all-composition arms, and appears to be the type with the composition legs clear to the hips; blonde painted hair; blue painted eyes, light brown eyebrows; wears Effanbee pin with the heart emblem and ''Effanbee'' on it. 1931. *Good Housekeeping*.

Illustration 253. 14in (35.6cm) Effanbee doll, name unknown, composition shoulder head, cloth body, composition arms, composition legs to the hips; brown mohair wig; green eyes, brown eyebrows, real upper eyelashes and painted lower eyelashes; open mouth with two teeth and a felt tongue. This leg shape was used on some early shoulder head *Patsy* dolls and some *Skippy* dolls. The shoes she is wearing are not original and are older than the doll.

Illustration 254. 14in (35.6cm) Effanbee doll of unknown name shown in *Illustration 252* wearing her original combination suit of soft pink cotton with half-slip attached.

Illustration 255. 14in (35.6cm) Effanbee doll of unknown name shown in *Illustrations 253 and 254* wearing a soft pink cotton batiste dress duplicated from the original. The bonnet is missing.

NOVELTIES

Fleischaker & Baum made every effort to appeal to the American buying public with its early presentations. Included were teddy bears, pull toys, rag dolls, toy dogs, bed dolls, Easter ducks and rabbits and much more. Sadly enough, collectors may never be able to locate authenticated examples of some of the advertised dolls and toys. We hope this book will cause more of them to be discovered and reported.

Careful comparison between old company catalogs, when available, reveal that the catalog designer often re-named items or dolls to his own preference, making things more difficult for researchers. *Dixie Flyer* in the 1915 Effanbee catalog becomes *Irish Mail Kid* in the *Mandel's Magazine*, Chicago, Illinois, 1915. In the same source, Effanbee's *Cycle Boy* becomes *Tricycle Kid*. Possibly this was done to give the seller the appearance of offering an exclusive or different item.

Rag dolls for younger children, prominently advertised in the July 1920 *Playthings*, were being manufactured at least as early as 1915. *Mandel's Magazine* in 1915 for Mandel Brothers, Chicago, Illinois, features Effanbee Reversible R/50 as *Topsy Turvy Doll*, with one face white and one black, 95¢ each. A complete black doll, R/26, was offered in 1920 as well. These dolls have not been identified in research but surely some of them still exist.

The Sears, Roebuck and Co. catalog, Chicago, Illinois, in 1920, features style R/15; boy, R/12 and girl in romper and bonnet, R/10. The faces were painted and the height is now given as about 16in (40.6cm). Montgomery Ward & Co. catalog, Fall and Winter, 1921, features *Sunbonnet Girly* R/16 in dress and bonnet, R/12 *Blue-Jean Boy* and R/50 *Sunbonnet Baby* or *Colored Mammy*. The single dolls were 98¢ each and the double version was $1.85. The Ward's examples are said to be 15½in (39.4cm) tall.

Playthings in May 1918 featured a half page photograph of a window display honoring *Sammie*, the "Win The War" Mascot; the display was by Adolph Reif for Best and Co.'s Fifth Avenue store.

Playthings, May 1918 proclaimed, ' "The Public is Going to the Dogs! They Happen to Be EFFANBEE Dogs, SAMMIE, THE "WIN THE WAR" MASCOT." The dog, a stuffed toy with serio-comic visage and a patched eye, was available in seven sizes, from $1.50 up. His circular tag reads: "Sammie//Mascot." We hope a few of them still survive.

The author has seen only one of *Little Miss Muffet* dolls, featured full page in *Playthings*, January 1921. Her lace-trimmed plump torso was orange, but 12 pastel colors were available. A metal Bluebird pin is affixed in front.

In May 1921, *Playthings* featured a *Mary Jane* ball-jointed doll pulling a "Hobbly Woobly" horse, said to be a great Dragabout toy. There were, no doubt, several versions of these animals on wheeled platforms. The cover of *Playthings*, March 1921, includes an elephant; as well as a horse.

No doubt, there were some teddy bears from 1915 on but the advertising for them is not available. In May 1921, *Playthings* featured a line drawing of a young boy playing with two teddies. Six sizes were made stuffed with kapok cotton. The bears were dressed in pretty rompers, "A Dear Little Bear, But Not A Bare Little Bear...A Distinct Novelty."

Buttons the Effanbee Monk was featured in *Playthings*, February 1923, full page. One wonders why so few have survived. This bellboy monkey has a red jacket trimmed in gilt braid, with a matching cap on his head. The three gilt buttons on the jacket read "Effanbee." He seems to have been somewhat influenced by the earlier *Puss-in-Boots* dolls, with red oil cloth boots. There were three sizes, the largest was 31in (78.7cm) tall.

Effanbee evidently was very proud of *Harmonica Joe*, as a full page advertisement appeared in *Playthings*, July 1924. A design patent was obtained by Hugo Baum for this doll. He came as a white or black doll. The metal harmonica is marked: "F. A. Rauner//Made in Germany" on one side and on the reverse: "My Little Charmer//D. R. W. Z. No 92551." A rubber ball in the center of the doll was squeezed to cause the doll to play his instrument.

Easter Novelties were advertised in December 1924. A rabbit doll which appears to have a composition head and plush hood with rabbit ears has never been located by this writer. Perhaps one will now be recognized.

The lowest survival rate of any doll is that made of cloth. When played with, they tended to soil and tear and were discarded. We have not located a *Kali-Ko-Kate* of 1933, with rubberized painted cloth face, 20in (50.8cm) and 25in (63.5cm). One can imagine how little girls would have loved her. Her golden tag calls her a doll for "Every Day Companionship."

The 1936 cloth version of *Popeye*, the sailor man, 16in (40.6cm) to 17in (43.2cm) high, is very hard to locate. The cloth arms were tatooed with anchors and the doll sold for $1.25.

We have always suspected, but cannot prove, that the composition *Buddy Lee* dolls were manufactured in the Effanbee factory. For many years, the featured dolls in *Good Housekeeping* magazine were strictly Effanbee. Eventually Alexander dolls were included, and these came out of the Effanbee factory at this period.

Golden Fleece animals were sold with *Tommy Tucker* dolls and possibly others, but evidently the animals were sold alone as well.

Effanbee advertised its second version of *Pat-O-Pat* in their 1939 catalog. (See M. Kelly Ellenburg's *Effanbee, The Dolls With The Golden Hearts.*) This was intended as a doll for infants and tiny tots. The doll was all-cloth with a wool wig. She patty-caked her hands when her stomach was pressed. There were sizes 15in (38.1cm), 16in (40.6cm) and 18in (45.7cm). In the same catalog soft rubber squeeze toys, *Boo-Hoo* (downturned mouth) and *Ha-Ha* (big smile) were recommended as bathtub toys. We have never seen an example. In 1940, a set of

Illustration 274. Advertisement for *Buttons,* The Effanbee Monk. Butler Brothers Catalog, 1923.

Illustration 275. Advertisement for *Harmonica Joe. Playthings,* July 1924.

Illustration 277. 14½in (36.9cm) *Harmonica Joe* as seen in *Illustration 276,* shown undressed and without his harmonica. The lower lip is chipped away, apparently by a child's playing with him and one eye has flaked away. He has a stationary shoulder head and the arms are fastened low. *Betty Johnsen Collection.*

Illustration 276. 14½in (36.9cm) *Harmonica Joe;* designed by Hugo Baum; composition shoulder head, cloth body, composition arms; brown cloth legs; black painted hair; brown eyes with black pupils and white highlight dots, black eyebrows, upper eyelashes only; open mouth with red rubber tubing which goes from inside over the harmonica; molded ears; rubber ball, in the center of the torso with the tube to the mouth, activates the harmonica when squeezed; wears red dotted shirt, tan overalls, black shoes with silver buckles but missing jockey cap; cotton twill label on shirt reads: "EFFANBEE (in blue ink oval)//TRADE MARK;" marked: "Effanbee" in script on back of shoulder. Patented on June 17, 1924. Harmonica marked: "F.A. Rauner//Made in Germany" on one side and on the reverse marked: "My Little Charmer (in script)//D.R.W.Z. No. 92551." *Harmonica Joe* shown here with his harmonica in place. His arms do not quite fit in to the musical instrument but the child owner could hold them in place. *Betty Johnsen Collection.*

Illustration 278. Original label on *Harmonica Joe.* *Betty Johnsen Collection.*

Special and different
—for bigger Easter sales

THERE'S nothing else on the market like the EFFANBEE Cuddly Easter Novelties. They are *distinctive and different*. Brightly-colored, they will catch the eye of practically everyone of your customers and make an irresistible appeal that will give you the largest Easter sales of any line you ever had.

The EFFANBEE Cuddly Easter Novelties have natural voices that every child loves to hear. They are cotton stuffed, and well made in every little detail. And—here's an important selling point—they are sold at *popular prices*.

Write for samples and prices

FLEISCHAKER & BAUM
General Office:
45 Greene Street, New York
Salesroom: 45 East 17th Street
NEW YORK

EFFANBEE DOLLS
They Walk—They Talk—They Sleep

Illustration 279. Advertisement from *Playthings* for December 1924 for Effanbee "Cuddly Easter Novelties."

LEFT: Illustration 280. An Effanbee rabbit doll shown in an advertisement, from *Playthings* for December 1924 for Easter novelties, which has never been seen in any book before.

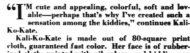

LEFT: Illustration 281. Advertisement from *Toys & Novelties* for April 1933 for *Kali-Ko-Kate.* Note the tag.

"I'M cute and appealing, colorful, soft and lovable—perhaps that's why I've created such a sensation among the kiddies," continues Kali-Ko-Kate.

Kali-Ko-Kate is made out of 80-square print cloth, guaranteed fast color. Her face is of rubberized cloth, painted with oil colors, and kiddies can wash her face without harming her pretty features.

Kali-Ko-Kate is made in two sizes, 20" (2 doz. carton, $4.50 doz.) and 25" (1 doz. carton, $7.45 doz.).

Send for a sample carton today and try Kali-Ko-Kate's popularity on your customers

FLEISCHAKER & BAUM
Creators of Dolls that are Different
45 East 17th Street   New York

Illustration 282. *HA-HA* and *BOO-HOO,* all-rubber novelty dolls by Effanbee. *HA-HA* has blonde hair and a red painted polka dot romper while *BOO-HOO* has brunette hair and a blue painted polka dot romper. The original tag on *HA-HA* reads: "HA-HA//Lucky Mascot//An Effanbee Product." and the original tag on *BOO-HOO* reads: "BOO-HOO//Lucky Mascot//An Effanbee Product," Both tags contain a sketch of the toys. They came packed in a box with a cellophane window and the box for *HA-HA* reads: "I am//HA-HA//I chase the BOO-HOO//An EFFANBEE Product." The box for BOO-HOO reads: "I am//BOO-HOO//Looking for a HA-HA//An EFFANBEE Product." These were called "Specialty Dolls" and were designed by an unnamed famous artist whose work was also shown on the sides of the boxes.

56. I'm Popeye the sailor man. Made of ground cork, covered with cloth, and 17" high. He wears white cotton pants, black-and-red middy, and is complete with his famous corncob pipe and anchor-tattooed arms; $1.25

57. Cowboy doll, authentic from his toes to his ten-gallon hat; 13" high; blue denim pants, rider's shirt, red bandanna neckerchief, light or dark brown felt replica of a ten-gallon cowboy hat, and regular lasso; $1.95

Illustration 283. Advertisement for 17in (43.2cm) *Popeye* and 13in (33cm) cowboy doll. *Good Housekeeping,* November 1936.

Illustration 284. Advertisement for 16in (40.6cm) *Popeye.* This was no doubt material sent out by Effanbee before the price had been set for the doll, which explains the price listed as $0.00.

EFFanBEE "Pat-O-Pat" dolls are very new and introduce an animated feature in soft dolls. They actually clap their hands and cry with delight at the accomplishment. An attractive little four-page booklet, with words and music to the Pat-A-Cake nursery rhyme, tells youngsters how to make dolly do her stunts. You just lift the doll up as you would a baby, press the chest gently, and the doll claps her hands and cries with delight! "Pat-O-Pat" is a soft body doll with mask face and movable head, dressed in dotted print costume, assorted colors. Made in 15 and 18 inch sizes, retailing for $2 and $3.

Illustration 285. Advertising for *Pat-O-Pat. Toys and Bicycles,* April 1940.

Illustration 287. 9¾in (24.9cm) *Mammy* and 3¾in (9.6cm) baby by Noma/Effanbee; *Mammy* is all-composition with painted black hair; brown eyes, black eyebrows; an open/closed mouth; wearing a red and white polka dot print cotton dress with a white sash and a yellow bandana around her head. The buggy is metal-framed with a composition body and has a red pull cord and wooden ball in the front. When pulled, the wide feet on the short legs caused the doll to appear to walk and push her infant charge along. The price was $2.97. Sears, Roebuck and Co. Christmas catalog, 1947.

2—The Cuddliest Toy we've seen in many a season is this member of the Golden Fleece family of furry animals made by Fleischaker and Baum, 200 Fifth Avenue, New York City. They are made of young lambskin, sterilized and processed until it is soft and non-irritating to tender skins and they are sanitary because they are washable. Price: about $2.00.

Illustration 286. Advertisement for a dog, named *Scotty,* a member of the Golden Fleece family of furry animals. Golden Fleece Toys were advertised by the Winchester Toy Co. in *Playthings* in September 1934. This was an alliance between Effanbee and the former company. *Parents* magazine, July 1940.

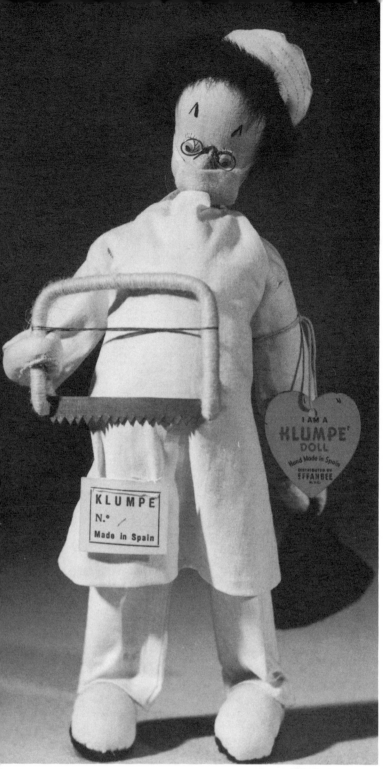

Illustration 288. 12in (30.5cm) *Klumpé;* handmade in Spain by Klumpe; distributed by Effanbee; all-cloth with felt soles; black cotton yarn wig; blue eyes with darker pupils, black eyebrows, black painted eyelashes; wears white surgeon's outfit, carries beige yarn-wrapped saw with gray blade and black doctor's bag; tag reads: "I AM A//KLUMPÉ//DOLL//Hand Made in Spain//DIS-TRIBUTED BY//EFFANBEE//N.Y.C." The tag is gold paper and "KLUMPÉ//DOLL" appears in red while the rest of the print is in black. These dolls were not actually made by Effanbee, but were distributed by them with the Effanbee heart tag. Circa 1950. *Barbara O'Brien Collection.*

Illustration 289. 12in (30.5cm) Klumpé; handmade in Spain by Klumpe; distributed by Effanbee; woven cloth head, cloth body arms and legs with cloth shoes and felt soles; brown cotton yarn wig; black pupils in eyes, painted eyelashes; red painted mouth; wears green felt coat with black buttons, red and black cotton cloth trousers and carries brown violin; tag reads: "I AM A//KLUMPÉ DOLL//Hand Made in Spain//DISTRIB-UTED BY//EFFANBEE//N.Y.C." The tag is gold paper and "KLUMPÉ//DOLL" appears in red while the rest of the print is in black. Circa 1950. *Barbara O'Brien Collection.*

The Mama Doll

The first Effanbee Mama dolls made their debut in 1919, yet few of them are found. The Butler Brothers wholesale catalog for this year offered *Christening Babies*, each with a composition head and hands, sleep eyes and a bobbed mohair wig. The name came from the voice box inserted in the doll which enabled it to cry "ma-ma" when tipped over.

By 1921 *Playthings* magazine advertised "another Effanbee triumph," a doll which had added "papa" to her vocabulary now that she was two years old. *Trottie Trulife* is first introduced at this time, and appears to be a painted-eye model with half composition arms, a romper and puff bonnet, half socks on cloth legs and strap slippers. Some models wore dresses. A paper tag read: "I say mama."

In 1920 Effanbee advertised "Dolls that walk and talk, Dolls that say 'Mama and Papa', Dolls that sleep and cry." Yet the typical chubby, solid type little **girl** is not illustrated until 1922. The "doll with the human voice" was said to be exclusively an Effanbee doll. The company claimed to control the all-metal voice device which had no rubber parts to rot or harden.

Some of these big Mama dolls of 1922 (which are depicted in *Playthings* magazine in line drawings) appear to be the lifelike 30in (76.2cm) models, judging by the size of the child shown "walking" it from behind. They were called *Dolly Dumpling* at this time.

The one doll illustrated next to the sketches has a puffed French bonnet with fancy ribbon bows, and much lace on the dress with lace-trimmed panties below. The shape of the hands are the earlier half-composition, wired-on type and the legs appear to be cloth. Half socks come up to lace-edged panties. Great pride was taken in the doll's voice, being metallic throughout. Headlines read: "Warning, All infringements will be vigorously prosecuted." The doll wore the metal Effanbee Bluebird pin plus a paper tag shown earlier.

Beach Baby was introduced in *Playthings* in June 1923 as a mid-season novelty designed for play at the countryside or seashore. The arms appear to be the half-composition , wired-on type. She wears a checked bonnet with matching collar and cuffs on the romper. The hood had a black patent leather brim, plus the doll wore an apron of the same material, with "Beach Baby" written on the front as well as the figure of a small child looking out to sea at a sailboat. The doll's name would be a **costume** title, as surely other models of the same mold came in **different** costumes.

The company offered a booklet, "How To Select The Proper Doll To Suit Your Child's Age," a new line of thought at this time (as far as the author is aware, no copy has survived). *Nancy Ann* and her many pretty sisters were shown therein. *Nancy Ann* was 23in (58.4cm) tall. The dress was organdy with edging and trimmings of imported crocheted lace with a matching bonnet. This year, 1923, these dolls had full composition arms and composition legs to above the knees. A big effort was obviously made for high quality in every aspect possible. In December *Playthings* advertised "The Best Doll In The Best Box." The golden locket came on some of the dolls for the first time. The oval symbol with "Effanbee//Dolls//They Walk.They Talk.They Sleep" is first used.

Butler Brothers in 1923 sold Mama dolls, in "Pollyanna" checked dresses, which are shown wearing the original circular paper tag suspended on a cord from metal Bluebird pin. (However, sometimes the same illustration is used in catalogs for two or more years.) A second doll in the same issue shows a newly designed paper tag, also shown in the August 1922 *Playthings*. The edges are fluted somewhat. Whether an example of either of these have survived on any doll is not known.

Honeybunch was introduced in July 1923 as an infant Mama doll. An inset shows the doll partially undressed to feature composition legs above knees, as though new at this time. This is not a character face doll, the name "Honeybunch" is not actually marked on the doll. An entirely different mold, the forerunner of *Bubbles* (shown elsewhere) **will** be found marked "Honeybunch." The company advertised heavily in 1924 and announced to the trade that they kept their factory running all summer to have enough dolls for last minute holiday rush orders.

Full page advertisements ran in the December *Good Housekeeping* magazine. The 29in (73.7cm) *Barbara Lee*, 23in (58.4cm) *Alice Lee* and 20in (50.8cm) *Betty Lee* are described. They were $15.00, $10.00 and $7.50, respectively. Others were said to cost $25.00, possibly due to a more elaborate wardrobe. One bonnet this year is more of a beret shape, edged in handmade crochet lace, which also generously trimmed the dress. So few survived in their original garments but with the illustrations now available many will be able to re-create the proper style for their doll.

It was claimed that *Betty Lee* and all her sisters in the Effanbee family were practically unbreakable. They were said to be made to be played with — not put away "for best." One was reminded to look for the golden heart necklace. The dimpled arms and legs were said to be just like a baby's, with a soft round body to hug.

Rosemary was said to be **the** Christmas Effanbee doll. This first *Rosemary* is not the famous one, marked on the shoulder "Rosemary." She is the typical Mama doll with same head mold as in 1923 and 1924, and the very chubby arms and legs. The only way to identify her would be to find an example in the exact costume shown. The advertising in ladies' magazines described only the 18in (45.7cm) size but surely there were others.

Illustration 291. Full page advertisement from the September 1922 *Playthings*. The same children are used as are seen in the advertisement shown in *Illustration 290* but the four dolls have all been redrawn as typical chubby Mama dolls. The legend "They Walk and they Talk" has been added.

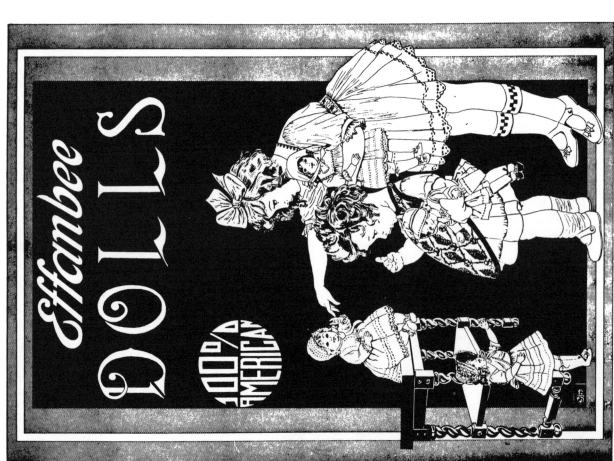

Illustration 290. Full page advertisement from the April 1920 *Playthings*. The artwork shows children playing with what appear to be ball-jointed *Mary Jane* types and one baby doll.

The following is a list of the Mama dolls manufactured from 1921 through 1931 by Effanbee.

1921: *Trottie Trulife*
1922: *Dolly Dumpling*
1923. *Beach Baby*
       Nancy Ann
       Honeybunch (infant Mama doll)
1924: *Barbara Lee*
       Alice Lee
       Betty Lee
1925: Rosemary (not so marked; slender Mama doll)
1926: *Rose-Marie* (marked "Rosemary;" slender Mama doll)
       Winifred (marked "Rosemary;" slender Mama doll)
       Rosemary (closed mouth)
       Lucinda (*Baby Dainty* girl with blonde wig)
       Lovey Mary (marked "Rosemary")
1927: *Mary Lou* (marked "Rosemary;" big sister to *Bubbles*)
       Naughty Eyes (marked "Rosemary;" flirting eyes)
1928: *Mary Sue* (marked "Rosemary;" light golden bobbed hair)
       Rose Mary (marked "Rosemary;" long dark brown curls)

1929: *Coquette* (marked "Rosemary;" flirting eyes)
       Laughing Eyes (marked "Rosemary;" flirting eyes)
       Mary Louise (marked "Rosemary;" long golden curls)
       Rose Mary (marked "Rosemary;" dark brown bob)
       Joan Carol (marked "Rosemary;" wind-blown bob)
1930: *Mischievous Eyes* (marked "Rosemary")
1931: *Dream Doll* (marked "Rosemary")

Rosemary (the first unmarked version), had blue eyes with real eyelashes, pink cheeks, a red rosebud mouth with little white teeth and a tiny tongue. The costume was organdy in a pretty color, with a matching rosebud-trimmed bonnet. Every Effanbee doll is now said to wear a golden heart necklace. The booklet "The Proper Doll for My Child's Age" is again offered and was said to contain helpful hints for using dolls for character-building play. Many doll sisters to *Rosemary* were shown from 50¢ to $25.00. One could obtain a golden heart necklace for 6¢ with the printed coupon, as well as the aforementioned booklet.

Illustration 292. *Trottie Trulife* dolls; composition heads, cloth cotton-stuffed bodies, composition wired-on arms to the elbows, cloth legs (later composition legs); painted hair; blue painted eyes, brown eyebrows, painted eyelashes; open/closed mouths with two teeth each; wearing quaintly colored gingham dresses and rompers, puff bonnets, cotton socks, patent leather "Mary Jane" slippers; have metal Bluebird pins and paper tags which read: "I Say Mama." *Trottie Trulife* was advertised as being able to walk and say "mama" just like a two-year-old child. The floppy legs were said to be something novel in construction at this time. *Playthings*, October 1921.

Illustration 293. Full page advertisement from the January 1922 *Playthings* showing the 26in (66cm) *Jumbo Mama* doll with a fabric face and stuffed with downy cotton. The doll cried "ma-ma" in a clear voice and was intended for a very young child. Composition head versions were made as well. She wears the Effanbee Bluebird pin at the waist and has on her red and white checked romper.

Illustration 294. The *Walking Doll* with the human voice as shown in the August 1922 *Playthings*. This doll was said to be one of 300 models which said "mama."

AMERICAN TOYS

Jumbo Mama Doll
26 Inches

A new Effanbee creation with a fabric face and a soft body stuffed with d o w n y cotton. Here is your big spring number. It will sell at a moderate price and keep you busy handing them out.

Jumbo Mama Doll
Talks and Walks

This wonderful doll is so light in weight that the youngest child can handle it. It says "Mama" in a clear voice (p a t e n t applied for) and cries like a real baby.

Send for Samples
Today!

Fleischaker & Baum
Effanbee Dolls
NEW YORK

45 East 17th Street

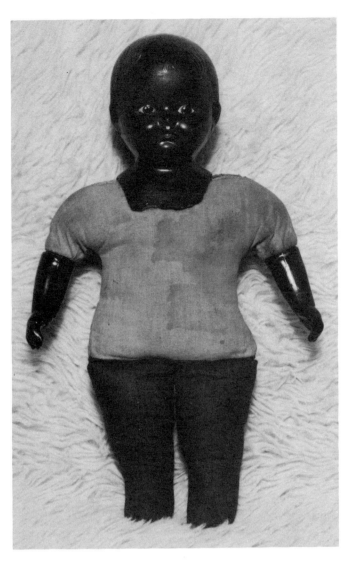

Illustration 295. 14½in (36.9cm) black Mama doll; composition head, white cloth body; black composition arms to the elbows, dark brown cloth legs; painted black hair; brown-black painted eyes, black painted eyebrows; open/closed mouth with two painted teeth; marked on back of shoulder plate: "Effanbee" in stylized script. This is a rare black version of one of the earliest Mama dolls. A checked gingham romper would be the appropriate clothing. *Merle Wehner Collection.*

Illustration 296. The back of the 14½in (36.9cm) black Mama doll seen in *Illustration 295,* showing the marking on the back of the shoulder plate and the location of the voice box. *Merle Wehner Collection.*

Mamma Dolls, sizes from 10 inches to 27 inches. Prices range 98c to $20.00.

Beautifully dress character Dolls. Composition bodies, bisque heads, moving eyes, says mamma—$6.50, 6.75, 8.95, 9.95.

Kestner Character Baby Dolls—dress in silk knit costume including bonnet beautiful hair, eyelashes, bisque head, open mouth showing teeth and tongue—$5.50, 6.50, 7.75.

Miniature China dolls dressed to represent different characters. Just the dolls for doll houses. Special price of 15c each.

Everything you can think of in doll clothes for dollie — stockings, knit union suits, bibs, wash cloths, towels, blankets, corsets, mittens, etc.

Don't fail to see our doll houses all fitted up.

EFFANBEE DOLLS

They Walk - They Talk - They Sleep.

Ma Ma Dolls

Walks and Talks

We are showing only the best makes of dolls including "Max Kestner," "Effanbee," "K and K," and many others. Owing to the heavy advance sale this year we are unable to illustrate each doll but give you a general list of prices and be glad to furnish you with minute description and price on any particular doll you have in mind. A visit to our doll section would be much more satisfactory as we are showing hundreds of different kinds. We have them from the smallest doll made in the world to the big life size dolls that walk, talk, sleep, some have movable tongues.

KIDLYNE BODY DOLLS

Height 11 inches	.50
Height 12 inches	.79
Height 13 inches	1.19
Height 15 inches	1.49

Kestner Character Baby Dolls. Undressed, high grade composition body, bisque heads, moving eyes, beautiful hair — $4.50, $6.75, $9.95.

Illustration 297. A page from an unknown catalog, circa 1923, showing five dolls. Note that the most prominently featured doll is the Effanbee Mama doll, the "rage" at this time.

THEY WALK, THEY TALK. THEY SLEEP

Illustration 298. Advertisement from the April 1923 *Playthings*. Fleischaker & Baum were now proudly exhibiting their "mark," shown here: "EFFANBEE DOLLS//THEY WALK.THEY TALK.THEY SLEEP" within an elongated oval. This claim referred to the **entire** group of dolls manufactured by the company, explaining why some painted-eye models are marked thus. Note the size of the doll in relation to the child drawn, emphasizing the deluxe big doll.

Illustration 299. Mama doll; composition shoulder plate, cloth body, composition arms, composition legs to above the knees; dark brown mohair wig over molded hair; blue metal eyes, brown eyebrows, real hair upper eyelashes, painted lower eyelashes; closed mouth; wears original metal heart necklace marked: "EFF-ANBEE;" marked on back of shoulder plate: "Effanbee" in stylized script. Circa 1923. *Nancy Carlson Collection. Photograph by David Carlson.*

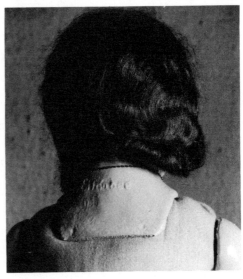

Illustration 300. Close-up of the back of the Mama doll seen in *Illustration 299,* showing the marking on the back of the shoulder plate. *Nancy Carlson Collection. Photograph by David Carlson.*

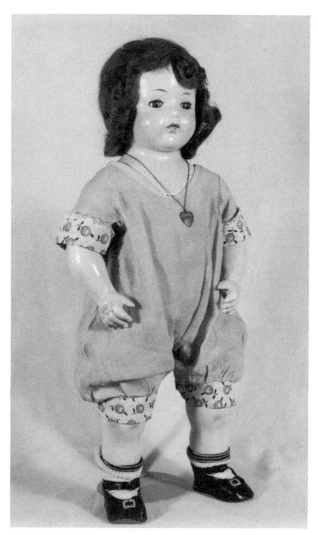

Illustration 301. Mama doll seen in *Illustrations 299 and 300*, shown wearing her original romper suit which is worn under her play dress. *Nancy Carlson Collection. Photograph by David Carlson.*

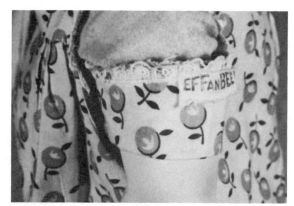

Illustration 303. Close-up of the woven label on the sleeve of the dress seen on the Mama doll in *Illustration 302.*

Illustration 302. Mama doll seen in *Illustrations 299, 300 and 301*, shown wearing her original dress over the romper suit and her bonnet. *Nancy Carlson Collection. Photograph by David Carlson.*

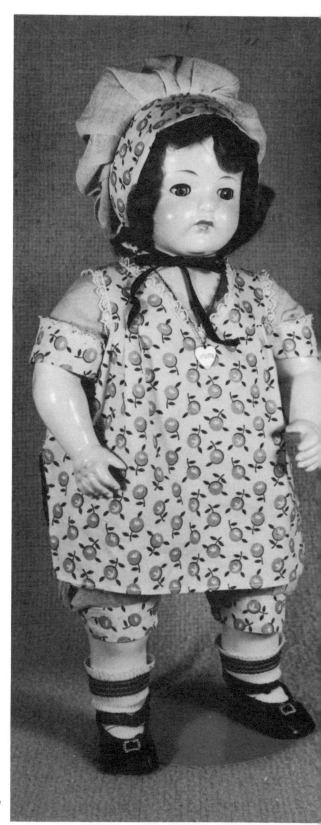

Illustration 304. An advertisement appearing in a December 7, 1923, unknown newspaper for Effanbee dolls. The Bluebird pin has been drawn on the doll and the logo "EFFANBEE//DOLLS//THEY WALK.THEY TALK.THEY SLEEP" in an elongated oval is prominently featured.

Illustration 305. This is the Bluebird (of happiness) pin used by Effanbee and advertised in 1920 but in use earlier.

Illustration 306. Original advertisement for 23in (58.4cm) *Nancy Ann;* composition shoulder head, cloth body, composition arms with disk joints, composition legs to above the knees; dark curly wig; blue-gray metal eyes, brown painted eyebrows, real hair eyelashes; open/closed mouth; molded ears; wears white sheer cotton dress with crocheted lace trim and matching trim on the bonnet; has a button pinned on the dress reading: "Effanbee." Her dress is said to have an Effanbee tag. *Ladies' Home Journal,* November 1923.

"Mother is going to wash dolly's face. It feels so good to have your face clean and it won't hurt dolly."

Illustration 307. Official Effanbee artwork advertising the 23in (58.4cm) *Nancy Ann* shown here wearing her Effanbee button. *Ladies' Home Journal,* November 1923.

WHEN *you lay her down, she closes her eyes and goes to sleep. She can say "Mamma"; she can walk, too.*

HERE *is dear little Nancy Ann all ready to dance with you.*

How to select the proper doll to suit your child's age

RIGHT: Illustration 308. 23in (58.4cm) *Nancy Ann;* composition shoulder head, cloth body, composition arms with disk joints, composition legs to above the knees; luxuriant curly brunette wig with bangs; blue metal eyes, brown painted eyebrows, real hair eyelashes; open/closed mouth; molded ears; wears a white sheer dress with crocheted lace trim; has a button pinned on the dress reading: "Effanbee." This doll sold for $10.00; a 20in (50.8cm) *Mary Ann* sold for $7.50 and was said to be exactly the same except for the size. *Ladies' Home Journal,* December 1923. **LEFT: Illustration 309**.

Close-up showing the 23in (58.4cm) *Nancy Ann* in her bonnet as well as the cover of the booklet Effanbee put out entitled "How to select the proper doll to suit your child's age." *Ladies' Home Journal,* December 1923. **MIDDLE: Illustration 310**. Official Effanbee artwork advertising the 23in (58.4cm) *Nancy Ann* shown here wearing her Effanbee button. The child is adjusting the bow on the bonnet and the doll wears her sheer dress. *Ladies' Home Journal,* December 1923.

Illustration 311. Advertisement which explains why
dolls were washable even though they were painted.
This is no doubt the source which Effanbee used since
only prominent firms advertised in *Playthings*. *Playthings,* April 1919.

Illustration 312. Advertisement for a 22½in (57.2cm)
composition shoulder head doll with molded hair. It
probably has composition arms to the elbows and the
legs are cloth. Montgomery Ward & Co. catalog, Fall and
Winter, 1921.

Illustration 313. Advertisement for a 13½in (34.3cm)
baby doll that says "ma-ma." The very basic clothing
shown being worn by the doll allowed it to be sold for
much less than it would have been otherwise. The
author has never examined an Effanbee Mama doll this
small. Sears, Roebuck and Co. catalog.

Step By Step and Day By Day
EFFANBEE DOLLS
Have Grown Better and Better in Every Way
THEY WALK—THEY TALK—THEY SLEEP

This is Number 232—It is a Handsome Little Doll about 14 inches in height and has a Mama Voice that is positively enchanting. Clad in Pastel Colored Rompers, it is an especially charming Easter item. A tiny pocket fashioned in the form of an Easter Chick or Rabbit is just large enough to hold a few bits of candy.

SEND FOR A SAMPLE DOZEN

Fleischaker & Baum
45 EAST 17th STREET, NEW YORK
We Specialize in Sleeping Eyes

Illustration 314. Full page advertisement for 14in (35.6cm) Effanbee dolls which are probably *Trottie Trulife* (numbered 232 by the company); composition heads, cloth cotton-stuffed bodies, composition arms to the elbows, cloth legs; blonde painted hair; blue painted eyes, brown eyebrows, painted eyelashes; closed mouths; both feature a mama voice; wearing pastel colored rompers designed especially for Easter. The pockets, in the shapes of an Easter chick or rabbit, were intended to hold a few pieces of candy. *Playthings,* January 1923.

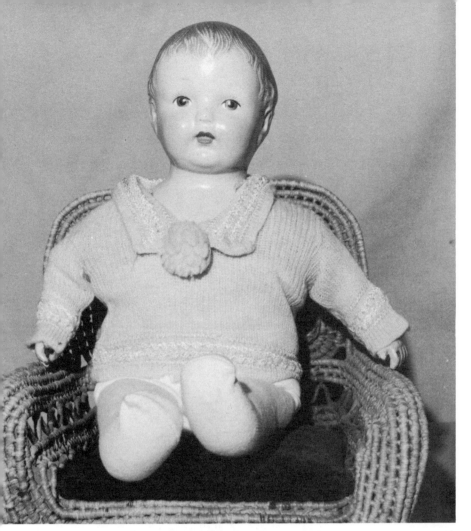

Illustration 315. 20in (50.8cm) *Mama Baby;* wood pulp composition head, cloth body, composition arms to the elbows, cloth legs; blonde painted hair; blue painted eyes, light brown eyebrows, painted upper eyelashes; closed mouth; marked on back: "Effanbee" in stylized script. 1924.

A Ma-ma Baby to Cuddle and Love
25½ Inches Tall

A cuddly, lovable Baby Doll, just learning to walk and say "ma-ma." She comes to her new mama in a crisp organdie dress and bonnet. With undergarments, socks and slippers you can take off. Head and arms of almost unbreakable composition. Body and legs stuffed. Painted hair.

449 N 2554 ..... $4.69
Postage, 16¢ extra

Illustration 316. Advertisement for 25½in (64.8cm) *Mama Baby,* similar to the one shown in *Illustration 315.* This doll is usually taken for a boy when found without original clothes. The legs in the advertisement are drawn as though they were shapely composition but they were actually cloth. Montgomery Ward & Co. catalog, 1924.

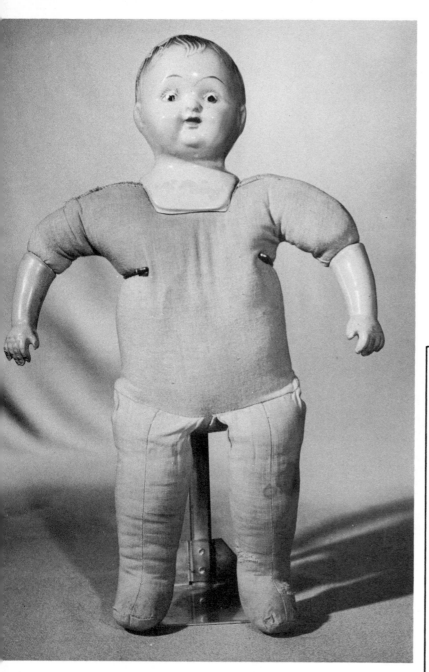

Illustration 317. 16in (40.6cm) Mama doll; composition shoulder head, cloth body, composition wired-on arms to the elbows, cloth legs; brown painted hair; blue painted eyes, brown painted eyebrows, painted upper eyelashes; open/closed mouth; molded ears; marked on back: "Effanbee" in stylized script. This doll appears to have been restuffed a bit too fully in the upper arms as these dolls were advertised as having "loosely jointed limbs." *Judy Johnson Collection.*

Illustration 318. Advertisement for the Mama doll shown in *Illustration 317.* Here one can see how much the original clothing gave a doll its true personality. "Star Value" offers made the price even more reasonable than usual; possibly the same design was available a year earlier. Butler Brothers catalog, 1923.

STAR VALUE

F 7 4 0 0 — "Effan-bee," loosely jointed limbs, strong crying voice, yellow, pink and blue organdie dresses, lace trim, lace trim bonnet to match, lace stockings, leatherette slippers, each in box. Asstd. ¼ doz. in pkg. Doz. **$12.50**

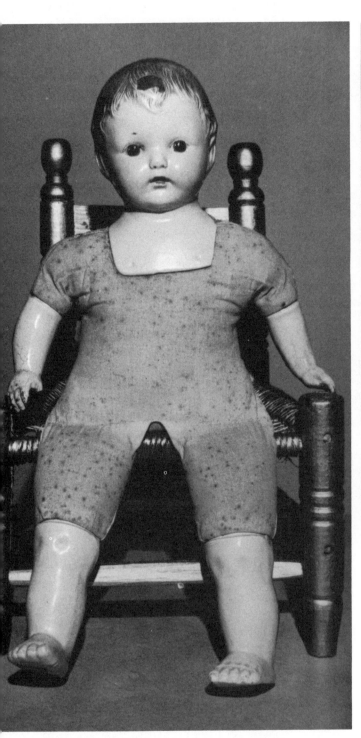

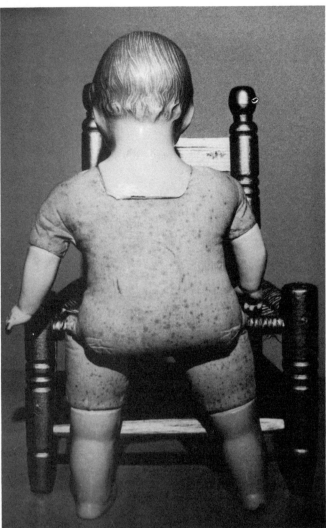

Illustration 320. The back of the 22in (55.9cm) *Mama Baby* seen in *Illustration 319,* showing the detail of the molded painted hair and the mark at the bottom of the neck.

Illustration 319. 22in (55.9cm) *Mama Baby;* composition shoulder head, cloth body, composition arms to the elbows, composition legs to the knees; brown painted hair; blue painted eyes, light brown eyebrows, painted upper eyelashes; closed mouth; marked at the bottom of the neck: "Effanbee" is stylized script. Somehow the head has received a hard blow but only the painted surface has chipped away, showing the darker wood pulp composition used at this time. There are two sew holes indented at the shoulder edge but not pierced through. Early 1920s.

PLAYTHINGS

Illustration 321. Original artwork showing the Mama dolls. *Playthings,* October 1923.

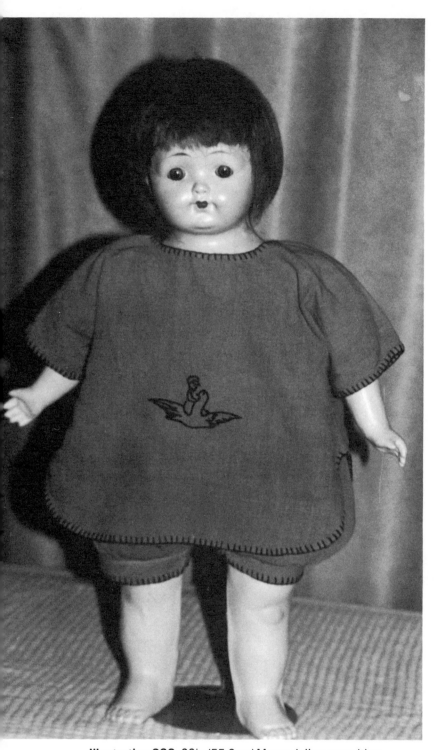

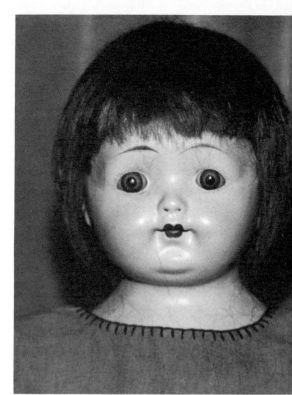

Illustration 323. **Illustration 323.** Close-up of the 22in (55.9cm) Mama doll seen in *Illustration 322. Alice Wardell Collection.*

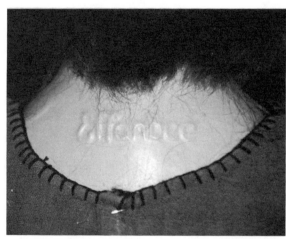

Illustration 322. 22in (55.9cm) Mama doll; composition shoulder head with a hole on top, cloth body, half composition arms, half composition legs; brown mohair wig; blue metal eyes, brown eyebrows, painted upper and lower eyelashes; closed mouth; wears an old pink cotton handmade dress with black embroidery; marked on the back of the shoulderplate: "Effanbee" in the early script writing. 1923. *Alice Wardell Collection.*

Illustration 324. Back of the 22in (55.9cm) Mama doll seen in *Illustrations 322 and 323*, showing the marking on the back of her shoulder plate. *Alice Wardell Collection.*

F7408—"Effanbee," 17 in. high, **loud voice**, painted hair, percale "Pollyanna" dress, organdie trim, puff crown bonnet to match, lace stockings, leatherette slippers. 1 in box.

Each, **$2.10**

Illustration 325. Advertisement for 17in (43.2cm) doll by Effanbee. Note the Effanbee Bluebird pin with the first circular guarantee tag hanging from it on a cord. This doll was available in 1922, also. Butler Brothers catalog, 1923.

"Effanbee" — **Moving eyes, mohair wigs,** voile "Pollyanna" dress, lace trim, bonnet to match with elastic, lace stockings, leatherette slippers. 1 in box.

F7414—17½ in.

Each, **$3.15**

F7415—21 in.

Each, **$4.25**

F7416—23 in., composition lower limbs.

Each, **$5.50**

Illustration 326. Advertisement for an Effanbee doll in three sizes. Note that she is wearing the second Effanbee paper tag with "Effanbee" the only discernible printing. The edges are slightly fluted rather than round. Butler Brothers catalog, 1923.

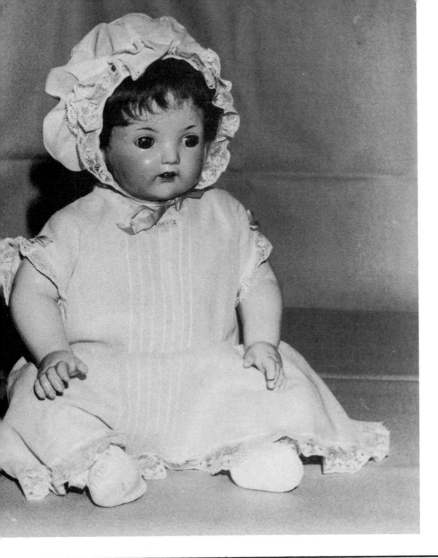

Illustration 327. 21 in (53.3cm) Mama doll; composition shoulder head, cloth body, composition arms, composition bent legs to the knees; brown mohair bob wig over molded hair; blue metal eyes, brown eyebrows, real hair upper eyelashes and painted lower ones; open mouth with two teeth and inset celluloid tongue; marked at the top of each arm: "Effanbee;" wearing cotton bonnet and dress trimmed with lace and ribbon bows with seven vertical tucks down the center of the dress, short kimono sleeves, cotton socks, real leather booties; blue silk woven label at neck reads: "EFFᴀɴBEE;" marked on back of head: "Effanbee." 1923.

Illustration 329. Advertisement featuring these dolls on a "stimulator page" at a special bargain price, lower than average. The artwork for the Effanbee doll shows the cloth Effanbee tag at the neck plus the Bluebird pin. The 15 in (38.1cm) baby sold for $12.00 per dozen whereas the 12½ in (31.8cm) German bisque doll with a wig and sleep eyes sold for $3.00 per dozen. Butler Brothers catalog, December 1925.

Illustration 328. Official artwork by Effanbee to advertise dolls for Christmas. This doll, which they show wearing slippers instead of booties, was sold by Butler Brothers in 1925. *Playthings,* December 1925.

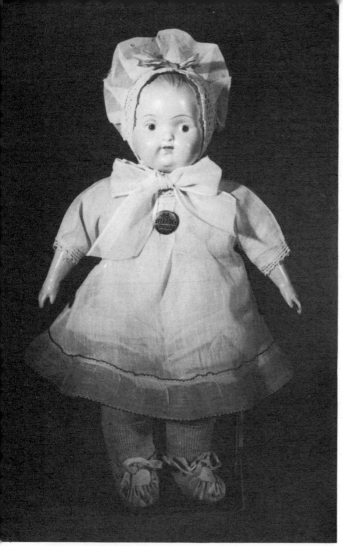

Illustration 330. 15in (38.1cm) Mama doll; composition shoulder head, cloth body, composition arms to above the wrists, cloth legs; light brown painted hair; blue painted eyes with dark pupils, brown painted eyebrows, painted upper eyelashes; closed mouth; wearing completely original yellow organdy dress over lawn bloomers, yellow poke bonnet trimmed in coarse lace, cotton socks, leatherette booties; Bluebird pin on front of dress; marked on back of neck: "Effanbee" in early script; cloth label at neckline of dress reads: "EFFANBEE//TRADE MARK" in an elongated oval. Due to the style of the arms and the cloth legs, the inception of this doll is probably earlier than 1923. 1925. *Darlene Payne Collection.*

Illustration 331. Close-up of 15in (38.1cm) Mama doll shown in *Illustration 330. Darlene Payne Collection.*

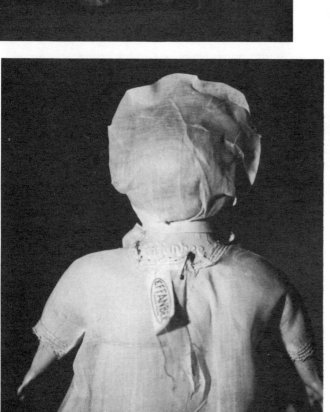

Illustration 332. Back view of 15in (38.1cm) Mama doll seen in *Illustrations 330* and *331* showing the cloth label at the neckline of the dress. *Darlene Payne Collection.*

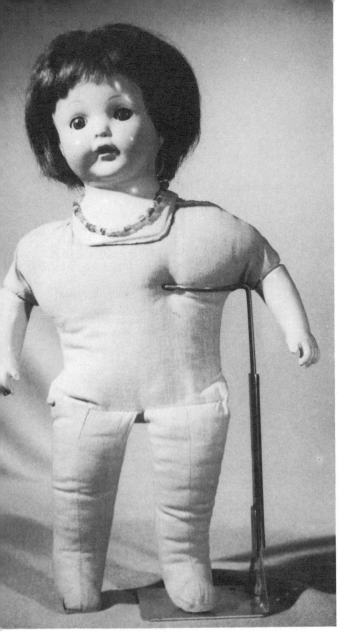

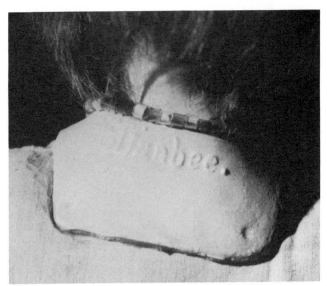

Illustration 334. Close-up of the back of the 18in (45.7cm) *Honeybunch* seen in *Illustration 333,* showing the marking on the back of the neck. Note the holes indicated as though to be punched for sew holes as in china dolls, but this head was simply glued onto the body.

Illustration 333. 18in (45.7cm) *Honeybunch;* composition shoulder head, cloth body, composition arms to the elbows, cloth legs a seam down each front; human hair wig; blue metal eyes, brown eyebrows, painted upper and lower eyelashes; closed mouth; molded ears; mama voice; wears old glass bead necklace made by a child; marked on back of shoulder plate: "Effanbee" in script. Circa 1922.

Illustration 335. 18in (45.7cm) *Honeybunch* seen in *Illustrations 333 and 334,* shown wearing her original old homemade pink voilé dress over a cotton slip, matching pink bonnet trimmed in old cotton lace, shoes are replaced.

Ilustration 336. Advertisement for *Honeybunch;* composition shoulder head, cloth cotton-stuffed body, composition arms to the elbows, composition legs to above the knees; mohair wig; metal eyes, brown eyebrows, painted eyelashes; closed mouth; wearing white lawn dress with Valenciennes lace at the neck, sleeves and hem, lacy bonnet trimmed with ribbon; note Bluebird button on dress. The composition bent baby legs were apparently new at this time. Effanbee called this doll "our latest handsome infant doll." *Playthings,* July 1923.

Illustration 337. Artwork prepared by Effanbee showing a small girl playing with her Mama doll. This was to be used in newspaper or magazine ad campaigns. Dealers were urged to "Doll up your shop windows with an EFFANBEE Display." *Playthings,* November 1923.

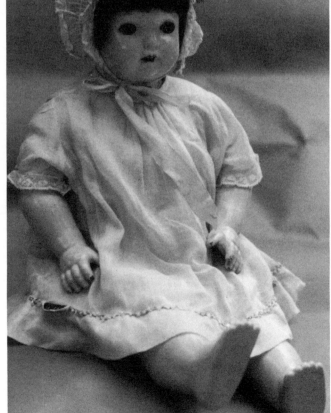

Illustration 338. 24in (61cm) Mama doll; composition shoulder head, cloth body, full composition arms with raised "Effanbee" at the tops, composition legs to the knees; brown mohair wig; blue metal eyes, brown eyebrows, real hair eyelashes; open mouth with two inset teeth and a celluloid tongue; marked on the shoulder plate: "EFFANBEE." 1923. *Sally Esser Collection.*

Illustration 339. 24in (61cm) Mama doll seen in *Illustration 338,* shown wearing her original yellow voile dress and bonnet, flower braid trim at hem top, lace on bonnet and sleeves; label sewn in top of dress hem reads: "EFFANBEE DOLL//FINEST AND BEST." *Sally Esser Collection.*

The doll YOUR child would choose

THE most perfect thing about Betty Lee is her precious adorable face —pink, dimpled cheeks, wee red mouth, big blue really eyelash eyes that go fast asleep. And dimpled arms and legs—just like a baby's— curly hair and a soft round body to hug.

She won't wear out

BUT the next-to-the-best thing is that like a real baby Betty Lee *won't wear out.* You can wash her face, dress and undress her, drop her on the floor. Of course she doesn't *like* being dropped, but it isn't likely to hurt her much. She is made that way—to last until daughter grows up.

For character-building play

BETTY LEE is so life-like she teaches gentle care and kindness. She wears clothes that can be taken off and put on again, washed and ironed. Her floppy legs dance with you like a real person. She really loves you and says "Mamma" in the prettiest way. Everything to a little girl that a real baby is to her mamma—just as absorbing and just as much loved.

Betty Lee is an Effanbee Doll— of course. If you want to know all about her, and all of her flocks and flocks of pretty sisters—a few of whom are sketched on this page—just drop into any good department or toy store and ask for Effanbee Dolls— the *"dolls with the golden heart."* You will know them by their darling little golden heart necklaces.

Every mother wants this booklet

SEND THE COUPON for our free booklet, "THE PROPER DOLL FOR MY CHILD'S AGE." It will tell you a lot about the best dolls for various ages, with a few hints on lessons children learn through doll play.

FLEISCHAKER & BAUM
Dept. 5, 45 Greene Street, New York City

BETTY LEE is 20 inches tall and costs $7.50. She has two bigger sisters, just like her, Alice Lee who is 23 inches tall and costs $10, and Barbara Lee who is 29 inches tall and costs $15. They wear the sweetest organdie frocks, trimmed with baby Irish lace. There are many, many dolls in the Effanbee Family—all sizes and from very moderate prices up to $25. If your dealer does not carry them write to us and we will see that you get what you want through him.

EFFANBEE DOLLS

FLEISCHAKER & BAUM, Dept. 5
45 Greene Street, New York City
Please send me your free booklet, "THE PROPER DOLL FOR MY CHILD'S AGE."

Name . . . .

Address . . . .

Illustration 340. Full page advertisement for *Betty Lee. Good Housekeeping,* December 1924.

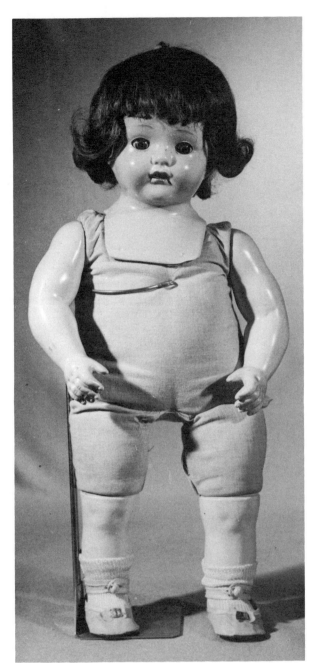

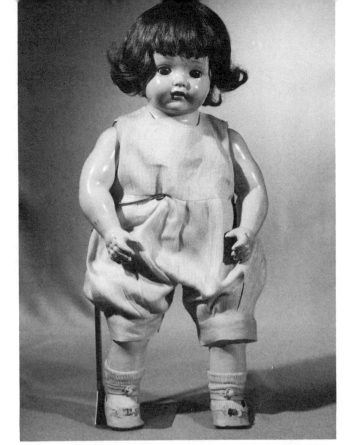

Illustration 342. 20in (50.8cm) Mama doll seen in *Illustration 341,* shown wearing her original pink cotton combination suit, seamed at the waist with fullness in the bloomers and open down the back. *Judy Johnson Collection.*

Illustration 341. 20in (50.8cm) Mama doll; composition shoulder head, cloth body, composition arms fastened by disks, composition wired-on legs to above the knees; molded hair under reddish-brown mohair; blue tin sleep eyes, light brown eyebrows, hair eyelashes; open mouth with two upper teeth and celluloid tongue; molded ears; head is marked: "Effanbee" in typical early script. *Judy Johnson Collection.*

Illustration 343. 20in (50.8cm) Mama doll seen in *Illustrations 341 and 342,* shown wearing her pink cotton slip trimmed with cotton lace over the combination suit. *Judy Johnson Collection.*

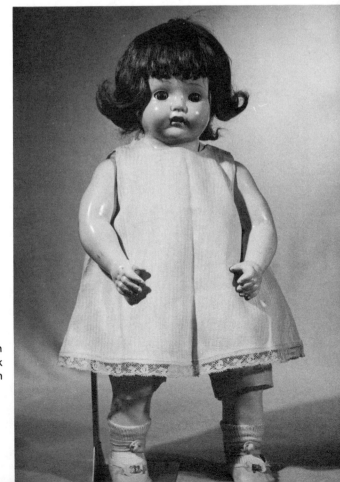

Illustration 344. 20in (50.8cm) Mama doll seen in *Illustration 341, 342* and *343*, shown in her original sheer pink mercerized cotton dress with lace net at the sleeves and skirt bottom, edged in scallops of material as in dress, woven braid trim on the dress at the neck, yoke and skirt of pink flowerets and green stems; tag on the front of dress at yoke reads: "EFFᴀɴBEE//DOLL//FINEST & BEST" within an elongated oval and "MADE IN USA" below the oval. *Judy Johnson Collection.*

Dainty solid color organdie
dress, val lace trimmed panels, edge of skirt, neck and
sleeves, lace trimmed poke
bonnet, combination petticoat and bloomers, socks,
leatherette strap slippers
with buckles, **sewed curled
mohair wig, moving eyes
with real lashes,** composition limbs.   **Each**
1F5126—18 in. high. **$3.75**
1F5127—24 " " **5.75**
1F5128—28 " " **6.95**

Illustration 345. Advertisement for an Effanbee doll;
composition shoulder head, full cotton-stuffed body,
composition arms, composition legs to above the knees;
sewed curled mohair wig; sleep eyes with real eyelashes;
each doll was said to have an Effanbee button. The
headline on the page read: "Effanbee Mama Dolls//This
brand is known wherever dolls are sold." Butler Brothers
catalog, 1924.

Dainty flowered crepe dress,
lace trimmed collar and
cuffs, 2 solid color felt pockets, poke bonnet to match,
mercerized socks, leatherette
strap slippers with buckles,
**sewed curled mohair wig,
moving eyes.**
                        Each
1F5121—17 in. high. **$3.00**
1F5122—21 " " **3.75**
1F5123—24 " " **5.25**

Illustration 346. Advertisement for an Effanbee doll
very similar to the one shown in Illustration 345. This
doll was also said to wear an Effanbee button and was
on the same page as the doll shown in Illustration 345.
Butler Brothers catalog, 1924.

Illustrations 347 and **348**. A two-page advertising spread with six styles of dolls in various costumes. The first doll in *Illustration 347* wears summer sandals and a play outfit. The infant doll next to her appears to be a smiling or serene version of *Baby Grumpy* (but the author has never located an example of this doll). The third doll in *Illustration 347* is a Mama doll in party clothes.

The doll on the left in *Illustration 348* is dressed for a party and has composition arms to below the elbows. In the center is a *Baby Grumpy* standing doll which the author has not located. He and the other Mama doll shown on the right have the full composition arms. Both light and dark slippers were used on the dolls. *Playthings*, June 1924.

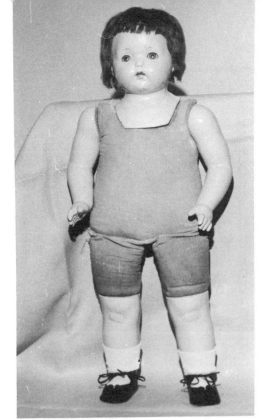

Illustration 349. 30in (76.2cm) Mama doll; composition shoulder head, cloth cotton-stuffed body, composition arms, composition legs to above the knees; mohair wig; blue metal eyes, brown eyebrows, real and painted eyelashes; closed mouth; marked on shoulder back: "Effanbee." This is a typical chunky Mama doll considered to be about age two, as often found, needing a complete costume replacement. Circa 1925. *Billie Nelson Tyrrell Collection.*

EFFANBEE Dolls that Walk and Talk

27 Inches Tall

The Queen of Toyland A Go-to-Sleep Dolly That Can Talk and Walk

The proudest, happiest little girl in all the world will be YOU when Santa puts this Dolly in your arms. It will be almost like having a real, live doll, for she can walk like a baby when you hold her hand, and can call you "Ma-ma." She is the most beautiful doll in Toyland; with soft, curly brown hair and blue go-to-sleep eyes with real lashes. And her beautiful clothes—a dress and bonnet of organdie, cunning petticoat and bloomers, half socks and slippers—and you can take them off. A genuine Effanbee Doll—chubby and dimpled like a baby. Her head, arms and legs are of composition, almost unbreakable. Body is stuffed and very well made, jointed at shoulders and sewed at hips. Mohair wig.

49 N 2553 .... $8.29
Postage, 20c extra

Illustration 351. Advertisement for the "Queen of Toyland." Note that the description says this girl doll is "chubby and dimpled like a baby." Today we would consider this a toddler or girl doll. Montgomery Ward & Co. catalog, 1924.

Illustration 350. Advertisement for an Effanbee Mama doll; wears a bonnet and a dress with a lace-trimmed square neck and sleeves, plain color band at the bottom of the skirt and on the bloomer bottom. Grunbaum Bros. Furniture Co., Inc., November 6, 1924.

Tested Leaders

Merchants' reorders indicate that these items are big sellers. How are your stocks

Jointed Body Character Babies

Turning bisque head, painted features, **SLEEPING EYES**, asstd. tosca and brunette mohair wigs, open mouth showing teeth and tongue, hardened pressed paper body, matte finish, flesh tinted, position limbs, hip and shoulder joints, lawn slips.

2F6427 — 12 in. high, silk dress, silk cap, lace trim underwear, rubber pacifier. 1 in box.
Each **$1.25**

2F6462—15¼ in. high, with sewed bobbed wig, ribbon bow, chubby body. 1 in box.
Each **$1.35**

"Effanbee" Baby Dolls

Dainty solid color organdie dress, val lace trimmed panels, edge of skirt, neck and sleeves, lace trimmed poke bonnet, combination petticoat and bloomers, socks, leatherette strap slippers with buckles. Sewed curled mohair wig, **SLEEPING EYES**, with real lashes, composition limbs. 1 in box.

1F5126—18 in. high. Each **$3.75**
1F5127—24 in. high. Each **5.75**
1F5128—28 in. high. Each **6.95**

Illustration 352. Advertisement showing large Effanbee Mama dolls referred to as "Baby Dolls." Note that the 18in (45.7cm) Effanbee doll sells for $3.75 while a 15½in (39.4cm) German bisque baby is priced at $1.35. Butler Brothers catalog, December 1925.

Dressed Mama—White corded dimity dress, novelty over-check fine quality gingham, square neck and border, pearl button trim, gingham band panties to match, matched poke bonnet, socks and slippers. Mohair wig, sleeping eyes, composition legs and forearms. 1 in box.

1F5117—18 in. high......Each **$3.00**
1F5118—21 in. high......Each **3.75**
1F5119—24 in. high......Each **5.25**

Illustration 353. Advertisement showing an Effanbee Mama doll in a different dress. This costume would be an excellent one to reproduce. The white corded dimity is trimmed with gingham bands at the neck and hem with matching panties. Butler Brothers catalog, December 1925.

Illustration 354. Advertisement showing a K & K German bisque doll selling for $1.25 and an Effanbee Mama doll selling for $2.25. The Effanbee doll was available in the same catalog in 1924 for $3.00. Even so, she still costs nearly double that of the imported bisque head German doll. Butler Brothers catalog, December 1925.

Illustration 355. 18in (45.7cm) *Rosemary* (not so marked); composition shoulder head, cloth body, composition arms with dimples at the elbows, composition legs to above the knees with dimples at the knees, cloth ''swing'' upper legs; blue-gray metal sleep eyes, painted eyebrows, real hair eyelashes; open mouth with white teeth and tiny tongue; molded ears; wears good quality organdy dress in a pretty color, rosebud-trimmed bonnet matches the color of her dress, real baby socks and slippers; every Effanbee doll was said to wear the golden heart necklace at this time. This doll sold for $5.00 and was said to be **the** 1925 Christmas Effanbee doll. She was advertised as having ''flocks and flocks of pretty sisters, prices ranging from 50¢ to $25.00 each.'' *Ladies' Home Journal, 1925.*

Illustration 356. The doll shown here represents a somewhat plainer costumed version made for the economy market. She is wearing a bloomer dress made deliberately shorter allowing the panties to show with the cuff on the leg of matching dress material. Sears, Roebuck and Co. catalog, circa 1925.

Illustration 357. 20in (50.8cm) and 16in (40.6cm) Effanbee Mama dolls; composition shoulder heads, cloth bodies, composition wired-on arms to the elbows, composition legs to above the knees; soft silky mohair wigs; blue-gray metal eyes, brown eyebrows, real hair eyelashes; open/closed mouth; molded ears; came in assorted pretty colored dresses with bonnets to match, cotton socks and removable patent leather slippers; had cotton tags at the necks of the dresses with "Effanbee" in an elongated oval. These were given as premiums for four subscriptions to *Junior Home* magazine. Premium dolls were usually older models and these resemble models that were new in 1923. *Junior Home* magazine, September 1926.

Illustration 359. Advertisement showing *Marilee* wearing a felt bonnet and soft cotton dress. *Ladies' Home Journal*, 1928.

Illustration 358. 22in (55.9cm) *Marilee*; composition shoulder head, cloth body, composition arms, composition legs to above the knees; dark human hair curled wig; blue eyes, brown eyebrows, hair eyelashes; open mouth with four teeth and a molded celluloid tongue; wearing all-original dimity dress. *Barbara Schletzbaum Collection.*

Illustration 361. 30in (76.2cm) *Marilee;* composition shoulder head, cloth body, composition arms, composition legs to above the knees; long brown human hair curled wig; blue metal eyes, light brown eyebrows, real and painted eyelashes; open mouth with four teeth and a celluloid tongue; wearing all-original pink silk dress with net ruffles; marked on back of shoulder head: "EFFₐₙBEE//MARILEE//COPYR.//DOLL" in an elongated oval. Came with her original box. 1928. *Jerri Peterka Collection. Photograph by Jerri Peterka.*

Illustration 360. Advertisement showing a doll that is probably *Marilee;* real human hair curled wig; sleep eyes, brown painted eyebrows, real hair eyelashes; open mouth with four teeth; wearing organdy frock and felt hat. The retail price was $4.95 and she was a new doll for Christmas. *Good Housekeeping,* 1928.

Illustration 362. Advertisement showing replacement heads by Effanbee and another unnamed company. A 5¼in (13.4cm) shoulder head by Effanbee sold for $1.19 while a 5½in (14cm) head by the other company sold for 49¢. The Effanbee heads were guaranteed not to chip or crack. Montgomery Ward & Co. catalog, 1928.

Mohair Ringlet Bob on This Composition Head

Her wide, blue eyes, cute little mouth and snub nose are painted on her pretty composition face, and she has the latest style curly bob with bangs. Wig of soft mohair. Read "How to Order" above. Ship. wt., 4 oz. to 1 lb.
48 C 2626—Height 4¾ in. Shoulder width, 2¼ in...**33¢**
48 C 2627—Height 5½ in. Shoulder width, 2¾ in...**49¢**
48 C 2628—Height 6 inches. Shoulder width, 3⅛ in...**65¢**
48 C 2629—Height 7½ in. Shoulder width, 4 in......**79¢**
48 C 2630—Height 8½ in. Shoulder width, 4½ in...**98¢**

Sleeping Eyes, *Mohair Wig*

Effanbee Doll Heads

Made exclusively for us by Effanbee with their name on back of each head. Stylish curly bob golden mohair wig. Sleeping eyes and thick lashes. Absolutely guaranteed not to check or crack. Read "How to Order" above. Ship. wts.: 6 oz. to 1 lb. 8 oz.
48 C 2595—Height 5¼ in. Shoulder width, 2¼ in...**$1.19**
48 C 2596—Height 5½ in. Shoulder width, 2¾ in...**$1.67**
48 C 2597—Height 6 inches. Shoulder width, 3¼ in...**$1.98**
48 C 2598—Height 8 inches. Shoulder width, 4 in...**$2.79**
48 C 2599—Height 8¾ in. Shoulder width, 4¾ in...**$3.39**

Dolls Marked Rosemary

By January 1926 the new dolls were marked "Rosemary." Strangely enough, the marked *Rosemary* debuted in *Playthings* as " 'Rose-Marie' Winsome and lovely, she wins every heart." She was said to have been tested in several stores at Christmas (1925), and proved an instant success. Again, one would know they owned *Rose-Marie* even if **marked** "Rosemary" only if found in the exact costume advertised.

Advertising stated that children were tiring of clumsy stuffed bodies. Actually, it was probably only good business technique to create something different. The solid chunky dolls of 1923, 1924 and 1925 were considered by the designers to be babies or very young children but appear older than that to our eye today. Effanbee stated that the new *Rose-Marie* was a little older than most "Mamma dolls."

Her long slim legs were said to dance prettily and easily. She had slender, graceful arms and beautiful natural curls of real hair, as well as real eyelashes, teeth and a tiny tongue. She said "mamma" and was said to be easier for a child to handle. First sizes were 18in (45.7cm) to 30in (76.2cm) and wore the golden heart necklace.

Surprisingly, there is a **marked** *Rosemary* with a closed mouth which may have been an early prototype since the head is one which has been cut off at the top to insert the eyes. Most *Rosemarys* (so marked) have a solid dome head, after a machine was invented to insert eyes without slicing the head at the top. The leg shape is slightly different than the regular model.

The finest "Rose Marie Doll Buggy" was illustrated in the Montgomery Ward & Co. catalog in time for Christmas. The copy verified it was actually tied in to Effanbee's *Rose Marie* or *Mary Sue,* 27in (68.6cm) tall. This was a high quality item as were the dolls. The entire buggy body could be reversed to face the "child-mother," if desired. The entire bed and hood were upholstered in dove gray velvet corduroy. The outside was two-tone silver over blue combination, with wheels and undercarriage in gray. Some collectors may own an example without realizing what they have! Lucky the fortunate child who received *Rose-Marie* and her buggy.

One ponders the "whys" of catalogs which do not use names of dolls for models known to have been named. Montgomery Ward & Co., showed two obvious marked *Rosemarys* but does not call them *Rose-Marie* as in *Playthings.* One had blonde human hair and one a brunette mohair wig, neither the long curls originally shown. Effanbee advertised *Lovey Mary,* in *Toys and Novelties* for June 1926 with heights from 18in (45.7cm) to 30in (76.2cm). The *Ladies' Home Journal,* December 1926, advertised *Lovey Mary* (along with *Bubbles*) in a 19in (48.3cm) size which cost $5.00. The hair on the doll illustrated is in dark ringlets. She has a charming dress and bonnet tied in black ribbon, which was chic at this period. The one-button "Mary Jane" slippers (inspired by the girl child in Buster Brown comics) are replaced by patent slippers with ties.

The *Seattle Daily Times* in November 1926, advertised *Lovey Mary* for $5.00 (along with *Bubbles* baby doll). Of course, *Lovey Mary* is marked "Rosemary." She was said to be the ideal playmate for every little girl. The costumes were organdy in pink, purple or blue. The French bonnet is organdy with rosette trim.

Many will be surprised to realize Effanbee offered a *Winifred,* never mentioned to date. Surely the costume determined the identity. Her dress (at least the version in the 1926 catalog) was sheer pink organdy piquoted in black. Blue silk rosettes trim the front of her dress. She wears the "Mary Jane" slippers.

We have an actual newspaper advertisement for 1927's marked *Rosemary.* She is named "*Big Sister*" *Mary Lou,* $5.00 for 18in (45.7cm) size. She is shown in the November 1927 *Ladies' Home Journal* in the same costume (there were others). "Mary Lou is Bubbles' big sister. She's so sweet and pretty in her little party clothes. Soft organdy of pink or lavender or blue, the latest Paris fashion with dainty frills and ribbon bows, with a lovely Paris hat to match. Mary Lou calls you 'Mamma' most adorably. She has blue eyes that go to sleep, real curly hair, and she can walk and dance with you," claims the magazine.

The 1927 Montgomery Ward's catalog featured the first version of the flirting eye *Rosemarys,* calling her "Effanbee's Masterpiece, Naughty Eyes, A Dancing Doll." The description reads: "Naughty Eyes just can't stop flirting! She rolls her big eyes naughtily from side to side in a most lifelike, tantalizing manner, a very accomplished miss. She'll dance with you, will go to sleep, and will say 'Ma-ma'." The dress was said to be pink organdy trimmed with ruching and ribbon. She wears an Effanbee locket and chain, and bandeau, with French flowers on her mohair wig.

Montgomery Ward & Co. in 1928 offered *Mary Sue* (light golden bob) and *Rose Mary* (dark brown long curls) from 18in (45.7cm) to 26in (66cm). The composition was said to be Hard-to-Break. The dress was sheer pink organdy with lace ruffles and gores. Six photographs came with the dolls, the idea being that one sent them out to friends, somewhat like a birth announcement, when receiving the doll.

The second flirting-eye models of *Rosemary* are offered in the Montgomery Ward & Co. catalog for 1928. The catalog has named her an "Effanbee Masterpiece, Laughing Eyes." The 14½in (36.9cm) and 16in (40.6cm) versions may be the *Baby Dainty* molds.

In 1929 Montgomery Ward & Co. offered two grades of *Rosemary.* These flirting-eye versions were called *Coquette* in the more deluxe edition and *Laughing Eyes* in the economy version. Either one would be superior to many other dolls, with seams finely sanded and beautifully painted.

This has never been explained but it is pretty certain some deluxe dolls received more coats of paint than others, depending on the market. Some catalogs designate a doll "Effanbee quality" and this seems to denote their finest product. There was $1.00 to $2.00 difference according to the size of the doll. It also seems policy often made a deluxe model 1 in (2.5cm) or 2 in (5.1 cm) different in size from the lesser version; elaborate costumes could make a **considerable** difference in price.

The St. Paul, Minnesota, 1929 Montgomery Ward & Co. catalog offered "Effanbee's Finest Feature Dancing Doll," *Mary Louise,* this year with long golden curls, or *Rose Mary,* with dark brown curls. Both said "mama." Sheer pink voile frocks were frilly with lace, finished with two-tone streamer ties and flower rosettes. The pink butterfly hair bows were of all-silk moire ribbon. The socks were now silky pink rayon, a first time mention. Earlier versions were cotton.

The Montgomery Ward & Co. catalog in 1930 advertised the flirting-eye dolls as *Mischievous Eyes* (marked "Rosemary") in two grades. The 14 in (35.6cm)

and 16 in (40.6cm) sizes are probably the *Baby Dainty* molds. "Laughing blue eyes roll naughtily from side to side....it's hard to be firm with such a fascinating little rogue! Created by EFFANBEE, world famous makers of fine dolls...better wig; better clothing; nothing short of perfection."

In 1931 dolls offered are called *Dream Dolls* in sizes 17 in (43.2cm), 19 in (48.3cm), 21 in (53.3cm), 23 in (58.4cm) and 25 in (63.5cm). The eyes do not seem to flirt. One could have a choice of golden or dark curls. These models were said to be "a sort of Fairy Princess of dolls that dwells in every small girl's imagination... actually brought into existence. To tell you the truth we don't know who else but the famous Effanbee could have really created her!" states the catalog. Her dress is ruffled pink silk crepe and she wears the Effanbee gold locket and chain.

Illustration 363. In this advertisement we see the very first appearance of the doll **marked** *Rosemary* but originally advertised as *Rose-Marie.* The new *Bubbles* is also mentioned. *Playthings,* January 1926.

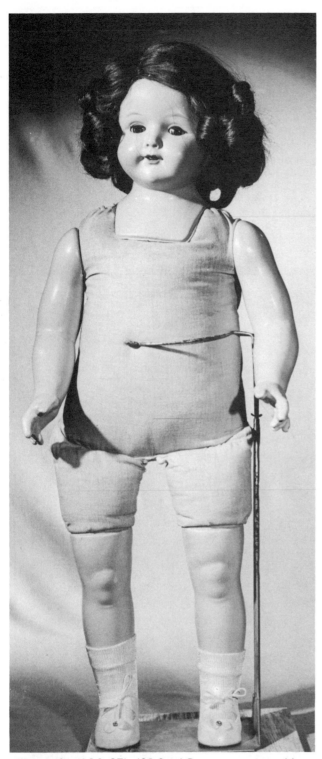

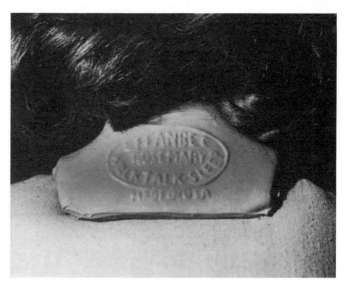

Illustration 365. Close-up of the back of the 27in (68.6cm) *Rosemary* seen in *Illustration 364*, showing the mark on the back of the shoulder plate. All *Rosemarys* or other named models of the same mold in various sizes seem to be marked the same. *Judy Johnson Collection.*

Illustration 364. 27in (68.6cm) *Rosemary;* composition shoulder head, cloth body, composition arms, composition wired-on legs to above the knees; dark brown human hair wig; blue metal eyes, light brown painted eyebrows, real hair eyelashes; open mouth with four teeth and a celluloid tongue; marked on the back of the shoulder plate: "EFFANBEE//ROSEMARY//WALK. TALK.SLEEP" in an elongated oval with "MADE IN USA" beneath it. Note the beautiful natural proportions and superior modeling of the arms and legs. This is the first mouth shape, a narrow little pursed mouth. Later the mouth was widened a bit. *Judy Johnson Collection.*

Illustration 366. 27in (68.6cm) *Rosemary* seen in *Illustrations 364* and *365*, shown wearing an old blue figured cotton print dress of a child, probably belonging to the former owner. The hem has been turned up on the bloomer dress. *Judy Johnson Collection.*

Illustration 367. 24in (61cm) *Rosemary;* composition shoulder head, cloth cotton-stuffed body, composition arms, composition wired-on legs to above the knees; light brown wig; blue metal eyes, brown painted eyebrows, real hair eyelashes; open mouth with four teeth and a celluloid tongue; wearing her original pink voile dress without a yoke, ribbon ruffles on the sleeves and dress bottom. Circa 1926. *Joyce Olsen Collection.*

Illustration 368. Close-up of the 24in (61cm) *Rosemary* seen in *Illustration 367,* shown in her pink ribbon-trimmed "French" puff bonnet. *Joyce Olsen Collection.*

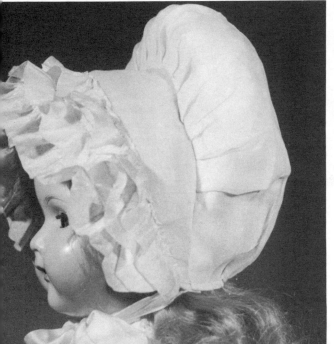

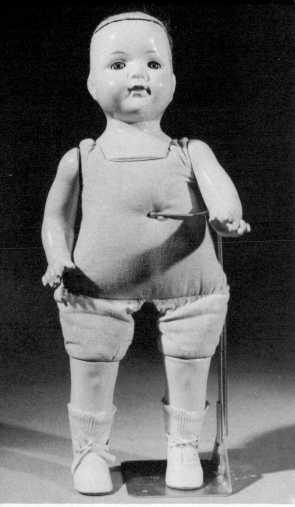

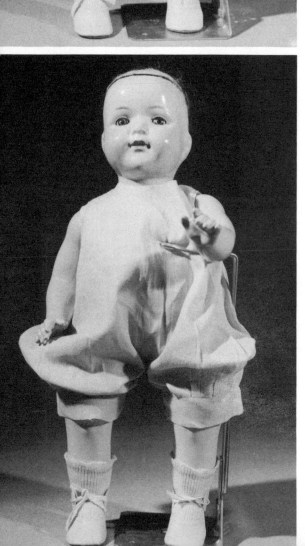

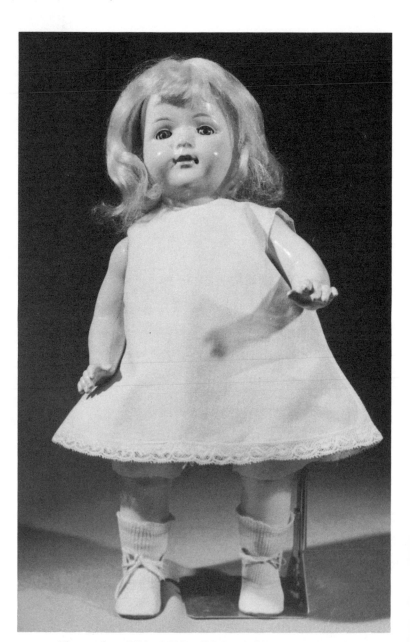

Illustration 369. 14½in (36.9cm) *Rosemary;* composition shoulder head, cloth body, composition arms, composition legs to above the knees; blonde mohair wig; blue metal eyes, light brown eyebrows, real hair eyelashes; closed mouth. This doll has legs of a different shape from others. *Joyce Olsen Collection.*

Illustration 371. 14½in (36.9cm) *Rosemary* seen in *Illustrations 369 and 370,* showing wearing her original blue cotton slip trimmed in cotton lace. *Joyce Olsen Collection.*

Illustration 370. 14½in (36.9cm) *Rosemary* seen in *Illustration 369,* shown wearing her original light blue cotton combination suit with leg bands of the dress material. *Joyce Olsen Collection.*

Illustration 372. 14½in (36.9cm) *Rosemary* seen in *Illustrations 369, 370 and 371,* shown fully dressed in her original soft batiste dress with unusual cotton trim in two rows on the skirt. The bonnet is a replacement. The same dress trim has been used on a *Bubbles* toddler doll. *Joyce Olsen Collection.*

Illustration 373. Close-up of the label at the yoke seam of the dress shown on the 14½in (36.9cm) Rosemary seen in *Illustration 372.* The label reads: "EFFᴀɴBEE//DOLL//FINEST & BEST" in an elongated oval with "MADE IN U.S.A." underneath. *Joyce Olsen Collection.*

Sleeping Eyes

Rayon Silk Dress

EFFANBEE
Slender
Body
Dollies

They Will Walk or Dance with You If You Lead

Girlish, slender figures, and beautiful-ly dimpled composition head, arms and legs. Her wig with a side part, is made of human hair, golden in color; you can just see the tip of her tongue. Appeal-ing "Ma-Ma" voice; cotton stuffed body. Golden yellow Rayon silk dress with underwear of same material; yellow hair bow; white French heel shoes and mercerized stockings. Effanbee locket and chain.

449 E 2594—24 inches tall **$9.39**
449 E 2593—19 inches tall... 6.98
Postage: 22¢ and 20¢ extra

22 Inches Tall

Dressed for a party in a canary yellow voile dress with rose figures and lace, with bloomer combination to match. On her mohair wig she has a yellow ribbon bandeau with a rose. Beautiful slender type of little girl body. Composition head, arms and legs; sleeping eyes with eye lashes; finest "Ma-Ma" voice. Cotton stuffed body. French heel shoes and mercer-ized stockings.

449 E 2613............. **$7.48**
Postage, 18¢ extra

Illustration 374. The Montgomery Ward & Co. catalog for 1926 offered the new girlish looking slender dolls actually marked "Rosemary" but not calling them that. Both mohair and human hair types were available. Since the earlier Mama dolls were very chubby and represented two-year-olds, the emphasis was now on being a slender young girl.

Best of all, these dolls *won't wear out!*

THE most wonderful thing about these dolls is that they won't wear out. That is because they are Effanbee Dolls. You can play and play with them, and they will last until you grow up. Ask Santa please to bring you Bubbles or Lovey Mary, whichever one you prefer.

Bubbles and Lovey Mary come in all sizes. Shown here they are 19 inches tall and cost $5. At all better-class department and toy stores.

You can tell them, in your favorite department or toy store, by their dear little golden heart necklaces. Every Effanbee Doll wears a golden heart.

A golden heart necklace for every child

Lovey Mary wants every child to have a golden heart necklace, too. If you would like one, mail the coupon and 6c to Lovey Mary Effanbee, 45 Greene St., New York City.

EFFANBEE DOLLS

Illustration 375. *Lovey Mary* was actually marked "Rosemary" so the name may have been used on dolls in certain costumes. Here is shown a coupon for a 6¢ golden heart necklace that could be ordered. Usually one outstanding baby doll (*Bubbles*) and one outstanding girl doll was featured. *Ladies' Home Journal,* December 1926.

"EFFANBEE" DOLLS *With Slender, Graceful Bodies*

Sleeping Eyes

Our Most Beautiful Dancing Dolls

Rose Marie's Sister Mary Sue

Two of the most wonderful Dolls in the world—Effanbee's best. They have slender graceful bodies like real little girls. Almost unbreakable composition heads, arms and legs, charmingly dimpled at knees and elbows. Sewed wigs of real human hair—Rose Marie's hair is medium brown and in long curls, Mary Sue has the latest ringlet bob and her hair is light. Both girls have sleeping eyes with real lashes and finest "Ma-Ma" voices. Cotton stuffed bodies. Either doll will dance or walk with you if you will lead.

Mary Sue

449 E 2523—26 inches tall	$10.50
449 E 2522—23 inches tall	9.50
449 E 2521—21 inches tall	7.98
449 E 2520—18 inches tall	6.98

Postage: 22¢, 20¢, 18¢ and 14¢ extra

Our Famous Rose Marie

Rose Marie's dress is pink voile with silk stripes and is trimmed with embroidered ruffles. Her sister Mary Sue's dress is pale blue sheer organdie with pin plaits in front and wide lace trimmed flounces. Both wear bloomer combinations and satin hair bows to match dresses, shoes with ribbon ties, knee length mercerized stockings and an Effanbee locket and chain.

With each of these dolls comes a set of six of her photographs.

Rose Marie

449 E 2623—26 inches tall	$10.50
449 E 2622—23 inches tall	9.50
449 E 2621—21 inches tall	7.98
449 E 2620—18 inches tall	6.98

Postage: 22¢, 20¢, 18¢ and 14¢ extra

Illustration 376. Advertisement for the larger, more deluxe models of marked "Rosemary" dolls. Both had human hair wigs, one in long curls, *Rose Marie,* and *Mary Sue,* in the latest style of blonde ringlet bob. Apparently, the wig and the costume determined the name of the doll. The *Rose Marie* costume is the same as that introduced in the January 1926 *Playthings.* Montgomery Ward & Co. catalog, 1926.

Illustration 377. *Mary Sue* doll (actually marked "Rosemary") in a portrait by Stone Van Dresser. Six copies of this portrait came with the doll for the child to give to friends. The six copies are shown between *Mary Sue* and *Rose Marie* in *Illustration 376. Loaned by Mrs. Robert E. Sweeney.*

Illustration 378. Advertisement for a high quality doll buggy made to fit the deluxe *Rose Marie* or *Mary Sue* dolls. The material was woven fiber reed in a fancy check weave. Montgomery Ward & Co. catalog, 1926.

Finest Rose Marie Doll Buggy

For Dolls Up to 27 Inches Tall

Handsome Doll Buggy, of splendid quality; large enough for our largest Rose Marie or Mary Sue dolls or any doll up to 27 inches tall. Its loom woven fiber reed sides and hood are in a fancy check weave. Beauty rolls with a peak on the hood and the bed. Notice the strong way in which the spokes are built into the round hubs of the 10-inch heavy wood (artillery) wheels with 9/16-inch rubber tires. These wheels slide onto axle, and a spring clip snaps over them exactly as on real baby carriages. The 5/8-inch tubular push bars extend all the way to the front axle. Windows in the hood in nickel plated frames 3 1/8 inches in diameter. Hood is on rod with sliding adjustment.

The entire bed and hood are upholstered in dove gray velvet corduroy. Reversible body. Extra strong frame; double foot brake; leather hold-in strap. Handsome turned wood push bar, black enameled; nickel plated hub caps; reclining back. Length of body, not including reclining back, 26 inches; width, 14 inches. Height to top of hood, 36 inches; to push bars, 29 in.

This buggy is a two-tone silver over blue combination, often called an **aluminum blue color.** Wheels and undergearing are gray. Ship. weight, 35 pounds. Can be shipped by freight or express only.
148 E 3522........$14.48

$14⁴⁸

CORDUROY UPHOLSTERY
SLIDING HOOD FIXTURE
HOOD WINDOWS
RECLINING BACK
TUBULAR PUSH BAR
ARTILERY RUBBER TIRE WHEELS
REVERSING BODY
BABY CARRIAGE WHEELS
BRAKE

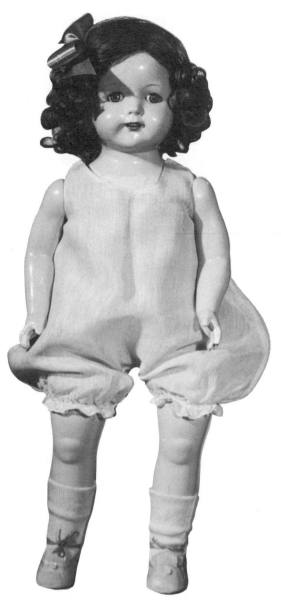

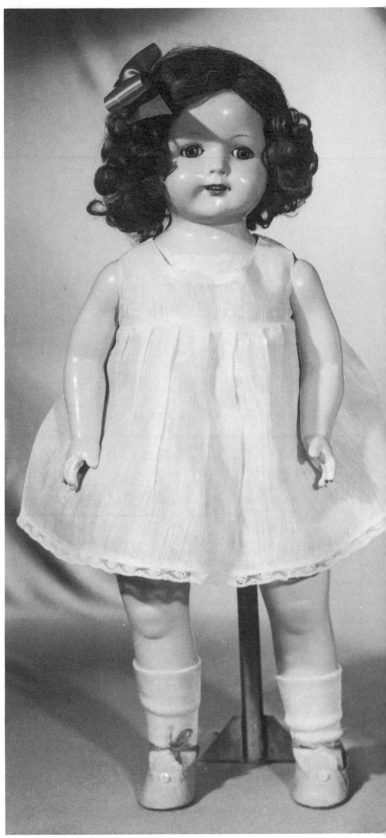

Illustration 379. 24in (61cm) *Rosemary;* composition shoulder head, cloth body, composition arms, composition wired-on legs to above the knees; brown human hair wig; blue metal eyes, light brown painted eyebrows, real and painted eyelashes; open mouth with four teeth and a celluloid tongue; shown wearing her original pink mercerized combination bloomer suit with lace at the panty legs, original shoes and socks. The emphasis on these dolls was that they were **American** dolls.

Illustration 380. 24in (61cm) *Rosemary* seen in *Illustration 379,* shown wearing her original separate mercerized pink slip trimmed in lace.

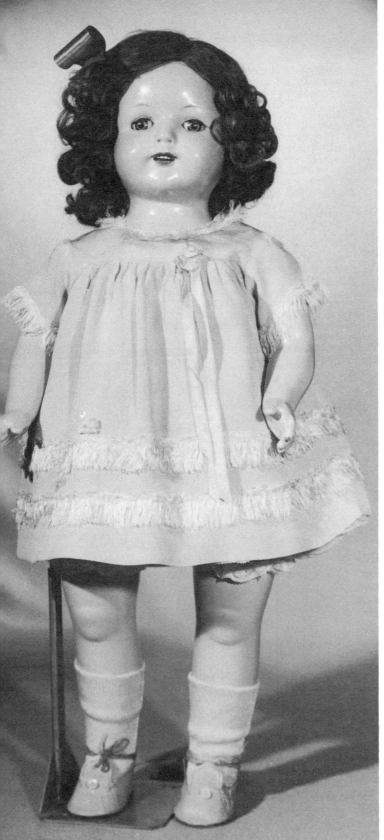

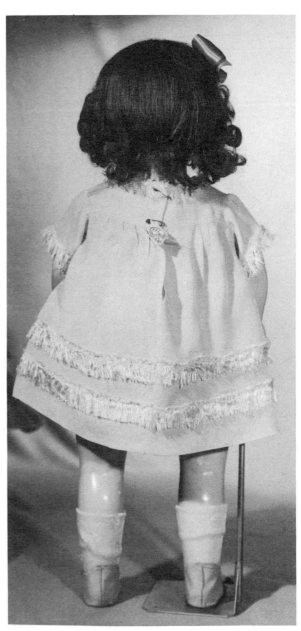

Illustration 381. 24in (61cm) *Rosemary* seen in *Illustration 379 and 380,* shown wearing her original pink silk crepe dress with a high yoke, fringed ribbon trim at the neck, sleeves and skirt, French flower on the yoke and skirt, ribbon streamers, original pink socks and shoes. This is one of the deluxe party dresses.

Illustration 382. Back view of the dress shown on the 24in (61cm) *Rosemary* seen in *Illustration 381.* The tag at the yoke seamline reads: "EFFᴀɴBEE//DOLL// FINEST & BEST" in an elongated oval with "MADE IN U.S.A." underneath.

She Goes to Sleep

She Will Walk or Dance With You If You Lead

EFFANBEE Winifred

"Miss Winifred" is slender and graceful like a real little girl. Her composition arms and legs are plump and dimpled. Her head is of Effanbee's famous practically unbreakable composition.

Her slender well shaped body is stuffed with cotton. She is jointed at shoulders and hips. You will like her pretty sewed mohair wig, real eye lashes and eyes that go to sleep. Her parted lips show a pink tongue and teeth. She says "Ma-Ma," and wears an Effanbee locket and chain.

Miss Winifred's lovely dress is made of sheer pink organdie with three ruffles daintily piquoted in black. Ruffles trim the neck, sleeves and her little bonnet, which has fine silk ribbon ties. Blue silk rosettes are on the front of her dress. She wears a pink lace trimmed petticoat, bloomer combination, pink button shoes and knee length pink cuff mercerized hose.

449 E 2512—
26 inches tall........ **$8.98**

449 E 2511—
21 inches tall........ **6.98**

449 E 2510—
18 inches tall........ **6.19**

Postage: 20¢, 18¢ and 16¢ extra

Illustration 383. Advertisement for *Miss Winifred* who has never been recorded previously in doll books. Her costume would be the clue to her identity. Montgomery Ward & Co. catalog, 1926.

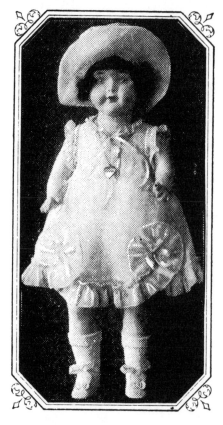

Illustration 384. 19in (48.3cm) *Mary Lou;* composition shoulder head, cloth body, composition disk jointed arms, composition legs to above the knees; dark curly mohair wig; blue metal eyes, brown painted eyebrows, real hair eyelashes; open mouth with four teeth and a celluloid tongue; molded ears; shown wearing an organdy dress of pink, lavender or blue in the latest Paris fashion with dainty frills and ribbon bows, lovely Paris hat to match, tie slippers with a bow and buckle. The doll shown wears the Effanbee golden heart necklace and sold for $5.00. She was said to be a big sister for *Bubbles. Ladies' Home Journal,* November 1927.

Illustration 385. Advertisement for a Seattle, Washington, newspaper for an 18in (45.7cm) "Big Sister" *Mary Lou.* December 4, 1927.

'Big Sister" Mary Lou, $5.00

The sweetest dolls—no wonder little mothers find it so easy to cuddle and love them! Dressed in the prettiest, latest style frocks—"Effanbee" unbreakable dolls, too—18 inches tall, call "Mama." Beautiful big blue eyes and lovely curly hair.

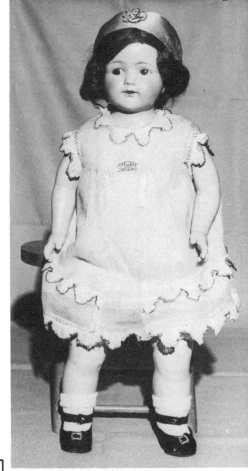

ABOVE: Illustration 386. *Naughty Eyes;* composition shoulder head, cloth body, composition arms, composition legs to above the knees; dark brown mohair wig; blue metal flirting eyes, brown eyebrows, real hair eyelashes; open mouth with four teeth and a celluloid tongue; wearing pink organdy dress trimmed with ruching and ribbon, pink bandeau with French flower on her hair; originally had an Effanbee locket and chain. Note label sewn at yoke seamline on front of dress. This doll is said to be a dancing doll. The leg shape is different from the typical version, more of a juvenile type. This same mold was used on some of the cloth-bodied *Patsy* Mama dolls. 1927.

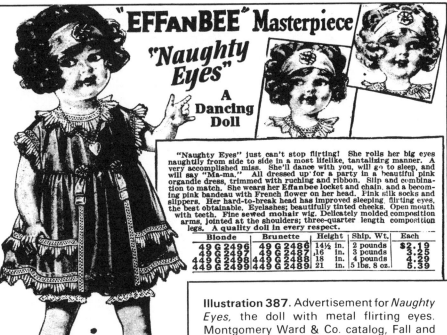

"EFFanBEE" Masterpiece
"Naughty Eyes"
A Dancing Doll

"Naughty Eyes" just can't stop flirting! She rolls her big eyes naughtily from side to side in a most lifelike, tantalizing manner. A very accomplished miss. She'll dance with you, will go to sleep, and will say "Ma-ma." All dressed up for a party in a beautiful pink organdie dress, trimmed with ruching and ribbon. Slip and combination to match. She wears her Effanbee locket and chain, and a becoming pink bandeau with French flower on her head. Pink silk socks and slippers. Her hard-to-break head has improved sleeping, flirting eyes, the best obtainable. Eyelashes; beautifully tinted cheeks. Open mouth with teeth. Fine sewed mohair wig. Delicately molded composition arms, jointed at the shoulders; three-quarter length composition legs. A quality doll in every respect.

Blonde	Brunette	Height	Ship. Wt.	Each
49 G 2496	49 G 2486	14½ in.	2 pounds	$2.19
49 G 2497	49 G 2487	16 in.	3 pounds	3.25
449 G 2498	449 G 2488	18 in.	4 pounds	4.29
449 G 2499	449 G 2489	21 in.	5 lbs. 8 oz.	5.39

Goes to Sleep

Illustration 387. Advertisement for *Naughty Eyes,* the doll with metal flirting eyes. Montgomery Ward & Co. catalog, Fall and Winter, 1927.

"EFFanBEE" Masterpiece
"Laughing Eyes"
Dance Doll

I FLIRT SLEEP WALK TALK

Goes to Sleep

$2.19 And Up

You Save a Third on These Dolls

LAUGHING EYES—just can't stop flirting! She rolls her big eyes naughtily from side to side in a most life-like, tantalizing manner. A very accomplished miss. She'll dance with you, will go to sleep, and will say "mama." All dressed up for a party in a beautiful flowered pink organdie dress, trimmed with lace. Slip and combination to match. She wears her **Effanbee** locket and chain, and a becoming pink bandeau with yarn flower on her head. Dainty socks and slippers. Her hard-to-break head has improved eyes that sleep and flirt—the best obtainable. Beautifully tinted cheeks. Open mouth with teeth. Fine sewed mohair wig. Delicately molded composition arms, jointed at the shoulders; ¾-length composition legs. A quality doll in every respect. 14½-inch doll has closed mouth and wig not sewed.

Height	Ship. Weight	Golden Curls	Brown Curls	
14½ inches	2 pounds	48 C 2496	48 C 2486	$2.19
16 inches	3 pounds	48 C 2497	48 C 2487	3.25
18 inches	4 pounds	448 C 2498	448 C 2488	4.00
21 inches	5 lbs. 8 oz.	448 C 2499	448 C 2489	4.98
23 inches	7 pounds	448 C 2491	448 C 2481	5.69

Illustration 388. Advertisement for *Laughing Eyes.* Note that this is the same doll previously named *Naughty Eyes* with her name changed to *Laughing Eyes.* The basic dress design is also similar to that of *Naughty Eyes* except that the ruching has been changed to dainty lace. 1928.

Sleeping Eyes

Both Can Say "Ma-Ma"

WE WALK TALK SLEEP

Each With Six Photos

Effanbee's Finest Feature Dancing Dolls

They dance or walk with just a tiny bit of help. Beautiful sleeping eyes with long lashes and fine human hair wigs sewed on cloth foundations! Hard-to-break-composition heads, arms and legs—jointed at shoulders and hips. Sleeping eyes; mama voices. Dressed in sheer pink organdie with lace ruffles and gores, pink petticoat, pink hose and slippers. Set of six photographs sent with each doll.

Mary Sue With Light Golden Bob

448 C 2817—Height 26 in. Ship. wt., 7 lbs.		$10.48
448 C 2816—Height 23 in. Ship. wt., 6 lbs.		8.98
448 C 2815—Height 21 in. Ship. wt., 5 lbs.		7.48
448 C 2814—Height 18 in. Ship. wt., 4 lbs.		5.98

Rose Mary With Dark Brown Curls

448 C 2821—Height 26 in. Ship. wt., 7 lbs.		$10.48
448 C 2820—Height 23 in. Ship. wt., 6 lbs.		8.98
448 C 2819—Height 21 in. Ship. wt., 5 lbs.		7.48
448 C 2818—Height 18 in. Ship. wt., 4 lbs.		5.98

Illustration 389. Advertisement for *Mary Sue* and *Rose Mary.* Montgomery Ward & Co. catalog, 1928.

Illustration 390. Advertisement showing, on the left, the deluxe version of *Laughing Eyes* but here named *Coquette!* Her party frock is designed by a famous Viennese modiste who is unnamed. See *Illustration 243* for a doll in the exact costume.

On the right is shown the economy version of *Laughing Eyes* wearing a sheer pale green voile dress with balloon clusters printed on it. The low price was possible because of a large purchase made in the off season. Montgomery Ward & Co. catalog, 1929.

Illustration 391. Advertisement for *Mary Louise* in golden curls and *Rose Mary* in dark brown curls. This is an example of a **wig** determining the name of the doll. Montgomery Ward & Co. catalog, St. Paul, Minnesota, 1929.

Illustration 392. 21in (53.3cm) *Mary Louise;* composition shoulder head, cloth body, composition arms, composition legs; blonde human hair wig which has lost its original curl; blue metal eyes, light brown eyebrows, real hair eyelashes; open mouth with four teeth and a celluloid tongue; wearing her original pink silk dress with much fine lace, streamer ties and flower rosettes, Effanbee locket and chain. 1929. *Luisa Gray Collection.*

OPPOSITE PAGE BOTTOM: Illustration 394. Advertisement showing an economy version of *Laughing Eyes* priced on special at $1.39 for a 14in (35.6cm) size while a 16½in (41.9cm) shoulder head German bisque doll with a kidiline body sold for $1.00. This advertisement came from a booklet type of catalog which was issued for last minute Christmas buying. The entire publication had bargains. In these Depression times the editorial ran: "It is going to be a Merry Christmas, after all, folks! Times are not nearly as bad as you thought they were going to be!" Montgomery Ward & Co. Christmas catalog, 1930.

Illustration 393. Advertising for two Effanbee dolls. The 16in (40.6cm) doll on the left is a *Baby Dainty* mold. The 18in (45.7cm) doll on the right is a marked *Rosemary*. The economy version, on the right, did not come with the Effanbee heart necklace, although the doll is from the Effanbee factory. Note that the same artwork goes around the advertisement for both dolls. Montgomery Ward & Co. catalog, 1930.

BELOW: Illustration 394. Special bargain catalog with rock bottom prices due to the great depression. Note shoulder head bisque girl is $1.00 to $1.39 for *Laughing Eyes*.

Merry, Mischievous Eyes

Nationally Known EFFanBEE $3.48

Never a serious moment! Laughing blue eyes roll naughtily from side to side. Indeed, this dolly is a problem. . . . it's hard to be firm with such a fascinating little rogue! Created by EFFANBEE, world famous makers of fine dolls . . . better wig; better clothing, nothing short of perfection.

Printed white dimity frock with wide ruffle at hem. Collar of crisp embroidered organdie; streamer ties match wider silk hair ribbon. White lace trimmed slip; pantie combination. Effanbee locket and chain. Composition head; improved eyes that sleep. Curly mohair bob sewed on cloth foundation. "Mama" voice on all sizes. Full length composition arms and legs. Cotton stuffed. We Pay Postage.

Golden Curls

Article No.	Height	Each
48 G 2930	16 in.	$3.48
48 G 2931	18 in.	4.59
48 G 2932	21 in.	5.69
448 G 2933	23 in.	6.79

Brown Curls

Article No.	Height	Each
48 G 2934	16 in.	$3.48
48 G 2935	18 in.	4.59
48 G 2936	21 in.	5.69
448 G 2937	23 in.	6.79

"Mischievous Eyes" at Lowest Prices $1.89

Not as fine as our Effanbee dolls at left, but splendidly constructed throughout. Almost unbreakable composition head with curly mohair bob wig **sewed on solid cloth foundation.** Her eyes go to sleep or roll coquettishly from side to side when dolly is moved. Crying voice. Full length composition arms, slim and gracefully formed, are jointed inside at shoulders. Walking type composition legs. **Soft cotton stuffed body.** Frock of pink organdie with lace collar and touch of blue embroidery. Satin hair ribbon, rosebud trim. White slip and combination. Slippers; blue and white socks. We Pay Postage.

Article No.	Height	Each
48 G 2618	14 in.	$1.89
48 G 2619	18 in.	3.00
48 G 2620	20 in.	3.75
448 G 2621	24 in.	4.75

Note Large Sizes

Dollies-Buggies-'N Everything"

$1.00 Each Water-Proof Kidiline Body
Was $1.39

A Lovely Doll to Dress

She's Fully Jointed

The most inexperienced little seamstress will find this pretty Doll easy to dress. Four sizes. Beautiful bisque head; sleeping eyes; eyelashes; tiny teeth and long soft curls of quality mohair. Body of fine white imitation kid, easily cleaned. She's jointed at knees, hips, elbows and shoulders. Her pyroxylin arms are hard to break. Removable buckle shoes and socks. Ship. wts. 2½, 3, 3½ and 3½ lbs.

48 M 2640—16½ in.
Was $1.39.
Now...........**$1.00**

48 M 2641—18¾ in.
Was $1.69.
Now...........**$1.29**

48 M 2642—20 in.
Was $1.89.
Now...........**$1.69**

48 M 2643—23¼ in.
Was $2.48.
Now...........**$1.95**

Rolling Laughing Eyes Walking Type Legs $1.39
Was $1.89

Curly Mohair Bob Crying Voice

Splendidly constructed throughout. Almost unbreakable composition head with curly mohair bob sewed on cloth foundation. Her eyes go to sleep or roll roguishly from side to side when she is moved. Crying voice. Full length graceful composition arms, jointed inside of shoulders. Soft cotton stuffed body. Pink organdie frock with lace collar and touch of blue embroidery. Satin hair ribbon, rosebud trim. White slip and combination. Slippers; blue and white socks. Ship. wts. on two smallest sizes 2 and 2½ lbs. We Pay Postage on Orders of $2 or More. See Page 32.

48 M 2618	14-in. ht.	$1.39
48 M 2619	18-in. ht.	1.87
48 M 2620	20-in. ht.	2.48
448 M 2621	24-in. ht.	2.79

We Pay Postage On Orders of $2 or More See Page 32

EFFan BEE'S FINEST
NATIONALLY ADVERTISED

The "Dream Dolls"

$4.25

Real Human Hair Curls Silk Crepe Dress

Here is the "dream doll" . . . a sort of Fairy Princess of dolls that dwells in every small girl's imagination . . . actually brought into existence! To tell you the truth we don't know who else but the famous Effanbee could have really created her!

Her lovely composition head is crowned with glorious curls . . . glittering gold ones or sleek shining brown ones of real human hair. This wig is sewed firmly on a cloth foundation. Her pretty eyes are the go-to-sleep kind with real hair lashes. **Mama voice.** Composition arms and walking type legs are jointed at shoulders and hips. Cotton stuffed body. Dressed in ruffled pink **silk crepe.** Pink undies lace trimmed. Big butterfly hair ribbon, silk socks and shoes. She wears the EffanBee gold locket and chain. **We Pay Postage.**

Height	Golden Curls	Brown Curls	Ward's Price
17 in.	48 C 2658	48 C 2653	$4.25
19 in.	48 C 2659	48 C 2654	5.25
21 in.	48 C 2660	48 C 2655	6.25
23 in.	48 C 2661	48 C 2656	7.75
25 in.	448 C 2662	448 C 2657	9.39

EFFAN BEE "The doll with the golden heart"

I Sleep
I Say
Ma Ma

Illustration 395. Advertisement for *Dream Doll.* Note that here a different name is now given to the blonde and brunette dolls. The dress is ruffled pink silk crepe this year. (Some models may have been *Marilee* examples.) Montgomery Ward & Co. catalog, 1931.

Illustration 396. 24in (61cm) *Rosemary;* composition shoulder head, cloth body, composition arms, composition legs to above the knees; blonde mohair wig; blue metal eyes, brown eyebrows, human hair eyelashes; open mouth with two celluloid teeth and a celluloid tongue. Note that she is wearing the Effanbee Bluebird pin. *Kerra Davis Collection. Photograph by Beth Hobbs.*

Illustration 397. 20in (50.8cm) *Joan Carol;* composition shoulder head, cloth body, composition arms, probably composition legs; gay windblown bob wig; came dressed in pink, blue, maize or green crisp organdy dress and bonnet to match; wears golden heart necklace marked: "Effanbee." This doll was available for $5.00 or $5.50 west of the Mississippi. *Ladies' Home Journal,* December 1929.

Illustration 398. 19in (48.3cm) doll, probably *Joan Carol;* composition shoulder head, cloth body, composition arms, composition legs; mohair wig; metal eyes, light brown eyebrows, real and painted eyelashes; open mouth with four teeth and a felt tongue. This view shows the basic doll without her wig and costume. The front shoulder plate has been broken. 1929.

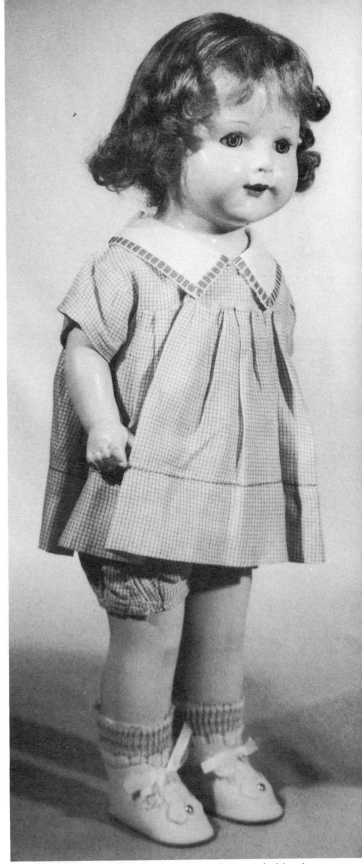

Illustration 399. 19in (48.3cm) doll, probably *Joan Carol,* seen in *Illustration 398,* shown wearing a red and white soft cotton dress with piqué collar over a one-piece combination suit of the same material. This version with the chubby all-composition legs seems a bit younger than some of the other models.

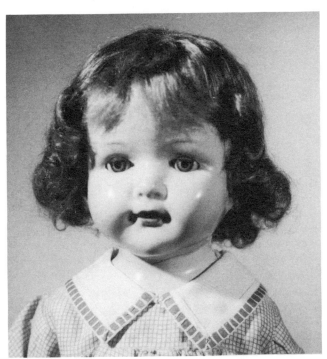

Illustration 400. Close-up of the 19in (48.3cm) doll, probably *Joan Carol,* as seen in *Illustrations 398* and *399.*

Illustration 401. This sketch accompanied a notice in a newspaper that "Toyland Opens Tomorrow" at Grunbaum Bros., Seattle, Washington. The date of the newspaper was November 15, 1931. The doll is an obvious *Rosemary* and will date those dolls found in similar costume. Note the two bubbles embroidered on the skirt.

Illustration 403. 24in (61cm) *Rosemary* seen in *Illustration 402*, shown wearing her original pink crepe de chine dress over the pink sateen combination suit and separate slip, shoes are replaced. *Georgia Van Wie Cannon Collection.*

Illustration 402. 24in (61cm) *Rosemary;* composition shoulder head, cloth body, composition arms, composition legs to above the knees; brown human hair wig; blue metal eyes, light brown eyebrows, real and painted eyelashes; open mouth with four teeth and a molded celluloid tongue. *Georgia Van Wie Cannon Collection.*

BUBBLES

One of the most famous and trend setting dolls ever created was the infant *Bubbles*. She sprang from the talented hands of sculptor Bernard Lipfert and was to become a classic. No other doll would inspire as many look-alikes by as many companies, yet *Bubbles* led the crowd in quality and appeal.

Although some unadvertised forms of *Bubbles* apparently existed in 1924, the superior version with the closed shoulder plate and one arm bent to allow a finger to go into her mouth, did not debut in *Playthings* until January 1926. There was **one size only,** 21in (53.3cm), when the doll was introduced. The prototype wore the Effanbee locket but was so new no round paper tag is shown on the doll. This model had real eyelashes which evidently were discontinued. Advertising copy claimed: "There is nothing like her in dolldom; the happiest smile in the world — created by a real artist." (Bernard Lipfert was not given name credit in the advertising.) The clothing is different from any subsequent edition, consisting of a fine muslin dress, an underslip with picoted edge, a cape of pique cotton with fancy picoted edging and a frilly matching bonnet.

By May of 1926 there were nine sizes of *Bubbles* with garments of organdy, lawn or silk. *Playthings* declared her "The Doll Sensation of 1926, she looks equally well dressed as a baby doll or as a regulation Mama doll with straight legs." (Collectors would call the latter version in toddler doll.)

This new creation was heavily advertised and caused most other major manufacturers to offer something similar quickly. In the early teen years many a German doll had served as a model for an American version, but as the United States became more proficient, year after year, in making more appealing composition dolls, Germany, and sometimes Japan, copied the outstanding models. Many American companies as well had their own version of *Bubbles* and later *Patsy.*

By January 1927 it was announced that the head and arms of *Bubbles* were registered under Copyright No. 75246 and the trade name of "Bubbles" was registered in the United States Patent Office, December 17, 1926, No. 241,611.

The next full page advertisement for *Bubbles* appeared in January 1927 and was repeated in later months with *Bubbles* in a brushed wool infant's suit, cap, jacket and booties of knitted fabric with silk embroidered edges, embroidered motifs on cap and jacket front turnbacks. The dress underneath had a plain yoke and was sleeveless though lace trimmed. She now has her paper tag: "This is Bubbles, bubbling over with life and laughter, an Effanbee doll." The February 1927 *Playthings* first shows an infant *Bubbles* in a long christening gown.

The first protests against whatever copies were rushed onto the market show up in February 1927 *Playthings* and March 1927 *Toys and Novelties:*

"The Personality And Charm Of People Simply Can't Be Copied. Take yourself for example. And then take an acquaintance or friend of yours. Let him be of the same height, weight, voice, and other general features. Dress him in your clothes. Go even further and have him 'made up' to resemble you in facial expression. In spite of all—he does not become you. Each one has his own personality, his own individuality. And it's the same with dolls.

"When a new doll of many excellent features and qualities becomes a best seller, imitations and copies are sure to spring up.* That has been the case with 'BUBBLES' the EFFANBEE doll that has been an instant success, because it sells on sight. But like the personality of an individual, or the creation of a skilled artist, copies are only poor imitations. They make the original stand out all the more — in striking contrast."

"*We have been granted several preliminary injunctions restraining and preventing the manufacture of a doll head with facial characteristics similar to 'Bubbles.' "

By December 1927 the brushed wool costume was replaced by the more familiar frilly bonnet and lawn dress edged in lace, with composition bare knees showing. The same photograph is used in March 1928, July 1928 and June 1929. August 1928 trade magazines show *Bubbles* in a white embroidered dress and bonnet, still shown in March 1929. For collectors with these models in original outfits, dating can be fairly accurate.

Bubbles truly was the sensation of 1926! No such doll existed before Bernard Lipfert created her. We do not know exactly why some models are marked 1924 when the doll first made her debut in January 1926. The Effanbee firm had issued a *Bye-Lo*-type doll marked: "Honeybunch" (*Bubbles* mold) in what may have been 1924. (In 1923 *Honeybunch* was used as a name for a Mama doll, but this was a name in advertising only and not actually marked on the doll.) If our supposition is correct, this would establish the **face mold** of this doll, if not the more deluxe model of the closed breastplate with arms strung on a metal spring.

A second 13in (33cm) version of the former *Honeybunch,* now marked: "Effanbee//Bubbles" with a flange neck, metal eyes and an open/closed mouth with two painted teeth, was issued. The rather heavy full composition arms are slightly bent but could not go into the mouth. There is no advertising for this type, which seems to be competing with some German bisque models of the period. One version of the German *Baby Gloria* with bisque head is very similar although there are differences in hair molding, and other features.

M. Kelly Ellenburg stated in 1973 in her book, *Effanbee, The Dolls With The Golden Hearts,* that Effanbee's $200,000 lawsuit filed in the courts against E. I. Horsman was concerning copying *Bubbles* expression of "bubbling over with joy." Effanbee is said to have petitioned to restrain Horsman from manufacturing a very similar doll, also modeled by Lipfert, the next year. The courts found in favor of Effanbee.

In March 1927 *Toys and Novelties* printed under "New Toys and Toy News" column, the article, "Fleischaker & Baum Obtain Injunctions Protecting Bubbles:"

"On application made by Max Shlivek, of 120 Broadway, attorney for Fleischaker & Baum, to Mr. Justice Lydon and to Mr. Justice Mahoney of the Supreme Court, New York County, two injunctions have been granted restraining the manufacturing or selling of dolls which simulate and are copies of 'Bubbles', the Fleischaker & Baum doll.

"The affidavits submitted with the application for injunction certify to the great popularity of 'Bubbles' and also to the fact that 'Bubbles' had been so widely and favorably known because of the vast amount of advertising and also because of the particular pleasing features. The affidavits of a great many buyers and representatives of some of the larger establishments throughout the United States were submitted to the court and set forth the fact that 'Bubbles' was absolutely a new and novel doll and was known as a Fleischaker & Baum product and that immediately upon observing the said doll anywhere, the trade generally and the public at large identified it as EFFANBEE's 'Bubbles'.

"It appears that this is the first time that a doll having no grotesque features or appearance has been protected by injunction and though the question seems rather novel, apparently the trade generally has acquiesced in Fleischaker & Baum's rights."

In spite of lawsuits, rampant copying seemed to go on and on among the various manufacturers. Many of the copies are equally collectible, but usually not of the high quality of Effanbee, when found in mint condition.

The following earlier research done by the author may repeat a few of the basic facts, but we have decided to include this material for the early advertising accounts and costume descriptions.

Bubbles was a new doll in 1925 although some of the earliest models are actually marked "1924" on the back of the composition shoulder head. Other examples are marked "1924" as well as "Bubbles," making these dolls especially desirable as collector's items. *Betty Bubbles, Charlotte Bubbles* and *Dolly Bubbles* were included in early advertising. Often times such identities are merely a matter of being dressed in a specific costume, illustrating a catalog.

Bubbles was one of its makers first big commercial successes. It was designed by Bernard Lipfert who also created *Patsy, Dy-Dee, Shirley Temple* and the *Dionne Quints*.

The earliest catalog we have acquired containing *Bubbles* advertising is a Montgomery Ward & Co. catalog for 1926. Just below the *Bye-Lo Baby* is "Bubbles--Our Ray of Sunshine! One year old." This advertisement will give a clear picture of how to dress the doll for those not fortunate enough to find her in original garments.

The *Bye-Lo Baby* and *Bubbles* were approximately the same age and, to a degree, in competition. Although it was the rage to own a *Bye-Lo* at this time, *Bubbles* might have been more appealing to many a child. She was not breakable (with reasonable care), she had composition arms completely to the shoulder and some versions had completely hard composition legs of a rosy hue. The expression was merry with dimples in the cheeks. Montgomery Ward & Co. offered sizes 25½in (64.8cm) at $11.48, 20½in (51.4cm) at $9.25, 18in

(45.7cm) with cotton legs at $6.25 and 15½in (39.4cm) with cotton legs at $4.29. There was also a separately listed Effanbee Walking *Bubbles* which was 20in (50.8cm) tall for $8.98. This is the less common toddler version. (The emphasis was on the babyhood of the doll.) Yet manufacturers usually managed to have more than one type to suit all tastes.

By 1927 *Bubbles* was featured as "Nationally Advertised." A sketch shows a young girl removing the bonnet to show the head. The sizes offered at this time have changed to 16in (40.6cm), 18in (45.7cm), 22in (55.9cm) and 24in (61cm). The two smallest were said to have cotton stuffed legs and bent knees like those of a real baby. To date a *Bubbles* in the dotted swiss dress with a plain yoke and lace trim shown in 1927 has not surfaced. The plain soft organdy material is much more commonly found.

In 1928 Montgomery Ward & Co. proudly headlined: "This is 'Bubbles' Effanbee" and boasted that they were the exclusive mail order distributors for *Bubbles* dolls. This, no doubt, referred to retail catalogs since a very informative advertisement depicting different types of *Bubbles* dolls ran in the Butler Brothers wholesale catalog of 1928.

More elaborate clothing could add considerably to the price of the doll. Montgomery Ward & Co. offered five sizes this year: 16in (40.6cm) at $3.98, 17½in (44.5cm) at $4.79, 20in (50.8cm) at $6.29, 22in (55.9cm) at $7.98 and 24in (61cm) at $9.98. The two large sizes had voices which actually said "mama" and real leather booties, and the smaller sizes had cry voices and imitation leather booties.

The 1929 Montgomery Ward & Co. catalog from St. Paul, Minnesota, carried a similar illustration with the headline: "I AM BUBBLES" and the same sizes were offered as in 1928. Effanbee's *Lovums* with the head that could be tilted from side to side or backward and forward would soon supersede *Bubbles*.

Good Housekeeping of November 1931 offered the 13in (33cm) *Bubbles* which cried and shut her eyes, in a white organdy dress and cap with a blue or pink jacket. Also, Pattern N-24 for a long dress, two long slips, bunting and sunbonnet was offered for 30¢!

Effanbee advertised in the *Ladies' Home Journal* in November 1926:

"Here they are, Children//The dolls with the golden heart//Santa has one for every little girl. Take your choice of these two adorable dolls. (*Lovey Mary* or *Bubbles*.) There is *Bubbles*, the wonder doll of her generation, just bubbling over with life and laughter. No little girl can cry or look cross with this darling doll in her arms. *Bubbles'* happy smile keeps you smiling too.

"*Bubbles* was modeled after an adorable real baby. She has rosy cheeks, the sweetest laughing face, beautiful big blue eyes that will go fast asleep, and precious little white teeth. And you ought to hear her cry for you!"

Also included is a description of *Lovey Mary* which appears to be a version of doll marked "Rosemary." No such marked doll as *Lovey Mary* has ever surfaced. The company publicity continues:

"The nice thing about these dolls is that they won't wear out. This is because they are Effanbee Dolls. You can play and play with them, and they will last until you grow up. Ask Santa please to bring you *Bubbles* or *Lovey Mary*, whichever one you prefer. *Bubbles* and *Lovey Mary* come in all sizes. Shown here they are 19" tall and cost $5.00. At all better-class department and toy stores.

Incredibly enough, any child could obtain a metal "gold" necklace marked Effanbee by clipping the magazine coupon and enclosing a six cent stamp.

By December 1926 the headline was changed to: "Here Santa, is the Doll I want! The Doll with the golden heart." The advertising must have been quite successful as by April 1927 (with the headline: "Oh Mother, how I'd love that doll for Easter or my birthday!"), the copy reads: "If your little girl was one of the many disappointed children because there weren't enough 'Bubbles' dolls for Christmas, you can now make her happy. There are thousands of new 'Bubbles' just sent out to foremost department and toy stores." The company again emphasizes that the dolls will not wear out and that every genuine Bubbles wears the golden heart necklace. The $3.00 size of 14in (35.6cm) is newly-mentioned. By October 1929, Bubbles is shown in Junior Home magazine. Most of the publicity is similar except for an over enthusiastic boast, "See her smile, see her pout." Clothing mentioned included "lace trimmed baby clothes with a gay bonnet to match and dear little white booties—and the cutest rubber panties! You will be so proud of her and she is so happy that she makes you happy too." The "playmate" doll at this time is Joan Carol—none of which have shown up, so marked. She appears to be a version of Rosemary, the special designation due to her costume of the period. Bubbles now offers children a golden heart necklace but the price has jumped to ten cents!

By April of 1931 Bubbles was offered under the headline: "Oh Mother, How I'd Love that Doll" (along with choice of Patsy) as a premium doll, sent free for three subscriptions of Junior Home magazine for $7.50 collected.

The advertising copy now reads: "Modeled after a real live baby who laughed and cooed all day. No little girl can be cross or unhappy with this doll in her arms. Rosy dimpled cheeks, beautiful big eyes that open wide or go fast asleep. She can put her little finger in her mouth — a rosebud mouth with tiny pearly teeth.

"Bubbles is 14 inches high, has a sweet little voice and eyes that open and close. Movable arms and legs. Attractively dressed with shoes and socks." In November 1931, a choice of three "gift Dollies" was given, Baby Lamkin, Bubbles or Patsy. "Little teeth in her tiny mouth" are mentioned as one of Bubbles' fine points.

For the full story of Bubbles you must be introduced to Honeybunch. She was a new doll in 1923, following the first copyright for the Bye-Lo Baby in 1922. Although the company created Baby Effanbee, its own composition version of a Bye-Lo, a flange-necked Bubbles was issued, identical as far as basic sculpture, eyes and mouth were concerned. Yet the original identity was Honeybunch, not Bubbles! The hands are composition, wired onto muslin cloth arms; the legs are cloth with a seam up the front and the back and there is a mama voice. The doll is marked: "EFFANBEE//HONEYBUNCH//Made in USA." The doll wore a long cotton slip with sleeves and a christening gown. Its height was 12½in (31.8cm) with a head circumference of 9⅜in (23.8cm). There was a molded tongue with open mouth, and two glued-in teeth with red felt behind them. It appears the model was discontinued in favor of the more deluxe Bubbles who

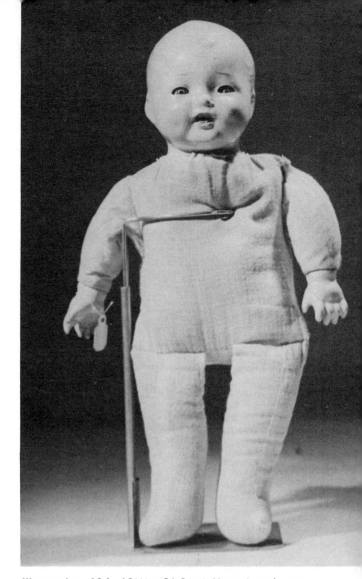

Illustration 404. 12½in (31.8cm) *Honeybunch;* composition head, cloth body, cloth arms with composition hands, cloth legs; glued-in teeth; originally wore a long christening dress; marked: "EFFANBEE//HONEYBUNCH//MADE IN USA." This was the same mold as the *Bubbles* doll. It is very rare and was made to compete with the German bisque dolls of the period. 1924. *Frances James Collection.*

Illustration 405. Close-up of the mark on the back of the 12½in (31.8cm) *Honeybunch,* seen in *Illustration 404:* "EFFANBEE//HONEYBUNCH//MADE IN USA." *Frances James Collection.*

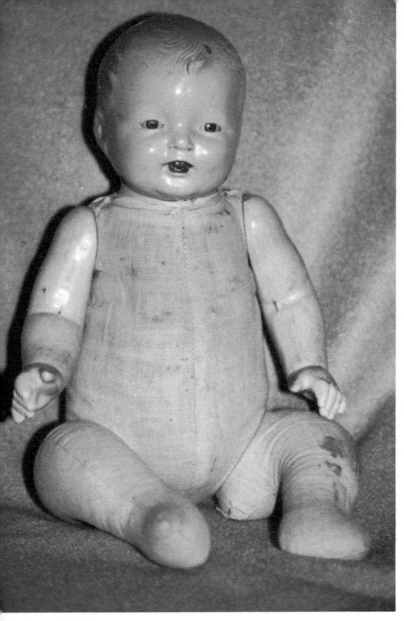

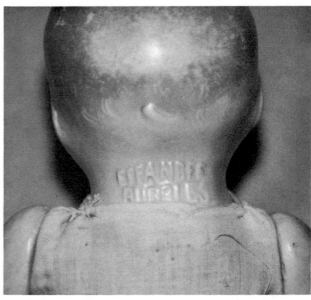

Illustration 406. 13in (33cm) *Bubbles;* composition head, cloth body, composition arms, cloth legs; golden hair; blue metal eyes; open/closed mouth with two painted teeth, molded tongue; inside jointed stuffed legs; marked on neck: "EFFANBEE//BUBBLES;" same mold as *Honeybunch.* Possibly dates from 1925. *Mary Lu Trowbridge Collection. Photograph by Mary Lu Trowbridge.*

Illustration 407. Close-up of the mark on the back of the 13in (33cm) *Bubbles,* seen in *Illustration 406;* "EFF-ANBEE//BUBBLES." *Mary Lu Trowbridge Collection. Photograph by Mary Lu Trowbridge.*

could wear short sleeves and pose her arms in various positions.

The following is from a publicity story originating with Effanbee describing *Bubbles:*

"It seems almost incredible that our loveliest, most childlike American dolls are made of such unromantic substances as wood flour, flake glue, rosin, starch, and other similar ingredients. But out of a doughlike mixture made of these ingredients manufacturers produce almost unbreakable composition heads. The mixture is put into heated steel presses to make the front and back of the head and shoulders, and then the two halves are glued together, the seam is ground smooth and, in the better quality of dolls, is covered with cement. The heads that are molded with the neck and shoulders, including the armpits, are less likely to break than those with the short neck and shoulders."

One drawback from the collector's viewpoint was that the steel-sprung arms sometimes unfastened causing the arms to be lost. A number of the dolls are found with replacement arms. The mechanism for inserting the eyes was unique, with a steel spring device making it nearly impossible to poke them out. Publicity pointed out that this often happened to imported dolls.

The smallest *Bubbles* (as opposed to the toddler), shown in *Illustrations 425* and *426,* is difficult to locate yet it was the least expensive.

Last of all in the *Baby Bubbles* are the 25½in (64.8cm) "superstars," in both black and white. This largest size does not have composition legs to the hip. The legs are wired onto a fitted muslin top beginning just above the knees. The black *Bubbles* were made to special order. The tin eyes are brown and the composition parts are painted a rich chocolate shade. The hair is black.

It would be hard to describe the tremendous appeal of this rare doll, larger than a newborn baby. The head circumference is 17¼in (43.9cm) and the teeth are celluloid. The right hand is bent and the thumb of the right hand is bent into the palm. It has the inverted brows of three strokes. There is a seam up the body front and the back is one-piece heavy muslin. An example of this black *Bubbles* is shown in *Illustrations 438* and *439.*

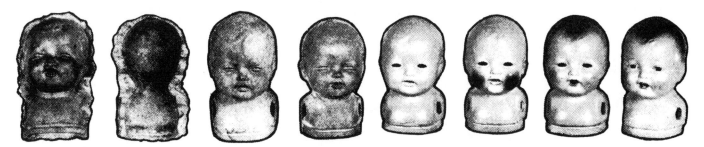

Eight phases in the life of a perfect doll.

Illustration 408. Early Effanbee publicity photograph for the new doll *Bubbles* showing the "Eight phases in the life of a perfect doll." From left to right: front half; back half; two halves glued together; head sanded and cement on seam; eyes punched out and enamel dipped; rosy cheeks and hair sprayed on; complexion coat added, brow and lips; complete with eyes, brows and teeth.

Santa has one for every little girl

Illustration 409. Advertisement showing early version of *Bubbles* with the bent cloth legs with long stockings and lace-trimmed combination suit. Paper label reads: "This is//Bubbles//Just Bubbling over with//life and laughter//An//Effanbee//Doll." *Ladies' Home Journal,* December 1926.

Illustration 410. An old photograph of a child showing an uncanny resemblance to *Bubbles*.

"Bubbles"—Our Ray of Sunshine! One Year Old

She Goes to Sleep

You know some real Baby just like her—some-year old baby with twinkling roguish eyes and one wet little finger that must always be pulled out of her rosy mouth before you can give her a kiss.

The forefinger on Bubbles' left hand just fits into her slightly opened mouth. Composition arms jointed at shoulders. Sleeping eyes. Sheer white organdy lace trimmed dress. Full length petticoat; bonnet with blue ribbon strings.

The two larger size "Bubbles" have composition legs, and they wear little combination suits, petticoats and soft pliable white leather bootees and half socks.

Six Photographs of Bubbles

With each Bubbles Baby we send six of her photographs. Grandma and Aunty will certainly want one.

449 E 2545—
25½ inches tall... **$11.48**

449 E 2544—
20¼ inches tall..... **9.25**

Postage: 22¢ and 20¢ extra

Two smaller sizes have cotton stuffed perfectly shaped legs. Diapers, long white stockings and shoes. Petticoats. Crying voices.

449 E 2543—
18 inches tall...... **$6.25**

449 E 2542—
15½ inches tall...... **4.29**

Postage: 18¢ and 16¢ extra

Illustration 411. Advertisement showing *Bubbles* complete with her own "Carte de Visite." Montgomery Ward & Co. catalog, 1926.

Bubbles, $5.95

A very gay infant all in white organdie, with a pretty cap. Just the right size for carrying when she's troublesome and cries.

Illustration 412. Advertisement for *Bubbles* from an unknown source in Seattle, Washington. 1926.

OPPOSITE PAGE: Illustration 413. Full page advertisement for *Bubbles*. Note that the photograph has been touched up to show two lower teeth. *Bubbles* actually had two upper teeth. *Toys and Novelties,* January 1927.

EFFANBEE DOLLS
The Dolls with the Golden Hearts

BUBBLES" Dolls have that indefinable charm that makes
TRADE MARK
them the year's best sellers.

FLEISCHAKER & BAUM

Sales Dept.
East 17th Street

NEW YORK, N. Y.

General Office
45 Greene Street

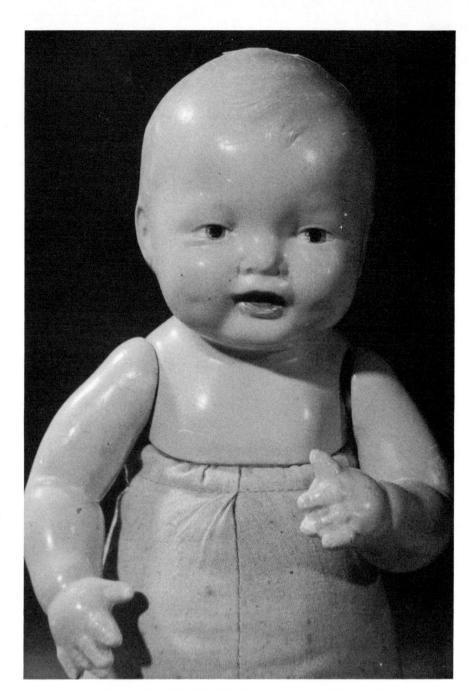

Illustration 415. 14in (35.6cm) rare painted eye version of *Bubbles* as sold by Montgomery Ward & Co. and shown in the advertisement in *Illustration 414*. The painted eyes were an economy measure at the time.

Genuine "Bubbles" Doll

Her face is just as cunning and her disposition as happy as our big Bubbles doll shown at the left. She's 14 inches tall. Has painted eyes. Crying voice. Cotton stuffed body. White organdie dress, lace trimmed cap to match. Underskirt, and flannelette diaper. White mercerized stockings and leatherette booties. Shipping weight, 3 pounds.
49 G 2633 . . . . **$2.59**

Illustration 414. Advertisement for a painted eye *Bubbles*. Montgomery Ward & Co. Fall and Winter catalog, 1927.

"Effan Bee" Famous "Bubbles" doll-Size 24 inches

Illustration 417. Advertisement in a rotogravure newspaper showing *Bubbles* with the Effanbee heart locket and the bubble-shaped paper tag on her arm. December 1927.

Mary Jane Sauter

Mary Jane and Her Doll

There is a legend in the toy trade that everybody connected with the industry keeps young, and undoubtedly there **is a** great deal of truth in this idea. There is something else about toy men, however, and that is the beauty of their children. As a proof of this assertion, Mary Jane Sauter, daughter of John F. Sauter, Buyer of Toys for the Carl Co., of Schnectady, N. Y., is presented herewith. Mary Jane is hereby welcomed into the toy trade as a fitting daughter of a toy man. It is whispered that she is pictured with an "Effanbee" doll.

Illustration 416. Advertisement showing Mary Jane Sauter, the daughter of a toy buyer for a store, with her *Bubbles* doll. *Playthings,* February 1927.

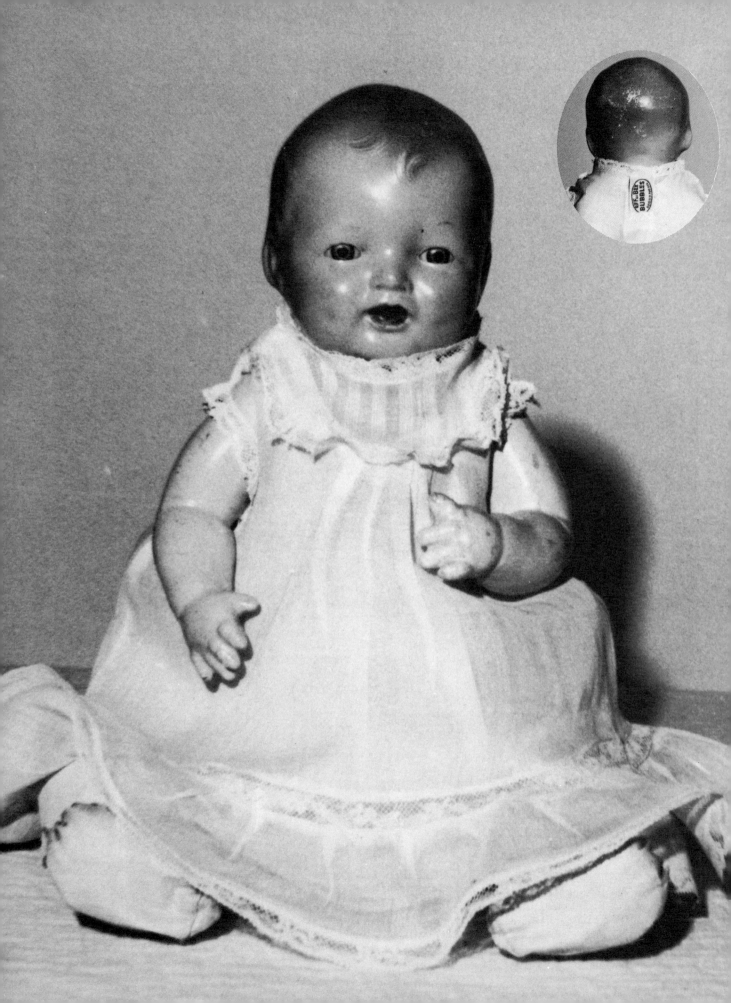

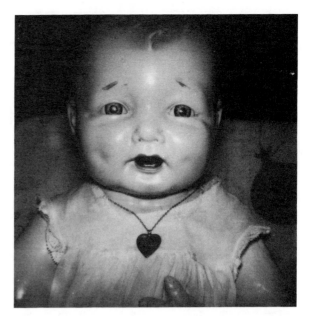

Illustration 421. 25½in (64.8cm) *Bubbles* showing the heart locket and the "fretting" brows of the early type. *Barbara DeVault Collection.*

Illustration 422. Advertisement showing *Bubbles* with composition legs. She had a new outfit in 1927 and it was still shown in 1928. She was billed as "THE NATION'S WONDER BABY" in *Playthings,* December 1927 and in *Toys and Novelties,* December 1927.

The dolls with the Golden Heart

Illustration 420. All-original *Bubbles* with label on her dress and the heart necklace, no longer on a metal chain but pinned to the dress. There are ribbon frills on her bonnet and dress and embroidered flowerlets on her dress front.

OPPOSITE PAGE: Illustration 418. 15½in (39.4cm) *Bubbles* with composition legs to the hips, in original outfit.

INSET: OPPOSITE PAGE: Illustration 419. Back view of the 15½in (39.4cm) *Bubbles,* seen in *Illustration 418,* showing the woven red, white and blue Effanbee label reading: "EFFᴀɴBEE//BUBBLES//REG. U.S. PAT. OFF" in an elongated oval. This is the label so desired by collectors but not mentioned in Effanbee's advertising.

"BUBBLES"

Each With Tag

Pink or Blue Fine Silk Short Dress — Curved composition legs, herringbone stitch insertion and trim cuffs, pleated ribbon and double row lace net collar, lace trim rayon slip, gum rubber pants, shirred elastic top and bottoms, double row lace ruffled cap with 2 large ribbon rosettes and mercerized bud trim, rayon tiestrings, mercerized socks, fabrikoid moccasins, locket and chain. 1 in box.

White organdie dresses with yokes, val lace trimmed, lace inserted skirt, ruffle edge, white organdie bonnet, white lawn slip, flannelette diaper, ribbed stockings.

With Long Dress—	With Short Dress—Soft legs.	With Short Dress—Composition legs. 1 in box.	With Brushed Wool Infants' Suit—Extra quality infants' knitted wool jacket, cap and bootees, locket and chain. 1 in box.	
1 F5432—(Mfrs 3191) 13½ in. ½ doz. in box ...Doz $22.00	1 F5445—(Mfrs 3161) 13½ in. ½ doz. in box...Doz $22.00	1 F5448—(Mfrs 3166) 20 in. .Each $4.50	1 F5453—(Mfrs 3296) 20 in....Each $6.25	1 F5473—(Mfrs 3696) 20 in....Each $6.25
1 F5433—(Mfrs 3193) 16 in. 1 in box. Each $2.75	1 F5446—(Mfrs 3163) 16 in. 1 in box. Each $2.75	1 F5449—(Mfrs 3167) 22 in....Each $6.00	1 F5454—(Mfrs 3297) 22 in....Each $8.00	1 F5474—(Mfrs 3697) 22 in....Each $8.00
1 F5434—(Mfrs 3195) 19 in. 1 in box. Each $3.25	1 F5447—(Mfrs 3165) 19 in. 1 in box. Each $3.25	1 F5450—(Mfrs 3169) 25 in....Each $7.50	1 F5455—(Mfrs 3299) 25 in..Each $9.75	1 F5475—(Mfrs 3699) 25 in....Each $9.75

Illustration 423. Advertisement for *Bubbles* with cloth or composition legs. The second doll from the left is shown with a round metal Effanbee pin with a heart design and "Effanbee" on it. Butler Brothers catalog, 1928.

The dolls with the Golden Heart

Illustration 424. Advertisement showing *Bubbles* in a dress with heavy woven embroidery trim and matching bonnet. She has a locket and a paper "Bubbles" tag. (This was also used in 1929 for advertising.) 1928.

Illustration 425. 13in (33cm) *Bubbles;* composition head and yoke, cloth body, composition arms, composition legs to the hips; blonde hair; metal eyes; open mouth with two molded teeth in the upper lip, molded tongue; wears dress with heavily embroidered yoke with drawn work, matching ruffle at dress bottom; label on the back of the right yoke; marked: "EFFANBBE (sic)//BUBBLES//COPYR. 1924// MADE IN USA." 1928. *Virigina Tomlinson Collection.*

Illustration 426. Side view of the 13in (33cm) *Bubbles,* seen in *Illustration 425,* showing the tag on the dress marked: "EFFANBEE//Bubbles//REG. U.S. PAT. OFF." 1928. *Virginia Tomlinson Collection.*

Illustration 427. Advertisement for *Bubbles*. The sketch of the child shown with the doll so greatly resembles *Bubbles* that one wonders if this could have been done from a photograph of the actual child who inspired the doll. Montgomery Ward & Co. catalog, Oakland, California, 1928.

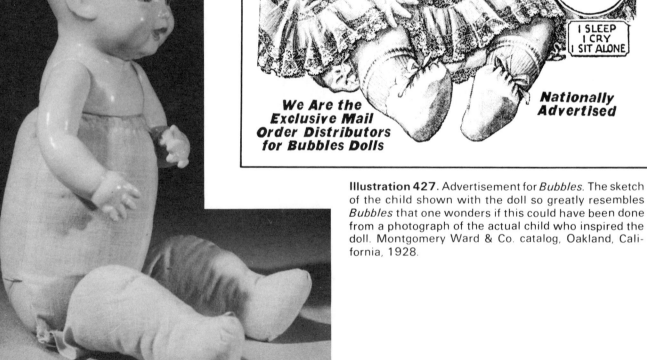

Illustration 428. 16in (40.6cm) "twin" *Bubbles*; composition shoulder head swing legs stitched flat with no inside joints; painted golden hair; sleep eyes, painted upper lashes; open/closed mouth with two painted upper teeth. 1927. *Ursula Mertz Collection.*

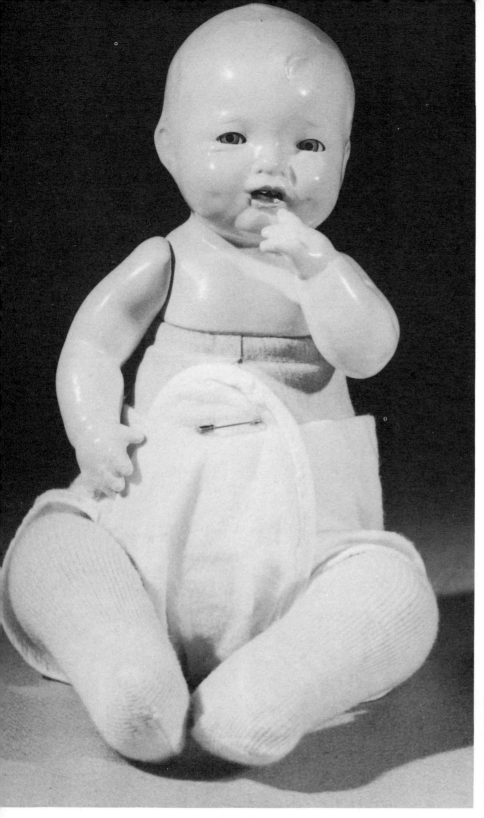

Illustration 429. 16in (40.6cm) "twin" *Bubbles* to the one shown in *Illustration 428*, except this one has cloth legs with inside jointed hips; open mouth with two celluloid teeth; wears original long cotton stockings, flannelette diaper with bound edge. 1927. *Ursula Mertz Collection*.

Illustration 430. Close-up of the 16in (40.6cm) "twin" *Bubbles,* seen in *Illustration 428.* Note the open/closed mouth with the two teeth and the painted tongue. She is wearing her original long muslin slip. 1927. *Ursula Mertz Collection.*

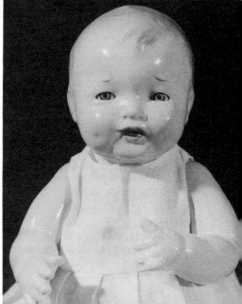

Illustration 431. 16in (40.6cm) "twin" *Bubbles* dolls, seen in *Illustrations 428* through *430,* shown together in their original christening gowns with two rows of lace above the ruffle which is edged in fine lace, and their white lace-trimmed bonnets. The "twin" on the left has the open mouth with the two celluloid teeth and jointed cloth baby legs while the "twin" on the right has the open/closed mouth with two painted upper teeth and stitched cloth swing legs with no inside joints. 1927. *Ursula Mertz Collection.*

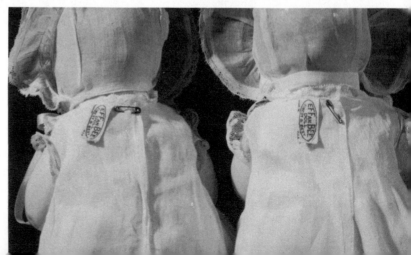

RIGHT: Illustration 432. Close-up of the backs of the 16in (40.6cm) "twin" *Bubbles* dolls, seen in *Illustration 431,* showing the labels on the original christening outfits which read: "EFFᴀɴBEE// DOLL//FINEST & BEST//TRADE MARK." 1927. *Ursula Mertz Collection.*

I AM BUBBLES! EFFanBEE

**I Cry
I Sit Alone
I Sleep**

WE PAY POSTAGE!

There goes that dimpled little finger again—straight into her rosebud mouth! Preciously like a real one-year-old baby with her twinkling blue eyes, face just puckering into an April smile, and chubby little active hands. **The widely advertised EFFanBEE BUBBLES.** No other doll so exactly reproduces a real baby's expression. Blue eyes that go to sleep. Open mouth with two little teeth. Composition arms, cotton stuffed body. Dainty white organdie dress trimmed in lace. Underskirt and real rubber diaper. Almost unbreakable composition head, arms and legs jointed at shoulders and hips. Legs are curved just like a baby's. Every doll has EFFanBEE locket and chain and six photographs which the little mother can give to her friends. The two large sizes have "mama" voices and real leather booties. The small sizes have crying voices and imitation white leather booties. Five sizes. **We Pay Postage.**

48 E 2890—Height 16 inches....	**$3.89**
48 E 2891—Height 17½ inches..	4.89
448 E 2892—Height 20 inches....	6.39
448 E 2893—Height 22 inches....	7.98
448 E 2894—Height 24 inches....	9.79

Illustration 435. Original advertisement for *Bubbles* showing five sizes. Montgomery Ward & Co. catalog, St. Paul, Minnesota, 1929.

BUBBLES

The Adorable Baby from Toyland

Illustration 436. Advertisement showing *Bubbles* "The Adorable Baby from Toyland." Here we see the heart necklace and paper tag, the frilly clothes, as well as the composition legs with short socks and shoes. *Junior Home* magazine, October 1929.

Illustration 437. Four sizes of *Bubbles* in original clothing. From left to right: 13in (33cm), 16in (40.6cm), 16½in (41.9cm) and 17¼in (43.8cm). The first doll has a head circumference of 9⅜in (23.8cm). The teeth and tongue are molded in the composition and the mouth is open. (One small toddler version was issued with an open/closed mouth with no opening.) The legs on this tiny baby are curved cloth. With this size only, it is the thumb rather than the forefinger which fits into the mouth, with all fingers extended out. The marking is surprising: "EFFANBBE (two Bs instead of another E)//Bubbles//Copr. 1924//Made in USA."

The second doll in the comparison has a head circumference of 10⅝in (27cm). The forefinger points up to the mouth and the thumb is modeled inward towards the palm. What seems to be celluloid teeth are applied behind the mouth opening. The marking is the familiar one: "EFFANBEE//DOLLS//WALK.TALK. SLEEP" within an oval with "Made in USA" beneath it.

The third doll has the same markings and characteristics as the second doll. She is in nearly mint condition except for the brows being worn away. The original painting of these was not the typical arched brow, but an inverted stroke with two shorter strokes just above it to denote a laughing expression. This costume is quite different with stitched ribbon frill at the neck and on the matching bonnet. The sleeves are a straight band with a row of pink embroidery trim. The skirt has no ruffle and the dress front is trimmed with two rows of pin machine-embroidered rosebuds and leaves. The original *Bubbles* woven label was sewn into the left back yoke seam. It has been clipped out carefully and resewn to the front yoke so that it may be seen when the doll is on exhibit. This doll once wore rubber pants.

The fourth baby has teeth glued into the open mouth. The forefinger goes straight out on the hand. The legs are all-composition. The doll is marked: "EFFANBEE//BUBBLES//COPR. 1924//Made in USA." The straight yoke of this dress is very plain making one suspect this model originally had the fancy knit bonnet and sweater or pink or blue silk jacket seen in the Butler Brothers catalog. There is no yoke in the back of the dress and the original label is attached at the neckline. The ruffle material is a dainty ribbed lace-edged organdy. Doll on right, *Virginia Tomlison Collection.*

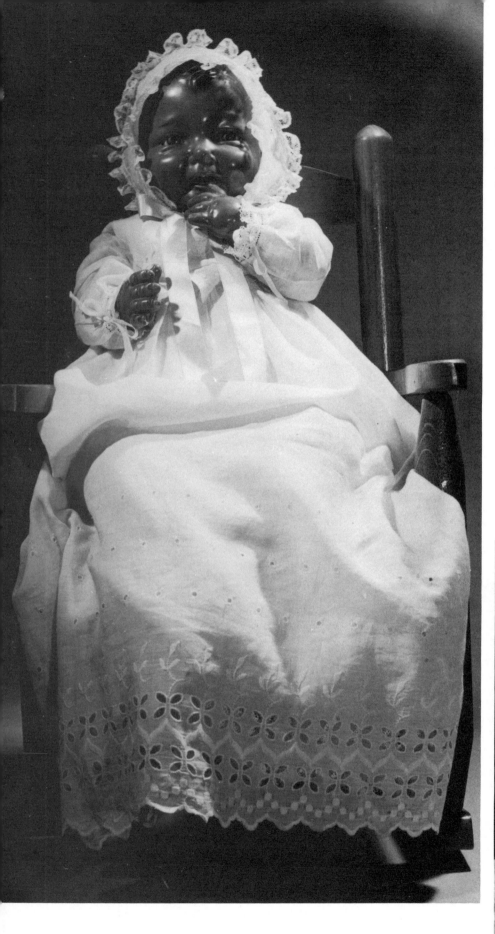

Illustration 438. 25½in (64.8cm) rare model of black *Baby Bubbles* shown wearing antique christening clothes. *Frances James Collection.*

Illustration 439. Comparative view showing the largest and the smallest models of *Bubbles*. The white doll is 13in (33cm) while the black doll is 25½in (64.8cm). Black doll, *Frances James Collection.*

THE TODDLERS

The much desired toddlers were actually advertised as Walking *Bubbles*. Collectors usually favor dolls which can stand since they are easier to pose in action and display very attractively. A 20in (50.8cm) size was advertised in Montgomery Ward & Co.'s 1926 catalog. The copy reads: "Bubbles is looking for a mother. She's standing with her finger in her mouth and feet wide apart, uncertain of her balance and very anxious to come to your arms. Perfectly proportioned, she looks like an adorable baby. Her unbreakable composition head has dimpled cheeks, painted hair and eyes that go to sleep. Her mouth is slightly open so that one of her fingers will just slip into it. She has full composition arms jointed at the shoulders, dimpled composition legs, a cotton stuffed body and finest quality voice that says 'Ma-Ma.' She's just right in size, not too large or too small to be a real playmate.

"You'll love her exquisite little blue silk crepe dress trimmed with white lace. She wears a hood to match with dainty lace ruching and pink silk ribbon ties; petticoat and bloomers to match; shoes and mercerized blue stockings. We never sold a more beautiful or lifelike doll at this price. Height, over all 20in ... $8.98." (The price of a 16½in (41.9cm) bisque *Bye-Lo Baby* was $8.25.)

An earlier 13in (33cm) version, shown in *Illustration 440*, has the open/closed mouth and two painted teeth. (This would have been a cost saving procedure at this time.) A painted-eye *Bubbles* was made as well.

There was also a 16½in (41.9cm) toddler, shown in *Illustrations 445* and *446*, with set-in teeth rather than molded composition ones and tannish blonde hair rather than the usual golden blonde. She does not say "Bubbles" in her marking but has simply: "EFFANBEE//DOLLS//WALK.TALK.SLEEP" within an oval and "Made in USA" beneath. The toddler legs are not as heavily dimpled and curved as a larger size but very appropriate.

The original costume of pink sheer china silk, shown in *Illustration 446*, is now very fragile but still intact. The length is much shorter than that of the 1926 version. Fine Valenciennes lace was used to trim the dress yoke and bonnet and net ruching was used about the face. The bonnet and dress yoke were embellished with a hand-embroidered daisy flowerlet and leaf design. Mercerized pink loop braid was utilized on the dress yoke and bonnet ruffle. From the center neck to the bottom of the hem is a bit more than 6in (15.2cm). The crown of the bonnet is gathered white lace. The very brief pink one-piece combination suit and slip is of mercerized cotton and trimmed in white lace.

A variation of the chubby leg toddler is a swing-leg Mama doll approximately 20in (50.8cm) tall, with a head circumference of 13¼in (33.7cm). The legs have two baby wrinkles above each knee, exactly suitable for this version. (This leg mold is also used on one *Rosemary* edition which had been a puzzler since that doll is an older version of a child.) This doll has a third variation of the marking with "1924" and a "C" within a circle (copyright) between "19" and "24." Below this is the familiar "WALK.TALK.SLEEP" within the oval, under "EFFANBEE//DOLLS," also within the oval, with "Made in USA" beneath. A similar doll in a very large size, possibly 30in (76.2cm), was seen at one time. The leg shape was like the solid fat ones of large Effanbee Mama

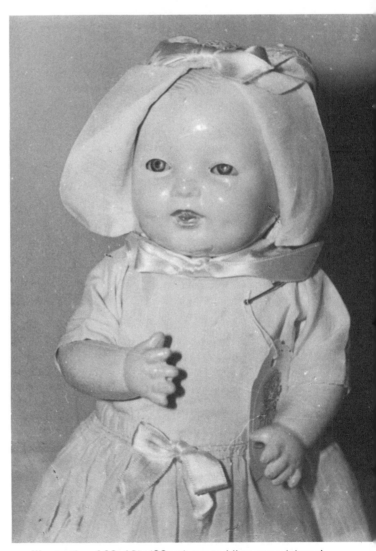

Illustration 440. 13in (33cm) rare toddler; open/closed mouth with no opening, two painted teeth. *Celina Carroll Collection.*

EVOLUTION OF WOOD PULP "GRUMPY"

FIRST TYPE: Shoulder head or breastplate, composition arms to elbows, cloth legs; 1923/1924.
  A. *Baby Grumpy Joan* — gingham clothes.
  B. *Baby Grumpy Gladys* — dainty white clothes.
  C. *Baby Grumpy Billie* — sailor suit, short trousers.
  D. *Baby Grumpy Peter* — unknown.

SECOND TYPE: Shoulder head or breastplate; 1923/1924.
  A. Same head as first type, **full** composition arms, composition legs to above the knees.
  B. Variant — same mold as above but as a socket head, date unknown.

THIRD TYPE: *Infant Baby Grumpy;* First use of continuous composition yoke and Hard-to-Break cold press arms, straight cloth legs; 1925/1926.
  A. Long white lawn dress.
  B. Mercerized pink knitted suit.
  C. Checked gingham romper.

FOURTH TYPE: *Grumpy Aunt Dinah;* Shoulder or breastplate head; 1925/1930.
  A. Red and white checked dress, 1925.
  B. Red and white dotted dress, 1930.
  C. "Aunt Dinah's boy" (no original advertising), circa 1926.
  D. *Grumpy* white boy — same size and type.

FIFTH TYPE: *Grumpykins;* Same head and continuous shoulder plate as *Infant Baby Grumpy,* same Hard-to-Break cold press arms but with short composition wood pulp legs; 1927/1928.
  A. *Grumpykins* girl — short dress and bonnet.
  B. *Grumpykins* boy — romper of cotton pique.
  C. *Grumpykins* sailor boy — variant with cloth legs.

Second version *Grumpykins;* (not so named on tag); mid 1930s. Redesigned arms and longer legs; mid 1930s.
  A. White girl — dimity clothes.
  B. Black girl — three black thread pigtails inserted into head, composition arms and legs — red dimity dress and bonnet.
  C. Black boy with no pigtails.
  D. Variant *Infant Grumpykins* — black **cloth** legs.
  E. Variant *Grumpykins* — same shoulder, second design arms, unjointed legs with molded shoes only.
    1. Fireman.
    2. Cowboy.
    3. Policeman.
    4. Sailor.
    5. Bellboy.

PENNSYLVANIA DUTCH DOLLS
  A. *Pop* or *Mom* doll with molded composition shoes.
  B. *Mom* doll with full molded legs, same as second version of *Grumpykins.*

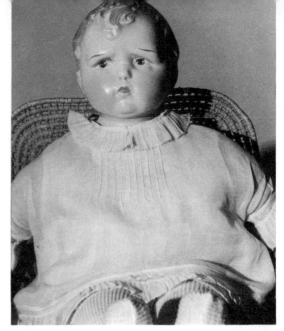

Illustration 471. 17in (43.2cm) *Baby Grumpy Gladys;* composition shoulder head, peach-colored cloth body, composition arms to the elbows, cloth legs; blonde painted hair; blue painted eyes, brown eyebrows, painted upper eyelashes; pouty mouth; mama voice; wears cotton dress trimmed with lace insertion, accordian pleated ruffles with pink edge at neckline, sleeves and skirt bottom, eleven vertical tucks on the chest, kimono sleeves, slip and drawers trimmed with lace elastic at the bottom of the drawer legs, white knit cotton stockings; strap slippers and bonnet and the ribbon rosettes on the dress are missing; marked on the back of the shoulder head: "EFFANBEE//BABY GRUMPY//COPR. 1923" in an oval. 1924.

"Grumpy"—Pin tucked organdie dress with lace headed plaited ruffle trim skirt, collar and sleeves, silk ribbon rosettes, lace trimmed matched poke bonnet, lace trimmed combination petticoat and bloomers, mercerized socks, leatherette strap slippers, attractive pouting baby face.

1F5120 — 17 in. high.
Each **$2.40**

Illustration 470. Advertisement for a 17in (43.2cm) *Baby Grumpy Gladys* identified simply as *Grumpy*. This was the first type with a composition shoulder head, composition arms to the elbows and cloth legs. This model was said to wear the Effanbee Bluebird pin and came in its own box. Butler Brothers catalog, 1924.

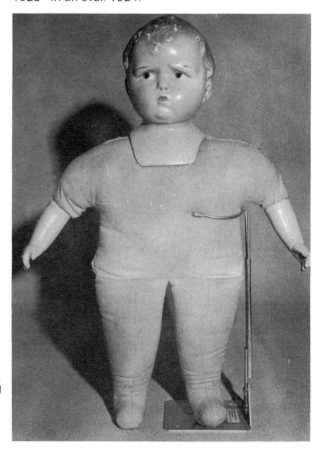

Illustration 472. 17in (43.2cm) *Baby Grumpy Gladys,* seen in *Illustration 471,* showing the body construction. Note the seam down the front of the leg and the shaped foot.

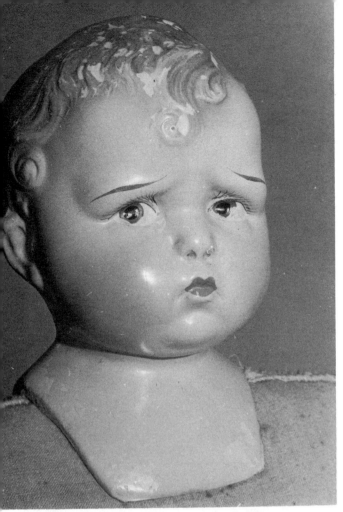

Illustration 473. Close-up of the head of the 17in (43.2cm) *Baby Grumpy Gladys,* seen in *Illustrations 471* and *472,* showing some flaking of the paint.

"Grumpy" in baby clothes plaited fine white lawn dres with yoke, lace trim neck cream cashmere jacket with blue silk hand crocheted edges, embroidered lawn bonnet, gold plated link chain and heart locket with "Effanbee" embossing, knitted vest, rubber panties, socks, **white kid moccasins, attractive pouting face, composition character limbs.** Each
1F5129—18 in. high. **$4.75**
1F5130—24 " " **8.25**

Illustration 475. Advertisement for an 18in (45.7cm) and 24in (61cm) *Grumpy* (a *Baby Grumpy).* This is a different costume from that shown on the cloth-legged *Gladys.* There is no record of whether or not the second type had specific names. This doll was said to wear the chain and locket with "Effanbee" embossed on it. Each doll came in its own box. The headline read: "Note the lifelike babies with the pouting faces, dressed like real infants." Butler Brothers catalog, 1924.

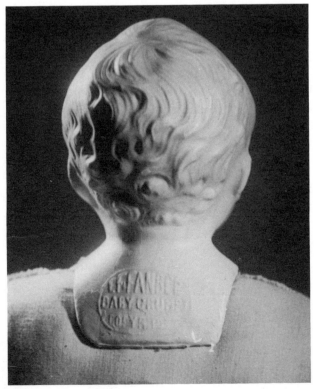

Illustration 474. The back of the head of the 17in (43.2cm) *Baby Grumpy Gladys,* seen in *Illustrations 471, 472* and *473,* showing the marking on the back of the shoulder head. Note the detail of the hair modeling.

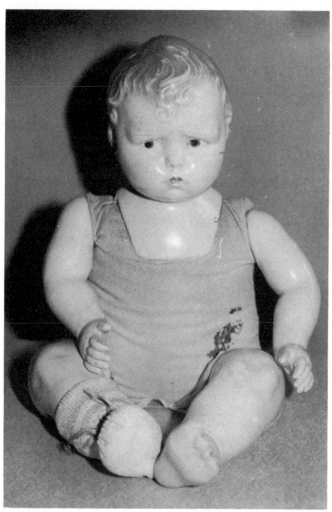

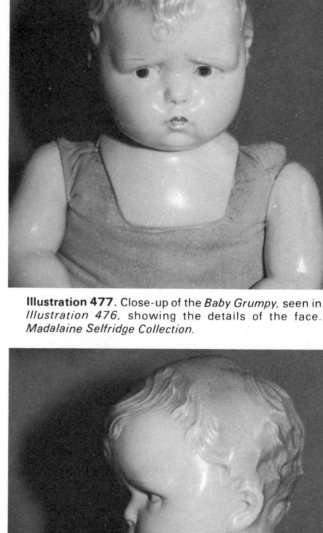

Illustration 477. Close-up of the *Baby Grumpy,* seen in *Illustration 476,* showing the details of the face. *Madalaine Selfridge Collection.*

Illustration 476. *Baby Grumpy.* This is the second type with molded, dimpled composition legs and full composition arms. This doll has the original white leather booties as shown in Butler Brothers catalog in 1924. 1923/1924. *Madalaine Selfridge Collection.*

Illustration 478. Side view of the *Baby Grumpy,* seen in *Illustrations 476* and *477,* showing the prominent brow and deep set eyes. *Madalaine Selfridge Collection.*

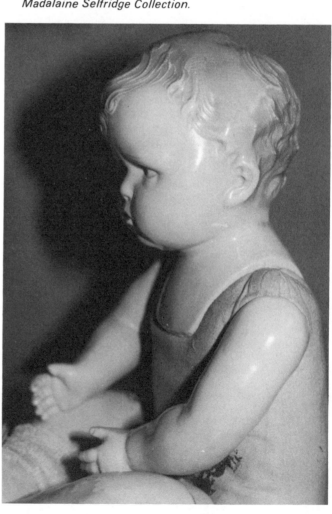

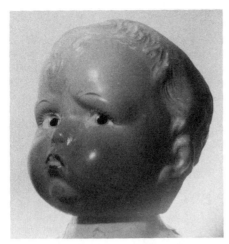

Illustration 479. 18in (45.7cm) *Baby Grumpy;* composition head which may have had a wig. This is a mystery socket head *Baby Grumpy.* The owner feels that the body is a replacement. The mold is that of the first shoulder head doll. He may have come on a separate shoulder piece. *Ursula Mertz Collection.*

Illustration 481. Advertisement for 11in (27.9cm) *Infant Baby Grumpy* shown wearing long baby clothes. The *Infant Baby Grumpy,* new at this time, was considered a novelty doll. It sold from $1.00 upwards. The doll is no longer a shoulder head but has a continuous breastplate with arms strung on springs. It is marked: "EFF-ANBEE//DOLLS//WALK.TALK.SLEEP" in an elongated oval. *Playthings,* December 1924.

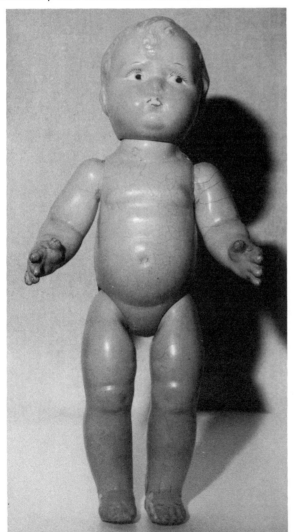

Illustration 480. Full view of the 18in (45.7cm) *Baby Grumpy,* seen in *Illustration 479,* showing the all-composition body which is believed to be a replacement. *Ursula Mertz Collection.*

Illustration 482. Advertisement showing an *Infant Baby Grumpy,* as seen in *Illustration 481,* as a doll and crib set. *Playthings,* December 1924.

36 B 924
$1.19

Cute Baby Doll with Crying Voice

36 B 924—This new Baby Doll has a cute face with painted hair and features and crying voice. Unbreakable composition head and arms are jointed at the shoulders. Cotton stuffed body and legs. White slip and white lawn long dress. Doll is about 11 inches tall. Entire length about 14½ inches............
Post. 9¢ extra. $1.19

Illustration 483. Advertisement showing a 14½in (36.9cm) *Infant Baby Grumpy.* This type of doll with the continuous breastplate and the arms strung through on a spring preceded the *Grumpykins* with the composition legs. Some catalogs omit the name of the doll. National Cloak & Suit Co. Fall/Winter catalog, 1926.

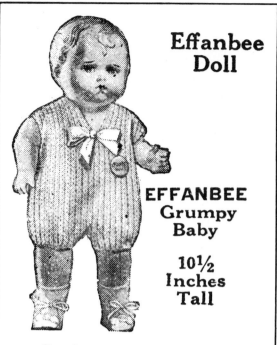

Effanbee Doll

EFFANBEE Grumpy Baby

10½ Inches Tall

Cunning pouting face with lips puckered and eyebrows raised in a complaining frown. Lovable and extremely popular with the children. Best quality composition head and arms, jointed at shoulders. Painted eyes and hair. Body cotton stuffed; crying voice. Mercerized pink knitted suit. **$1.29**
49 E 2669.........**$1.29**
Postage, 8¢ extra

Illustration 484. Advertisment for a 10½in (29.2cm) *Infant Grumpy Baby;* composition head, cloth body, composition arms, cloth legs; blonde painted hair; blue painted eyes, light brown eyelashes; closed mouth; wearing mercerized pink knitted suit with the Effanbee Bluebird button. Some versions were listed at 10½in (29.2cm) while others were listed at 11in (27.9cm). Montgomery Ward & Co. catalog, 1926.

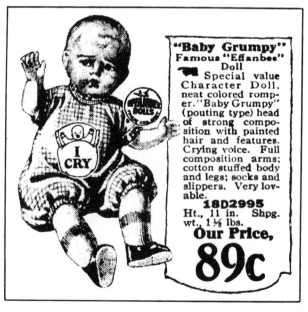

"Baby Grumpy"
Famous "Effanbee"
Doll Special value Character Doll, neat colored romper. "Baby Grumpy" (pouting type) head of strong composition with painted hair and features. Crying voice. Full composition arms; cotton stuffed body and legs; socks and slippers. Very lovable.
18D2995
Ht., 11 in. Shpg. wt., 1⅛ lbs.
Our Price,
89c

Illustration 485. Advertisement for an 11in (27.9cm) *Infant Baby Grumpy.* Note the Effanbee Bluebird pin. THe artist has shown the cloth legs as curved but they are actually straight. Sears, Roebuck and Co. catalog, 1926.

LEFT: Illustration 486.
14½in (36.9cm) *Grumpy Aunt Dinah;* composition shoulder head, cloth body, composition arms and legs; black painted hair; brown eyes, black painted eyebrows; tag on apron reads: "EFFᴀɴBEE//FINEST & BEST" in an elongated oval with "MADE IN U.S.A." beneath it. Note the Bluebird Effanbee pin. 1925. *Anita Wright Collection.*

14½ Inches High

EFFANBEE Grumpy Aunt Dinah

Grumpy Aunt Dinah is 14½ inches tall. Effanbee has made in their usual splendid quality a real colored mammy with a heart of gold back of her frown. You need a maid to help you with dollies' teas, keep dolls' clothes mended and see that the doll house is always in order. She wears a colored checked dress, an apron and a red bandana handkerchief around her head. Head and hands are of an almost unbreakable composition, her body is full cotton stuffed an she has a "Ma-Ma" voice. Shoes and stockings come off.

49 E 2607..$2.29
Postage, 12¢ extra

Illustration 487. Another view of the 14½in (36.9cm) *Grumpy Aunt Dinah,* seen in *Illustration 486. Anita Wright Collection.*

Illustration 488. Advertisement for 14½in (36.9cm) *Grumpy Aunt Dinah;* composition shoulder head, cloth body, composition arms and legs; painted black hair; brown eyes, black eyebrows; wears red and white cotton checked dress with bandana kerchief and an Effanbee tag on the apron with the Bluebird pin on the collar. Montgomery Ward & Co. catalog, 1926.

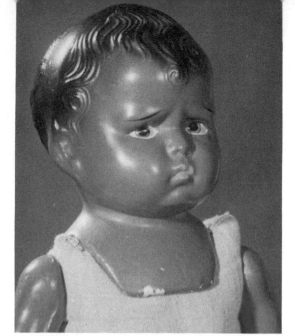

Illustration 489. Close-up of the head of 13½in (34.3cm) *Grumpy Aunt Dinah* or "Aunt Dinah's boy;" shoulder head with black painted hair; brown eyes, black eyebrows, painted upper eyelashes; closed mouth; marked on the back: "EFFANBEE//DOLLS//WALK.TALK.SLEEP" in an elongated oval. 1926

In the Children's Land of Make-Believe

▲ *"Aunt Dinah" chocolate-colored doll is cotton stuffed and dressed in Mammy style with white apron, red kerchief, and speaks, 15"; $1.95.*

Illustration 490. Advertisement for a 15in (38.1cm) *Grumpy Aunt Dinah;* composition head, cloth body, composition arms and legs; dressed in "Mammy" style with white apron, red kerchief, red and white dotted cotton dress, white cotton shawl; Effanbee label is on the apron near the doll's right hand. Note that the pin is now the heart with "Effanbee" printed on it rather than the Bluebird pin. *Good Housekeeping,* 1930.

Illustration 491. Comparative view showing 13½in (34.3cm) swing-leg *Baby Grumpy,* on the right, with the earlier version of 12in (30.5cm) *Baby Dainty,* on the left, with the same leg mold of molded shoes and socks.

Illustration 492. 13½in (34.3cm) *Baby Grumpy* (a black toddler); composition head, cloth body, composition arms, composition legs to above the knees; black painted hair; brown painted eyes, black eyebrows; closed mouth; wearing original pink and white cotton romper with separate shirt of plain pink trimmed in the same material as the romper. Note the Bluebird pin. These dolls came with shoes and socks over the molded ones. Circa 1925.

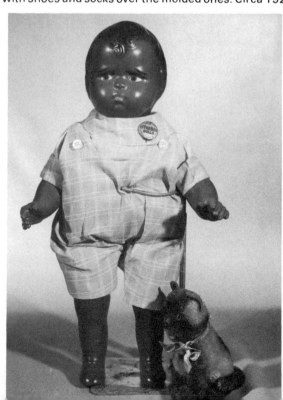

Illustration 493. Comparative view of 13½in (34.3cm) *Baby Grumpy* shoulder head doll with 14½in (36.9cm) *Grumpy Aunt Dinah* showing the differences in height and arm shape. Doll on right, *Anita Wright Collection.*

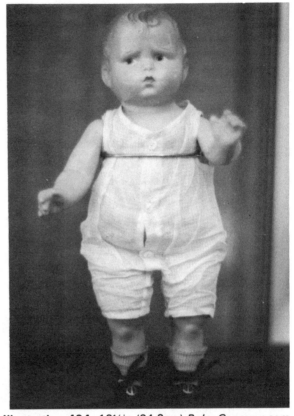

Illustration 494. 13½in (34.3cm) *Baby Grumpy;* composition shoulder head, cloth body, composition arms, composition legs to above the knees; brown painted hair; blue eyes, brown painted eyebrows; wearing original underwear, shoes and socks over molded shoes and socks; marked: "EFFANBEE//DOLLS//WALK.TALK. SLEEP" in an oval. Circa 1925. *Rhoda Gage Collection. Photograph by Rhoda Gage.*

Illustration 495. Advertisement for *Grumpykins.* "Kin" designated a small size of a doll. *Grumpykins* was 12in (30.5cm) tall. *Playthings,* March 1927.

LEFT: **Illustration 496.** 12in (30.5cm) *Grumpykins,* the first type; composition head, cloth body, composition cold press type arms, composition legs; blonde painted hair; blue side-glancing eyes, blonde frowning eyebrows; closed mouth; wearing a combination suit, lace-trimmed slip and green organdy dress and bonnet with green mercerized embroidery at the hem top and on the bonnet ruffle, lace at the neck and sleeves; marked on the back shoulder: "EFFANBEE//DOLLS// WALK.TALK.SLEEP" in an elongated oval. *Ursula Mertz Collection. Photograph by Ursula Mertz.*

RIGHT: **Illustration 497.** Advertisement for *Grumpykins.* This seems to be the earliest catalog advertising for *Grumpykins.* The dresses came in blue, canary, pink, orchid and soft green. Butler Brothers catalog, 1928.

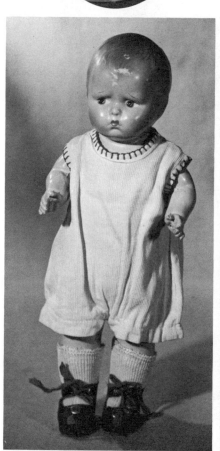
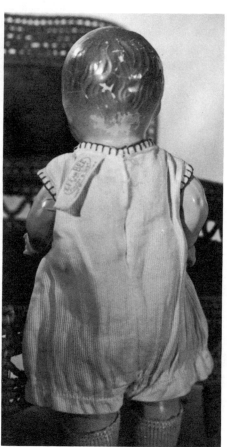

FAR LEFT: **Illustration 498.** 12in (30.5cm) *Grumpykins* (first type); composition head, cloth body, composition cold press type arms, composition short toddler legs; brown painted hair; blue eyes, brown frowning eyebrows; closed mouth; wearing white pique romper with red embroidered tape at the neck and arms, (elastic in the romper legs was once snug to the legs); tag at neck back reads: "EFF-ANBEE//DOLL//FINEST & BEST" in an elongated oval with "MADE IN U.S.A." beneath it. 1927. *Gerri Voorhees Collection.*

LEFT: **Illustration 499.** The back of the 12in (30.5cm) *Grumpykins,* seen in *Illustration 498,* showing the tag. *Gerri Voorhees Collection.*

Illustration 500. 12in (30.5cm) *Grumpykins;* composition head, cloth body, wood pulp composition arms, cloth legs; blonde painted hair; blue painted eyes, blonde painted eyebrows; closed mouth; wearing original white sailor suit with tie; tag on doll's left wrist reads: "This is //GRUMPYKINS//TRADE MARK//A doll so cute, you //just want to hug her//AN//EFF-ᴀɴBEE// DOLL" inside a gold heart. *Pidd Miller Collection.*

Illustration 501. Detail of the gold paper heart tag from the 12in (30.5cm) *Grumpykins* shown in *Illustration 500. Pidd Miller Collection.*

RIGHT: Illustration 502. *Grumpykins,* the second type; continuous composition shoulder head, cloth body, composition arms and legs; painted hair, blue two-tone eyes, brown eyebrows; closed mouth; wears original blue batiste combination suit, original shoes and socks; marked on back of shoulder head: "EFFAN-BEE//DOLLS //WALK.TALK.SLEEP" in an elongated oval; gold paper heart tag has been changed to read: "I AM AN//EFFANBEE// DURABLE DOLL//THE DOLL//WITH//SATIN-SMOOTH//SKIN." Circa 1925. *Alice Wardell Collection.*

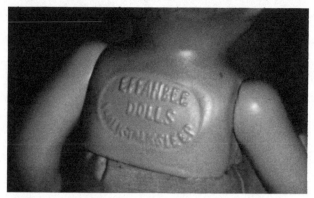

Illustration 503. The back of the *Grumpykins*, seen in *Illustration 502*, showing the mark on the back of the shoulder head. *Alice Wardell Collection.*

RIGHT: Illustration 504. *Grumpykins*, seen in *Illustrations 502* and *503*, shown wearing her orignal blue dimity dress with white organdy ruffles on the yoke and bonnet frill, white organdy bonnet ties; tag on doll's right hand. *Alice Wardell Collection.*

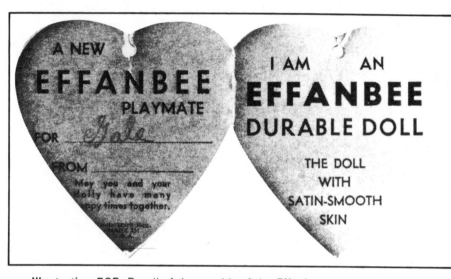

Illustration 505. Detail of the outside of the Effanbee tag shown on the *Grumpykins* in *Illustration 504*. Obviously the doll was given to a girl named Gale whose name is on the tag. The tag reads, on the left: "A NEW//EFFANBEE//PLAYMATE//FOR Gale//FROM //May you and your//dolly have many//happy times together.// Trade Mark Reg.//MADE IN//U.S.A." On the right it reads: "I AM AN//EFFANBEE//DURABLE DOLL//THE DOLL//WITH//SATIN-SMOOTH// SKIN." *Alice Wardell Collection.*

A note to the proud owner of this

New EFFANBEE Doll

You will find your Dolly a wonderful playmate, with her dainty clothes, her satin-smooth skin and pretty eyes. You will have lots of fun caring for her.

EFFANBEE dolls are like real healthy, happy children. They are strong and beautifully finished. That is why they are called EFFANBEE Durable dolls. Their clothes are always stylish and well-tailored and can be washed time af'er time, as they are made of the finest color-fast fabrics.

Illustration 506. Detail on the inside of the Effanbee tag shown on the *Grumpykins* in *Illustration 504*. *Alice Wardell Collection.*

Illustration 507. 12in (30.5cm) *Grumpykins* dolls. Comparative view to show the first type (on the left) with the cold press composition arms and short toddler legs compared with the second type (on the right) with more shapely arms and legs of wood pulp composition. Doll on the left, circa 1927; doll on the right, circa 1930s. No black doll has been located at this time with the original tag.

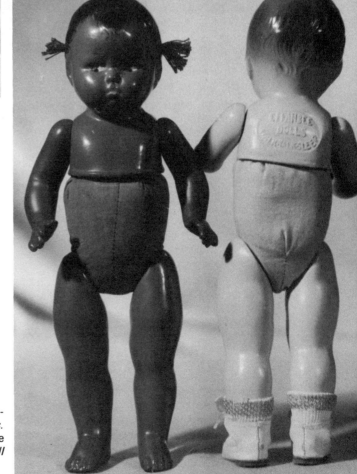

Illustration 508. 12in (30.5cm) *Grumpykins* dolls. Comparative view showing the second type of *Grumpykins*. Note that the black doll is slightly smaller than the white doll. Circa mid 1930s. Doll on the right, *Alice Wardell Collection.*

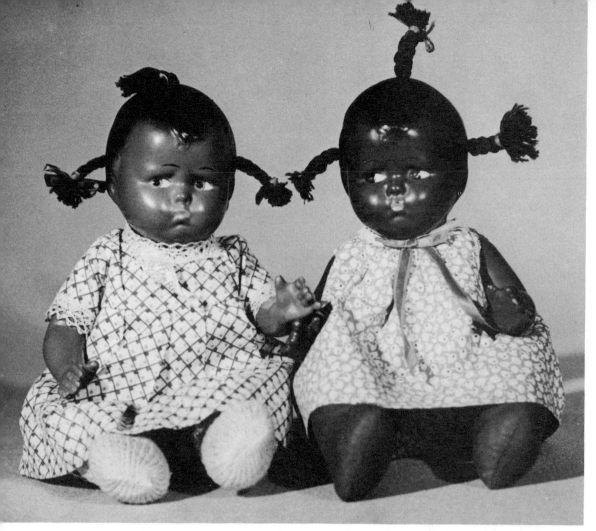

Illustration 509. 10½in (26.7cm) *Infant Grumpykins;* composition heads, cloth bodies, composition arms, cloth legs; black painted hair with three braids; closed mouths. The doll on the left has brown eyes with black pupils and is circa 1926. The doll on the right has non-frowning heart-on-the-side eyes and is circa mid 1930s. Note that the doll on the left is chocolate colored while the doll on the right is much darker with the different eye painting. *Frances James Collection.*

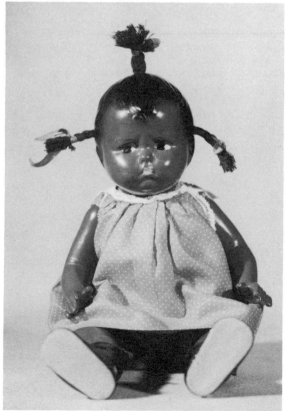

Illustration 510. 10½in (26.7cm) *Infant Grumpykins;* composition head, cloth body, composition arms, replaced composition legs instead of the original cloth ones; painted black hair with three thread braids; heart-on-the-side eyes, black eyebrows; wearing original red and white dotted swiss cotton dress with lace at the neck and sleeves. Circa mid 1930s. *Frances James Collection.*

Illustration 512. 12in (30.5cm) *Grumpykins,* seen in *Illustration 511,* in his complete cowboy outfit including a removable metal gun. Satin label sewn to shirt reads: "Effanbee Durable Dolls." Christmas 1936. *Christine Lorman Collection.*

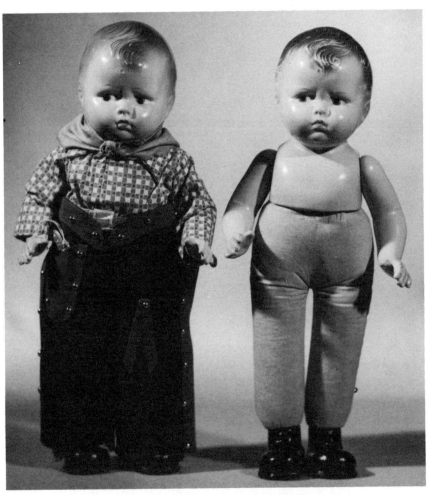

Illustration 511. 12in (30.5cm) *Grumpykins* dolls; composition heads, cloth bodies, wood pulp composition arms, cloth legs with composition feet; brown painted hair; blue eyes, non-frowning eyebrows; closed mouths. Comparative view showing the one doll dressed and the other undressed. The doll on the right has a navy blue sailor suit. Besides the cowboy and sailor there was a policeman, fireman, a bellboy and possibly others in the group. 1936. Doll on left, *Christine Lorman Collection.*

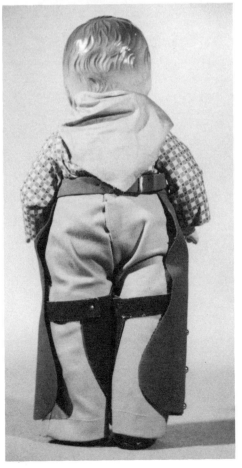

Illustration 513. Back view of the 12in (30.5cm) *Grumpykins,* seen in *Illustrations 511* and *512,* showing the back of his outfit. *Christine Lorman Collection.*

PENNSYLVANIA DUTCH DOLLS
By Marie Polack

Upper Picture: Mennonite.   Lower Picture: River Brethren.

at the
Pennsylvania Dutch Gift Shop

*A Miniature Museum of the Dutch Country
featuring authentic Pennsylvania Dutch Dolls.*
Mennonite — Amish — Dunkard — River Brethren.
ALSO LOCAL GIFTS AND ANTIQUES.
Route 30, 2 miles East of
York, Pa., at Valley Inn.
Mail Address: 25 E. Market St., York, Pa.
Wholesale and retail price lists on request.

jlyp

Illustration 514. Advertisement for the *Pennsylvania Dutch Dolls* by Marie A. Polack. The *Mom* and *Pop* were *Baby Grumpy* dolls, sold undressed by Effanbee and apparently costumed by Marie A. Polack. The children are not believed to be by Effanbee since they are not up to their quality. It is thought that the doll sets were orignally available in 1936, according to a dated leaflet packed with the dolls. *Hobbies,* July 1941.

Illustration 515. 9in (22.9cm) *Sister,* 12in (30.5cm) *Mom* (a *Baby Grumpy* doll by Effanbee) and 9in (22.9cm) *Brother* from the *Mennonite Family* of *Pennsylvania Dutch Dolls;* costumed and distributed by Marie A. Polack. *Mom* has a composition head, cloth body, composition arms and feet; brown hair; blue eyes, eyebrows not painted in the *Grumpy* frown. *Sister* is wearing a blue and white checked dress with a dark head scarf and removable shoes and socks. *Brother* has on a blue woolen suit, thread buttons, and painted bare feet. The paper tags are marked: "Mennonite." Original advertising shows *Mom* with white hair, so each set was not completely identical. 1941. *Linda Mazer Collection.*

Illustration 516. 9in (22.9cm) *Sister,* 12in (30.5cm) *Mom* (a *Baby Grumpy* doll by Effanbee), 12in (30.5cm) *Pop* (also a *Baby Grumpy* doll by Effanbee) and 9in (22.9cm) *Brother* from the *River Brethren Family* of *Pennsylvania Dutch Dolls;* costumed and distributed by Marie A. Polack, *Mom* and *Pop* have composition heads, cloth bodies, composition arms and composition feet; *Mom* has a dark brown wig while *Pop* has a light wig and beard; blue eyes, tan painted eyebrows. The children are wearing a denim type of clothing; *Mom* wears dark rayon and *Pop* has a wool type of suit and coat. *Pop* and *Brother* are also wearing black hats. The children have removable shoes and socks. Circa 1936. *Linda Mazer Collection.*

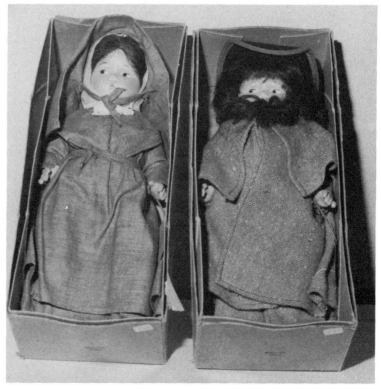

Illustration 517. 12in (30.5cm) *Mom* and *Pop* (*Baby Grumpy* dolls by Effanbee) from the *River Brethren Family* of *Pennsylvania Dutch Dolls;* costumed and distributed by Marie A. Polack. Both have composition heads, cloth bodies, composition arms, molded shoes; brown wigs; blue eyes, brown painted eyebrows. *Mom* is wearing a gray cotton shawl, an apron, headdress and white cotton cap. *Pop* wears a gray wool coat over a suit and a dark hat. According to a leaflet which came with the dolls the "white bonnet worn by the women and adopted when receiving church membership is esteemed as a covering of the head at prayer." *Linda Mazer Collection.*